THE
COMPACT HISTORY
OF THE
UNITED STATES
ARMY

COL. R. ERNEST DUPUY

USA, RET.

• • • •

Illustrations by Gil Walker

HAWTHORN BOOKS, INC.

PUBLISHERS / NEW YORK

Second Revised Edition

· · · ·

THE

COMPACT HISTORY

OF THE

UNITED STATES

ARMY

I see these things, still am I slave,
When banners flaunt and bugles blow,
Content to fill a soldier's grave
For reasons I shall never know.

MAJ. GENERAL CHARLES T. LANHAM,
USA, Ret.

CONTENTS

PREFACE TO SECOND REVISED EDITION

In presenting this second revised edition, the author is glad to have the opportunity to record the life of our Army from its beginnings up to the final quarter of the twentieth century. It is a soldier's survey and also, to some extent, a personal reminiscence, since the author has in one way or another been linked to the Army's fortunes during the past seventy years: in military school, in the National Guard and, since 1917, in the Regular Army.

The United States Army, or the Army of the United States—for in their broadest sense the terms are synonymous—is a throbbing entity, possessing both body and soul. Its body includes all the elements of physical being: personnel, weapons and supply. Its soul is that intangible flame we call *esprit de corps:* the will to win, which gives it life.

An army lacking that vital spark is no army at all. It is merely an armed mob, gathered momentarily through fleeting patriotism or in the valor of ignorance. Under stress such an aggregation dissolves through the basic urge of its individual members to seek self-preservation.

The will to win—the team spirit—on the other hand is no momentary flash. It is compounded of leadership and discipline, tinctured with tradition. Solidified into a storage battery of dedication, this amalgam galvanizes the individual soldier to team action above and beyond his personal norm.

A national army such as ours is also affected spiritually by the mass motivation of the people whose servant it is, and who serve in its ranks. None of this motivation is necessarily permanent, although the basic principles involved may be. The urges change in accordance with the character of the national life, and they reflect the national mood of the moment.

In 1937 the late Major John H. Burns, Inf., brilliant editor of the *Infantry Journal* (now *Army*), raised this point when he wrote: "The officer who believes that American civilization as it is evolving will give him the same human material that fought at Gettysburg or in the Argonne is living in a fool's paradise. . . . Whether this American will make a different or better soldier no one can say. . . ."

Major Burns did not live to see his Army tested during World War II, the Korean War or the agony of Vietnam; but history proves the validity of his prophesy

So let's look at the record.

ACKNOWLEDGMENTS

Chapters 11 to 17 inclusive are based, with much elaboration, upon an article entitled "Pass in Review," copyright 1954 by the Association of the United States Army, and published in the October, 1954, issue of *Combat Forces Journal* (now *Army*), written at the request of its editor, John B. Spore, for the *Journal's* fiftieth anniversary. Sincere thanks are due to the Association and to *Army* for permission to use this article.

Major General Charles T. Lanham, USA, Ret., graciously permitted publication of a verse from his poem, "Soldier," as dedication.

The late Major General Anthony Drexel Biddle, Adjutant General of the Pennsylvania National Guard, was most helpful in furnishing vital information pertaining to the lineage of certain Pennsylvania units.

The Office of the Chief of Military History, Department of the Army, and in particular Mr. Charles A. MacDonald, cheerfully furnished much essential data.

Colonel Roger Willock, USMCR, was most helpful with advice and suggestions pertaining to leaders, arms and character of the Indian campaigns of 1866-1891.

Harper & Row, publishers of *Global Mission,* by the late General Henry H. Arnold, USAF, graciously permitted reproduction of the quotation from that book appearing on page 235.

Colonel Trevor N. Dupuy, USA, Ret., son of the author, gave most valuable assistance from his store of military historical knowledge.

The late Laura N. Dupuy, Army wife and Army mother, who during her lifetime untiringly furnished inspiration, guidance and encouragement to the author, was more of a collaborator than a patient editorial counsellor.

In acknowledging his gratitude for all this assistance, the author takes full responsibility for any errors or omissions. The opinions expressed and conclusions drawn are his and his alone, and not attributable to the Department of Defense, the Department of the Army, or to the service at large.

R. ERNEST DUPUY,
Colonel, U.S. Army, Ret.

Arlington, Va.

THE
COMPACT HISTORY
OF THE
UNITED STATES
ARMY

IN THE BEGINNING

There was little outward evidence around beleaguered Boston town on the hot, muggy day of July 3, 1775, that the soul of an Army was aborning. Certainly British General Thomas Gage and his disciplined red-coats manning the defenses along Charlestown Neck and up in the works on Bunker Hill north of Charlestown knew nothing of it. No more, probably, did the great majority of that New England rabble in arms—clustered in the hamlets and fields of the countryside ringing Boston from Roxbury to Chelsea—know that this day would be any different from the other days of this still young rebellion against the British King.

On Cambridge Common a few people knew something was up. They had seen a tall man of imposing appearance, riding gracefully and well, and clad in the buff and blue of the Virginia militia, draw rein there. They heard General George Washington take command, at the behest of the Continental Congress then gathered in Philadelphia, of "all the continental forces, raised or to be raised, for the defense of American liberty."

Actually this Army that Washington was sparking could be called neither the United States Army nor the Army of the United States. There was as yet no United States; a year and one day would have to pass before the amended Declaration of Independence would be approved by the Congress. But this force—the New England troops already in the field, together with the first contingent authorized by the Congress on June 14 and now raising—a total of six companies of riflemen from Pennsylvania, two from Virginia and two more from Maryland, comprised the first body of troops assembled to defend the thirteen United Colonies as a whole. It was the nucleus of the Continental Army.

Let's look at this aggregation of Americans hemming in the British in Boston; this crowd of individuals, arms in hand, who had already met their enemy at Lexington, Concord and on the bloody slopes of Bunker Hill, and who were yapping, like clumsy puppies around a porcupine, in front of Gage's defenses. This was the raw material from which Washington must fashion an Army. They could shoot a gun, most of these men, and as individuals they could fight—when they thought it necessary. But they couldn't stand up in the open against a disciplined bayonet charge. They couldn't—or most of them wouldn't—obey orders; they were individualists and they could be pretty obstinate about it. As a matter of fact, few among their leaders could give an order or command sufficient respect to be obeyed when they did; it was a case of the blind leading the blind.

And yet these were men of a people who had been fighting Indians continuously for more than a century, and who had already been involved in no less than four major wars.

To understand them, we must go back to the beginning of Anglo-Saxon immigration in North America. Only then can we see why a certain latent military spirit burned in some of these men, and why also it was almost smothered in a welter of basic taboos upon things military—taboos some of which persist to this day. We will get some idea of the task which Washington faced in moulding this mass of iconoclastic, stubborn individuals into an Army. And we will, perhaps, better appreciate the value of leadership.

What manner of men were these who made up the conglomerate which George Washington was about to weld into an army? These men might have been descendants of one of the well-to-do grantees, but more probably they were from one of the other three classes of immigrants—the poor, the indentured who had sold their bodies to labor as price of passage to the promised land, or the deported law-breakers. And these last-named ran the gamut from the criminal to the unfortunate whose sin lay in that he had espoused the wrong cause in England's stormy civil wars of the seventeenth century, and as a result found himself thrown as a chattel on an American beach.

But most of these people had come over voluntarily, seeking something freer than the life they had known in Europe. The great majority were of Anglo-Saxon origin, although of course by 1775 several well-defined minority groups had taken root. There were the Pennsylvania Dutch from the Rhinish Palatinate, the Hollanders in the Hudson valley, the few Swedish settlers along the Delaware coast, and the French Huguenots who had flocked to the lower Hudson valley.

Whatever their origin or their previous station in life, these people all shared one hatred: standing armies. The King's livery to them stood for all they had gladly left behind: oppression, repression, grinding submission to the "divine right" of royalty, and the whim of autocratic rulers. The better-educated among them could visualize, too, from historical example, the threat of military despotism subverting civilian rule. All this combined to instill in them a distrust for all things and men military.

So, when they had to take up arms in their new land—as they were obliged to do from the very beginning—they did so grudgingly for the most part, or at best in the spirit of "here's a chore to be done, and as soon as it's over let's get back home and go to work."

The colonial had early found that most of the simple things to which he had been accustomed in Europe were lacking over here. The paltry trickle of supply from overseas was entirely insufficient. Food had to be grown, materials had to be fashioned, and tools to accomplish the task had to be extemporized or even, in some cases, invented. One has only to glance at the collections of wood and metal-working and agricultural tools on display in the various colonial museums extant to discover the lengths to which necessity had developed the ingenuity of these people. There was real meaning—and some very bitter irony, too—in the early Americanism, "Root, hog, or die!" It didn't take long for such men and women as these, thrown on their own and succeeding, to develop a spirit of individualism and a certain scorn for the more orderly conventions and limitations imposed upon the people of the highly-populated areas abroad from which they had migrated.

It was natural, then, that with their predominantly Anglo-Saxon background, the military expedient seized upon was the fundamentally civilian concept of military life, which had from time immemorial been part and parcel of England's life and the hard-won rights of English freemen. This was the train band or militia, the able-bodied citizenry of each county, subject to call only for home defense when necessity arose, under a county lord lieutenant.

It began over here when the Pilgrims in 1620 hired Captain Myles Standish, a professional soldier, to "organize a train band" from among their number to defend their new-found domain. So, from the onset, the American soldier was a part-time warrior, and any attempt at a permanent organization was frowned upon.

Since the enrollment was a part of the processes of local government, the train bands speedily mushroomed in every township in New England. They were called out sporadically in the Plymouth, Massachusetts Bay and Connecticut colonies for the Pequot War of 1636-1637. By 1636 the Massachusetts Bay colony incorporated a number of train bands in the North Regiment, later the Regiment of Middlesex. Reorganized in 1775 as Gardner's Regiment, it took part in the investment of Boston. And there we have the beginnings of today's 182nd Infantry, the former 5th Massachusetts, granddaddy of all existing National Guard units.

In Virginia the train bands first coalesced in 1652, when the Charles City-Henrico Counties Regiment of Militia came into existence. Elements of this formation were constituted for active service in January, 1754, as the Virginia Regiment, which four years later was expanded into Colonel George Washington's 1st and Colonel Richard Byrd's 2nd Virginia Regiments. And in July, 1775, reconstituted, the grouping became Colonel Patrick Henry's 1st Regiment of Virginia Regulars, later of the Continental Line, which has come down through the years as today's 176th Infantry, second senior unit of the National Guard.

In 1662, Massachusetts produced the Hampshire Regiment, from which in early 1775 flowered "minute companies" and later part of the Massachusetts Line. This regiment, known in later years as the 2nd Massachusetts, is today's 104th Infantry. In 1672, Connecticut militia units were fused into two organizations—the Regiment of Hartford County and the Regiment of New Haven County. The former, becoming the 1st Connecticut, is now the 169th Infantry; the latter, once the 2nd Connecticut, is the present-day 102nd Infantry.

Thus, albeit reluctantly, did our militia tradition emerge, by the end of the seventeenth century, in a colonial civilization still convinced in general that it wanted no part or parcel of any permanent military establishment.

There were exceptions to this way of thinking, of course. The young bloods of the growing towns, excited by adventure or fancying themselves parading in showy uniforms, began to gather into volunteer units which were incorporated in the respective colonies. First of such was the Ancient and Honorable Artillery Company of Boston, organized in 1638 by a former member of the English militia unit of similar name—the Honorable Artillery Company of London.

Characteristic of the general animosity to such militaristic trends was the reaction of Governor John Winthrop to the petition of this group for a charter of incorporation:

"Divers Gentlemen and others being joined in military Company desire to be made a Corporation, but the Council considering from the example of the Pretorian band among the Romans and Templers (*sic*) in Europe how dangerous it might be to erect a standing authority of military men which might easily in time overthrow the civil power, thought fit to stop it betimes; yet they were allowed to be a Company but subordinate to all authority."

In fact organizations of this sort presented but little danger to the civil government. Nor did the militia in general. Training was of the most meager character. Officers were political appointees, favorites of the colonial royal governors, or else they were elected by their men on a popularity basis. Most of them were entirely unfitted for any military task.

Even had they been adequately trained and led, these units in time of major conflagration formed only a collection of separate colonial militias without common head or central command. They were filled with all the suspicions and jealousies of the respective colonies toward one another. The seeds of future states' rights contentions were already sown by sectional and religious differences.

The New Englanders, filled with the so-called "leveling influence" of democracy, looked askance upon the Virginians and Marylanders, suspect—without too much foundation in fact—of Cavalier and Papist tendencies. The Virginians, growing up in an atmosphere already markedly different from that of New England, looked down their noses at the Northerners as being straitlaced Puritanical traders. Out on the frontiers of the Carolinas, Georgia and Kentucky, where the lawless and adventurous elements had begun to drift, the hard-fighting, hard-drinking, roistering frontiersmen took little stock in their more domesticated Eastern neighbors. And up North in the New Hampshire grants internecine warfare between New York and Vermont was beginning.

In this atmosphere, bickering on command status was common on the few occasions when militia levies of several colonies were massed for a momentary military undertaking. Not only did the militiamen themselves resist being put under command of officers from colonies other than their own, but the respective colonial governments actively sided with them.

The first of these combined military efforts was in 1675, when New England levies from the Massachusetts, Connecticut and Plymouth colonies were massed to fight the Indians in King Philip's War, which ended with the final collapse of Indian resistance in that area. Here, as in the constant clashes with the Indians further south and to the west, the colonists learned one particular way of war—stealthy, individualistic guerrilla warfare against elusive foes who drifted through the woods noiselessly, whose sensitive eyes, ears and noses could follow the faintest trail, and who never gave battle in the open as did Europeans.

Here, too, in all this Indian fighting the settlers learned the value of individual marksmanship. Powder and shot were scarce; one had to make do with what was in hand. Woe to the unfortunate who discharged his firearm carelessly; arrow, knife or tomahawk would find him before he could reload again. So, even if short on tactics and ignorant of strategy, the colonist, particularly the frontiersman, was learning something priceless—the value of aimed marksmanship. Learning it, he was fostering what would become a great American tradition.

The patient Pennsylvania Dutch emigrants from the Palatinate and the Swiss Alps played an enormous part in this. They had brought over with them a weapon far superior in range and accuracy to the ordinary smooth-bore musket; they had brought the rifle. Their transplanted gunsmiths, working with loving care in steel, had done something to this heavy, short handarm so prized by the *jagers*—the huntsmen of the mountainous regions of their native Europe. They lengthened the barrel to a full five feet, they reamed the grooved bore to carry a half-ounce ball instead of the one-ounce bullet of the smoothbore, and they produced what the world was later to know as the Kentucky rifle.

New Englanders at first didn't know much about the rifle. But the border men—in western Pennsylvania, along the Virginia Blue Ridge, in Kentucky and the Carolinas—knew it. Their experts could funnel ball after ball into a seven-inch group at two hundred and fifty yards, much to the dismay of the musketeer whose wobbling bullet dropped harmlessly to the ground at a lesser distance and who, except by good luck, could not expect to hit a man a hundred yards away.

It was well that the colonists were learning this woodlore and marksmanship and the craft of Indian fighting. Not only was it to stand them in good stead when the French use of Indian allies grew, but it was in fact to radically affect—after it had been learned the hard way—the pompous, rigid tactical formations of eighteenth century European armies.

Under such conditions Anglo-Saxon North America found itself involved in four successive wars. Massachusetts militia levies under Sir William Phips, the royal governor, captured Port Royal in Nova Scotia from the French in King William's War, 1689-1697. New York militia went up there to capture it once more (the British having meanwhile returned it to France) in Queen Anne's War, 1702-1713.

King George's War, 1740-1748, involved the English colonies against both Spain and France. There was bickering along the Florida border and a composite provincial regiment, in which Virginians predominated, went with Admiral Edward Vernon in his unsuccessful Cartagena expedition. Not only did the colonial officers present receive some war experience here, but one of them, Lawrence Washington, perpetuated his admiral's name by christening his Potomac estate "Mount Vernon."

Up North, against France, provincial militia levies from Massachusetts, Connecticut and New Hampshire, under Sir William Pepperrell of Kittery, learned something more about amphibious warfare in the capture of Fort Louisbourg on Cape Breton Island, in 1745. The commander of the colonial artillery, who was also chief engineer of the expedition, was one Richard Gridley, a half-pay English officer living in Massachusetts, who was later to lay out the American earthworks on Bunker Hill and then command the Massachusetts artillery regiment before Boston.

The martial spirit, activated by none other than Benjamin Franklin, struck Philadelphia during the latter part of this period. The Associators, a military organization founded by him in 1747, became the Associated Regiment of Foot of Philadelphia, which fought through the Revolutionary War and exists today as the 111th Infantry of the National Guard.

The next upsurge of war was to affect not only the fortunes of the colonies, but also their military spirit. Westward expansion of the English colonies was waxing by mid-eighteenth century. Virginians and Pennsylvanians drifting into the Ohio Valley clashed with French-Canadian exploitation of the region. To forestall French encroachment, Governor Robert Dinwiddie of Virginia in 1754 sent a serious-minded young militia officer, Major George Washington, with a force to construct a fort at the junction of the Allegheny and Monongahela Rivers, a site previously selected by Washington as a key point.

French forces seized the site before Maj. Washington and his Virginia militiamen arrived, and established Fort Duquesne where Pittsburgh stands today. Washington, hurriedly erecting Fort Necessity at Great Meadows, near the present site of Uniontown, Pa., in an effort to check further French advance toward the Potomac Valley, was overpowered by superior French forces and had to surrender. Thus was the curtain raised on the French and Indian War, which was to develop into Europe's Seven Years' War ending in France's final defeat and surrender of all her North American mainland holdings.

When George Washington first tasted the bitter tea of defeat in the wilderness at Fort Necessity, the French claimed and held the major part of the land area of the present United States. Between their two fortified bases of Quebec City and New Orleans stretched a chain of some sixty posts. The Hudson Valley was dominated by French forts at Crown Point and Ticonderoga on Lake Champlain, while Fort Niagara blocked a British outpost at Oswego. Fort Duquesne controlled the Ohio Valley. Kingston, Erie, Detroit, St. Louis and Natchez were French strongholds; the Great Lakes and the Mississippi in French hands. The English colonies were threatened by this encirclement. Both sides were wooing the powerful Indian tribes along the wide frontier.

England, alarmed by the situation, dispatched General Edward Braddock to Virginia in 1755, to command all British forces in North America. With him came two regiments of British regulars, all pipe-clay and precision. With about one thousand of these fine troops, reinforced by more than four hundred colonials—mostly Virginians—Braddock marched westward to Fort Duquesne to meet disaster, death, and the birth of an American tradition.

By July 9, 1755, Braddock's little army was only eight miles short of its destination, marching precisely along a trail beside the banks of the Monongahela. The column was alert and prepared for battle—European style. Suddenly attacked from front and flank, its well-ordered ranks riddled by the fire of an unseen enemy, most of the army dissolved in panic. A few gallant officers were able to re-establish some control over small bodies of men and these—mostly colonials—fighting loosely from tree to tree, from tussock to tussock, in accustomed Indian-fighting style, saved the survivors from annihilation. Young Colonel George Washington, serving as a volunteer on the staff of General Braddock, was conspicuous for his bravery and his leadership in organizing bands of confused men during this crucial phase of the withdrawal.

Out of the disaster, and a welter of confused and misleading reports, grew that dangerous illusion that the American frontiersman and the militiaman were somehow superior to the British regular; that enthusiasm could outfight discipline—an illusion that unfortunately was to last long after it had been disproved in fact on the battlefield.

What Braddock's defeat did prove was that European eighteenth century battle tactics—precise linear masses of soldiers fighting shoulder-to-shoulder—had no place in the wilderness. Also, that aimed fire of individual marksmen making every shot count was superior to the massed unaimed volley-fire in which the British soldier of that time was schooled. What was needed, it seemed, was a combination—disciplined soldiers trained to fight in loose formation. The lesson was not lost on the British Army.

Within a year a new regiment was on the army list—the Royal Americans, the 60th Foot. Organized on Governors Island in New York, its personnel were mostly enlisted from Pennsylvania (there were imported Germans, too), and its officers were a conglomeration of British regulars and soldiers of fortune. Drilled in an entirely new fashion of open-order fighting, it not only was to prove its effectiveness almost from the beginning, but it was also to become a forcing bed for leaders of the future. It exists today, as the King's Royal Rifle Corps, bearing more battle honors than any other British regiment.

Light companies, to skirmish in the American fashion, were also added to existing English regiments. And a new type of soldier was born when Robert Rogers of New Hampshire organized the famous Rogers' Rangers—trained woodsmen who became a unit of the

British Army. It is interesting to note that Rogers' second-in-command was John Stark, who would later win fame during the Revolution by his victory over British forces at Bennington, Vt., and by his slogan: "We'll beat them before night, or Molly Stark will be a widow!"

The new organizations and tactics showed their value in the campaigns of 1758 and 1759 against the French along the St. Lawrence, Lake Champlain and the Ohio River. They played an important part in General Jeffrey Amherst's campaign against Louisbourg, in General James Wolfe's famed assault upon Quebec, and at Bushy Run against Pontiac in 1763.

But the martial spirit ebbed at conclusion of the war when France had been driven from all her holdings on the North American mainland and Canada won for the British crown. The colonial levies were disbanded and their veterans scattered and submerged in the conglomeration of separate militias whose continued existence was sketchy and whose discipline was almost non-existent, despite the workable machinery for calling the men out.

The militias were now divided into two categories—"minute-men," approximately twenty-five per cent of each unit, pledged to turn out like volunteer fire companies on alarm, and the "regular" militia, existing mostly on paper. In most of the colonies these men turned out only once a year for muster, the occasion being more a combination of barbecue roast and whiskey-guzzling than anything else.

But the leaven was there. So, available to Washington in 1775 were such men as Henry Knox, the Boston bookseller who had learned about artillery in the Ancient and Honorable Artillery Company, and John Stark who had learned about war in Rogers' Rangers. There were three ex-British regular officers—Arthur St. Clair, who had served at Louisbourg and Quebec; Horatio Gates, veteran of the Braddock campaign and later a major in the Royal Americans; and Charles Lee, Seven Years' War veteran both in America and Portugal. There were such men, too, as "Mad Anthony" Wayne and "Light Horse Harry" Lee, natural leaders whose sole thought in battle was to seek out and destroy the enemy. There was Daniel Morgan, backwoods' rifleman, another Braddock veteran. There were Richard Montgomery, who had been on the second Louisbourg expedition, and Nathanael Greene, the volunteer militiaman from Rhode Island.

Available, too, was a brilliant soldier and audacious leader who as a seventeen-year-old boy had first run away to war and whose name, had he died in battle at Saratoga, would have been carried today on the roll of great American soldier patriots. Unfortunately he was to live and to trail the name of Benedict Arnold into the mire as a synonym for basest treachery.

One may sum it up by stating that of thirteen general officers who were to be appointed by the Continental Congress in 1775, all but two had seen war service, and eight of these in the grade of lieutenant colonel or higher.

All this points up the fact that when the break with Britain did come, and the "embattled farmers" swarmed like angry bees about British-held Boston, there was in the American Colonies a proportion of men who had some military experience. But taken as a whole, the available man-power lacked organization, lacked almost all the essential rudiments of discipline and training, and above all lacked adequate numbers of experienced leaders, particularly in company officers and non-commissioned officers.

What these men did share was a military concept stemming from civilian sources; from a matrix as English as John Bull himself—the militia concept. It was exemplified in this Virginia planter who had now ridden up from his estates at the call of his country to give them leadership.

How Washington accomplished the task, how he breathed a soul into this mixed bag of reluctant dragons, is all part and parcel of the story of the United States Army.

*   *   *   *   *

• • • •

BLUE AND BUFF

"I found a mixed multitude of People here, under very little discipline, order, or Government . . . Confusion and disorder reigned in every Department." Such was Washington's first impression as he inspected his new command in 1775. The men, he remarked, "regarded their officers no more than broomsticks."

It was to be expected. What did discipline mean to an angry mob which had been exposed to Sam Adams' rabble-rousing oratory? To his pronouncement that "the natural liberty of man is to be free from any superior power on earth, and not to be under the will or legislative authority of man, but only to have the law of nature for his rule"?

So many things had to be done, the commander-in-chief found. In the first place, the only uniforms in this crowd were the variegated regalia of a few volunteer militia companies and the almost-uniform appearance of the riflemen of the new units authorized by Congress and now arrived; their frock-like brown hunting-shirts of common pattern were to come into widespread use. Insignia of rank had to be extemporized; ribbons and cockades of various colors had to serve to identify the officer and his grade.

There was no uniformity of arms, either. Each man carried whatever weapon he had at home—musket or fowling-piece. There was no uniformity of supply; a commissariat and quartermaster system had to be evolved, including, of course, some sort of transport. Records were non-existent; it took a week to compile returns showing that the new Army comprised 16,770 men, of whom 1,592 were absent—which meant that they had gone home—and 1,598 others were sick.

Powder and shot were lacking. Cannon were to be few until the energetic Henry Knox and his artillerymen later dragged 58 guns from Fort Ticonderoga—captured by Ethan Allen—all the way across the mountains and down to Boston.

Worst of all, the enlistments of most of the militia were to expire in December, and the homesick amateurs had not the slightest intention of remaining a single day longer than their time. Their wives and their farms needed them. They were being pushed about by this new-fangled idea of discipline. Appeals to their patriotism by Washington were unheeded. When canvassed to re-enlist for a year under new Continental regulations, less than a thousand of the six thousand men due for discharge responded.

"Such a dirty, mercenary spirit pervades the whole," wrote Washington at this time, "that I should not be surprised at any disaster that may happen."

There was indeed good reason why Washington in those early days felt frustrated as he strove to bring order out of this chaos. Wholesale desertions were one of the principal banes, and were to continue throughout the war. These men could not understand why they should not go back home when they felt the necessity. There were crops to be sown and reaped, there were families to be fed. Every man absent on military service was a handicap to agricultural communities. There were also, of course, the malingerers, who deserted not from personal necessity but simply because they wanted to get away from obviously dangerous service.

The most rudimentary concepts of cleanliness had to be instilled, and punishment applied to violators of all parts of the elementary discipline Washington promulgated. Desertions were at times punished by death, but the lash and the pillory were the most common forms of punishment for this as for other derelictions. Running the gantlet—the culprit being driven between lines of his comrades who were free to beat him with sticks or with their fists—was another form of penalty. In addition there was the wooden horse, a peaked device on which the victim sat strapped with the weight of his body supported by the tip of his spine. But this was so severe and injurious that Washington discouraged its use. The times were violent, it must be remembered, and the punishments inflicted were no more severe than those applied in the British service.

There were a few bright spots in this crazy-quilt of amateur soldiering. For instance, there was the Rhode Island militia, a brigade of three regiments of infantry and a company of artillery. Nathanael Greene who commanded it was a quiet young man who liked to read Caesar and Turenne and who had been playing soldier in the Kentish

Guards, a volunteer organization chartered in October, 1774. Rhode Island had done pretty well for its militia in the way of camp equipment and tentage. Its neat cantonments were in vast contrast to the ramshackle array of hutments and hovels in which most of the Army had gathered and which were more like hobo "jungles" than anything else.

And there was, too, Colonel John Glover's Marblehead Regiment, composed of deep-water fishermen and sailors from the Massachusetts coast who were as much at home on land as they were on water. They were apparently a pretty clannish group, these Marblehead men, whose nautical pea-jackets and rolling gait drew some caustic comment from Morgan's roistering Virginia riflemen when that hunting-shirted confraternity camped near them in Cambridge. The resultant free-for-all was quelled by General Washington himself, who, so the story goes, waded into the fray to seize two ringleaders and bang their heads together.

The most pressing need was to improve the quality of the officers. Fortunately, the Congress, when it authorized the first increment of really national troops on June 30, 1775, had also adopted a code to govern its armed forces. As might have been expected, this was nothing more or less than an adaptation of the British regulations—the so-called Mutiny Act and Articles of War governing the King's troops. This code contained one unique article which imposed on the military officer a higher obligation, it would seem, than upon any civilian official:

"Whatsoever commissioned officer shall be convicted, before a general court martial, of behaving in a scandalous, infamous manner, such as is unbecoming the character of an officer and a gentleman, shall be discharged from the service."

Here was the cornerstone of a code of honor which for years to come governed the conduct of an officer of the United States Army. At the moment, however, it was a potent weapon in Washington's hands to assist in elimination of the many trimmers, rogues and pilferers who had wangled commissions in the militia.

Washington firmly felt that the only way to recruit an Army, and to appoint the officers of that Army, would be by means of a system purely national—independent of the whims and politics of state control. He was not entirely successful. His recommendations that the men be enlisted for the duration of the war were bitterly contested. He had to be content with a part-measure—enlistments for one year predominating. The resultant continuous recruitment and replacement badly hampered all long-range planning.

The states countered this Congressional threat to their prerogatives by giving bounties to recruits enlisting in their short-term militias. Thus was born a pernicious system of competition which was to impede the cause of liberty throughout the war.

In spite of half-measures, Washington's efforts brought about the firm establishment of the Continental Line, a corps of comparatively long-term soldiers about which the short-term militiamen raised by the states could be clustered and strengthened. On January 1, 1776, the Line came into being. On that day, too, in front of Boston was raised the first flag of the United Colonies—thirteen alternate white and red stripes, with the crosses of St. George and St. Andrew in the canton. The first step had been taken to build an Army whose naked, bloody footprints were to trace the road to freedom under fantastic circumstances.

It must be remembered that the thirteen colonies presented no united front. A good third of the American population was, for one reason or another, allied in sentiment to Britain. While the poor man welcomed relief from taxation and, with no stake involved, was ready for revolt, many rich men quite naturally veered towards the side promising security and ordered government. This was particularly true in the New York area, where the great landed proprietors stood to lose their all by rebellion. So men bearing such names as De Lancy, De Puyster and Robinson were to be found actively leading Tory troops, fighting for the Crown.

As for the South, there the war was to take on the aspect of a civil war indeed, with all the bitterness and savagery of such struggles of neighbor against neighbor. In the Carolinas entire communities of Scottish settlers fought solidly for the King. A sharp contrast was this to the patriotic attitude of the Pennsylvania Scotch-Irish and Protestant Ulstermen and Cromwellians who had fled the reprisals of Charles II. Many landed proprietors in the South, too, fearing for their estates should the Revolution succeed, joined the Tory ranks.

These Southern Tories made up a sizeable proportion of the British forces engaged in the Carolina campaigns of 1780-1781. At

King's Mountain, for instance, on October 7, 1781, of all the opposing forces engaged only one man was not an American. He was Major Patrick Ferguson, British regular who had made a name for himself both as an able—if bloodthirsty—leader of Tory partisans and as the inventor of a breech-loading rifle. Ferguson, commanding the British troops atop King's Mountain, fell there.

In the large communities, such as New York and Philadelphia, Tory sentiment was rampant—its power fluctuating as the fortunes of war affected the issue—and careful self-seekers altered the trim of their sails to catch the breeze most favorable to their personal fortunes.

This division of allegiance from the very beginning of the struggle hampered the call-up of the various colonial militias, for the Tory sentiment affected both officers and men, contributing to the further dislocation of the already nebulous command status.

Other than in parts of New England, the patriot soldier could never have the feeling that he was fighting in the midst of a friendly population. He frequently found himself in hostile territory, where enemy eyes were spying upon him, enemy tongues were ready to betray his presence, and enemy partisans—all as American in origin as himself—were waiting to take pot-shots at him. Nor could he be certain that while he was away fighting for this new-fangled thing called liberty, other white Americans and their red-skinned allies would not be raiding his home and butchering his family. The Mohawk and Susquehanna Valleys in particular were scarred by such atrocities, as Tories and Indians again and again brought fire and sword on the settlements.

Further than that, the Continental soldier had real reason to feel that his government, such as it was, did not appreciate his efforts. Irregularly paid, and then only in Continental currency—backed only by the ink of its paper and so depreciated as to give rise to that expression of complete worthlessness, "not worth a Continental"—officers and men were entirely dependent on what they might themselves lay hands. Clothing and shoes always lacked. So, too, did food during many periods. Only the combination of leadership tinctured with discipline could conquer such psychological encroachments on the Continental soldier's mind.

Leadership Washington furnished; an amazing quality of personal leadership which dragged his men behind him through the harrowing days and years to the end of 1777 and the grim despondency of Valley Forge. His troops had been defeated at Long Island and saved only by his quick ingenuity and personal direction of a remarkable evacuation. They had gone through the agony of the retreat to the Delaware. They had risen to the heights in the following ten-day campaign when the river was crossed again, the Hessians crushed at Trenton and Cornwallis foxed at Princeton—the campaign dubbed by Frederick the Great as the most brilliant in military history.

They were warriors, these men, but they were not yet soldiers. Their leader's lofty spirit soared high above his tatterdemalion array, above the slime of political skullduggery and self-seeking politicians, the intrigues of Tories and the breastbeatings of the faint-hearted, in times which Tom Paine said "tried men's souls." But Washington could not single-handedly ignite the spark of troop leadership in the subordinate units.

These men could rebound from such defeats as the Brandywine and Germantown. But they could not, either in victory or defeat, withstand the British bayonet-charge. At Princeton, Gen. Hugh Mercer's troops had quailed before Col. Charles Mawhood's bayonets; on the Brandywine, Gen. John Sullivan's men melted before cold steel; so, too, had Gen. Anthony Wayne's ranks collapsed at Paoli. They lacked the cohesion and steadiness which only basic training and discipline could provide.

Something more was needed, and this the officers could not yet provide. Although Washington's program of selection and discard had taken some shape, it was hampered by the insistence of state governors of their right to appoint whomsoever they chose—often unfit and untrained—to command their own men.

Silas Deane, American commissioner and purchasing agent in Paris, solved the problem—unwittingly, perhaps. For Deane in 1776-1777 had started sending over a drove of self-seeking foreigners with promise of commissions in the American Army. Major-generalships were promised in abundance and not a few were confirmed by the Congress, much to the bewilderment and resentment of Americans who now rightly or wrongly felt themselves qualified by their war experience for such posts.

However, Deane's misguided generosity also bore some magnificent fruit, such as Lafayette, De Kalb, Du Portail, Kosciusko, Pulaski, and Poniatowski. Lastly—on him we will linger—there was that mysterious, merry, sagacious tactician Baron von Steuben. As Christopher Ward remarked, von Steuben "was one of God's best gifts to America in its struggle for liberty." What George Washington was as creator of the soul of our Army, von Steuben was in building its body; framing a system of tactical discipline.

He was, true, a soldier of fortune. But he came to America offering his services as a volunteer, and asking only that his necessary expenses be defrayed. And he discovered, at Valley Forge, in 1778, what makes the American tick; a fact as true today as it was when von Steuben found it out, and the key opening the door to the military education of the American.

"The genius of this nation," wrote von Steuben to a friend (Baron von Gaudy), "is not in the least to be compared with that of the Prussians, Austrians or French. You say to your soldier, 'Do this,' and he doeth it; but I am obliged to say 'This is the reason why you ought to do that,' and then he does it."

We must examine von Steuben and his procedures, for here we have the making of the American soldier. This transplanted German adaptation of military discipline and tactical training became the keystone to an arch built upon the rugged foundations of a British military system and buttressed by a rough-hewn individualism typically American.

Von Steuben found the remnants of an Army that had no regular formation, where discipline did not exist, and where such rudiments of military training as were present differed between regiments and even between companies in a regiment. They were ragged and shoeless, these men, and frequently hungry.

Von Steuben felt he could do something to this mass, and Washington, recognizing his capability, agreed. First as acting inspector-general and later inspector-general, the pudgy, spluttering newcomer went to work.

A manual of regulations was written—in French, for von Steuben knew no English. Translated by his aide, Pierre Duponceau, and polished by John Laurens and Alexander Hamilton, the manual was to be our Army's bible for more than thirty years, as it turned out. The first copies at Valley Forge were laboriously scribed, piecemeal, in long-hand—there was no printing press in this man's Army—and von Steuben began his task.

A model company, selected from various outfits, was organized. This von Steuben drilled in person, beginning with one squad, and beginning at the beginning—the "position of the soldier"—as other officers and men looked on. He taught them how to handle their arms, he taught them the use of the bayonet, and he taught them how to march. The squad was split among the rest of the company and later the company among the rest of the Army in an ever-widening circle of instruction, with precision the keynote.

Von Steuben's earnestness and his pyrotechnic outbursts in German and French with occasional good English "God Damns!" brought a note of comedy at times, and Valley Forge was a place where a touch of comedy was sorely needed. But it brought good will, too, and it brought the swing and lilt of cadenced soldiery, of men confident in themselves and their officers. The pay-off was to come the following summer at Monmouth, where for the first time the Continental Army used the bayonet to meet and hold the elite of the British Army, including the Guards Brigade. There, under the personal leadership of Washington, William Alexander (called Lord Stirling) and von Steuben, the Continentals came wheeling into line under fire with parade precision. Never, until he had seen this, said Alexander Hamilton, had he "known or conceived the value of military discipline."

Wayne's later storming of Stony Point, accomplished without a shot fired by the assaulting light infantry whose fixed bayonets swept the slope, was further proof of von Steuben's training. Never again was the American Regular to blench from cold steel. The native fluidity of individual Indian-fighting had been married to the controlled discipline of tactical formations; the valor of ignorance replaced by the confidence that only training and leadership can induce.

It should be noted, too, that while von Steuben had made men march and fight in cadence and with precision, he had done nothing to impede or stultify the basic instinct of the American to "call his shots" in action. On the contrary, individual marksmanship training was stressed; a marksmanship which so frequently concentrated upon key individuals of the enemy array—officers and gunners.

Nor was there anything in von Steuben's doctrines resembling the caste-conscious brutality we have come to know as "Prussianism"—

the degradation of the individual soldier to the status of an automaton kicked about at the whim of a superior.

"A Captain," wrote von Steuben in his regulations, "cannot be too careful of the company the state has committed to his care. He must pay the greatest attention to the health of his men, their discipline, arms, accoutrements, ammunition, clothing and accessories.

"His first object should be to gain the love of his men by treating them with every possible kindness and humanity, inquiring into their complaints, and when well founded, seeing them redressed. He should know every man of his company by name and character." He should, von Steuben stressed, visit the sick and see that they were being well tended, for "the attachment that arises from this kind of attention to the sick and wounded is almost inconceivable; it will, moreover, be the means of preserving the lives of many valuable men."

The lieutenant, who was also "to gain the love of his men by his attention [to their] health and convenience," was enjoined to make frequent inspections of living quarters and of meals, as well as investigating complaints which, if well founded, should be redressed, but he was to "discourage them from complaining on every frivolous occasion."

As for the ensign—that is, the junior subaltern in the company—his especial charge was inspection of arms, accoutrements and clothing. He was, too, to ensure that the non-commissioned officers "support a proper authority, and at the same time do not ill treat the men through any pique or resentment."

This remarkable German soldier overlooked little in his manual or his personal instruction . . . from camp sanitation to the manual of arms, from bed-check to face-washing. He instituted the system of Saturday-morning inspections which has lasted in our Army to today. He drilled officers as he drilled men. And he made an Army.

Von Steuben's product took the brunt of battle in the vital Southern campaigns in the last phase of the war. One remarks this without reflecting upon the military qualities of Daniel Morgan, of Col. Andrew Pickens and his Virginia militia, or of Col. Francis "Swamp-Fox" Marion's guerrilla hit-and-run tactics. As a matter of fact, the Continentals held Col. Banastre Tarleton's attack at the Cowpens and permitted Morgan to accomplish his American Cannae—a double envelopment that crushed the British leader.

Greene, in those bitter days, losing every battle, yet won the campaign which set the stage for Gen. Cornwallis' surrender at Yorktown. Only the ordered discipline and steadiness of his Delaware, Maryland and Virginian Continental Line units held his battered army together.

It was a fast-marching, competent Continental Army, too, that Washington then brought down from the Hudson Valley to close in on Yorktown, beside its spick-and-span French allies. Virginia militia made up but a small part of the force into whose lines on October 19, 1781, Cornwallis' red-coats marched to lay down their arms, to the tune of "The World Turned Upside Down." The Revolution was won, then, to all intents and purposes. It had been won by force of arms, by an Army pitiably small in number but held together in spirit by an indomitable leader from Virginia and forged and sharpened into an instrument of precision by a Prussian soldier of fortune suddenly become American.

It must not be imagined that the Continental soldier's nature had been changed by this training and discipline. He was still an American, cantankerous when he felt he was being pushed about, vocal in his objections, and, in last resort, he could be mutinous, too.

At Morristown, in the bitter period of 1780-1781, when the fortunes of the Americans were at lowest ebb, several serious mutinies took place among the unpaid, starving troops. Pay—such as it was in the depreciated Continental currency—was five months in arrears, and the men were reduced to half-rations by the inability of the quartermasters to obtain provender.

The first outbreak took place on May 25, 1780, when two regiments of the Connecticut Line paraded under arms, with drums beating, and announced that they would either go home or hunt for their food at the bayonet's point. The tumult was finally controlled by their own officers.

Again at Morristown, this time on New Year's Day, 1781, more serious trouble broke out. The soldiers of the Pennsylvania Line had enlisted to serve "for three years *or* during the war." Their three years were up; they claimed their discharge. When refused it, riots broke out. An officer and several men were killed. This was Wayne's command, but even that strict disciplinarian could not regain control.

Six regiments formed in column and marched out of camp, determined to demand from Congress at Philadelphia all arrears of pay and discharge for every man who had served three years.

They marched in order, under command of their sergeants. Wayne followed them. They bivouacked at Princeton and waited answer to their demands, sent ahead to Philadelphia. The timorous Congress, after debating whether to leave town before the mutineers arrived, thought better of it. Joseph Reed, President of the Congress, with a committee, went to Princeton to argue with the men. It was agreed that arrears of pay should be made up as soon as practicable and that men who had enlisted under that dubious "either . . . or" clause should at once be discharged.

Nearly the entire group was discharged. But having won that victory a great proportion of the men at once re-enlisted, and the Pennsylvania Line was again a loyal corps. However, the news flew. Three New Jersey regiments at Pompton also started off for Trenton on January 20. This was too much for Washington, then at West Point. He sent Major General Robert Howe, a North Carolinian, south with a detachment of the New England Line; the mutineers were to be compelled to unconditional submission and "a few" of the ringleaders to be executed.

Howe, surrounding the mutineers' camp, selected one man from each of the regiments, tried them by court martial, hanged the two most involved and reprieved the third. The mutiny ended.

The Pennsylvania outbreak had a most interesting repercussion. Sir Henry Clinton, commanding the British forces, got word of the mutiny and sent two Tory emissaries to Princeton to offer the malcontents his protection, free pardons and payments of all their arrears.

The mutineers seized Clinton's emissaries and turned them over to Wayne. They were promptly tried, condemned as spies and hanged. When Wayne offered a reward in gold to the mutineers, their leader, Sergeant William Bouzar, declined, his men having agreed that they were not entitled to "other reward but the love of our country."

That, it seems, gives clear insight to the character of the Continental soldier. Malcontents might be many; they did have provocation. But the individual was innately a patriot, and "Benedict Arnolds" were few.

In 1782 General Washington, searching stimuli to raise the soldier's pride—little official pats on the back for work well done—instituted our first military decoration, the Badge for Military Merit. But the American people were worshipping the fetish of democratic simplicity. They were to frown even on the Order of the Cincinnati, the association later formed by ex-officers of the Continental Army. It was, people said, an indication of that bugbear of caste. So the Badge for Military Merit, bestowed for any singularly meritorious action or service, promptly fell into disuse. It was not to be reactivated —as the Purple Heart—for more than a century to come.

Congress, however, from the very beginning had never hesitated to bestow its thanks—usually accompanied by a sword or special medal—on commanders for singularly distinguished service. The crux of this matter of military decorations seemed to rest upon this Congressional jealousy of its prerogative as well as on the national dread of the perpetuation of professional military cliques.

The war was finally won; the United States became a nation. So, even before the formal signing of peace, before Washington took leave of his officers at Fraunces Tavern in New York, the American people began bit by bit to disband its Army—the first of many such dismemberments. The pattern and the argument was always to be the same—the instinctive revulsion to the professional soldier, a revulsion cast irrevocably in the mold established by Governor Winthrop's words in 1638:". . . how dangerous it might be to erect a standing authority of military men which might easily in time overthrow the civil power."

Agriculture, commerce and industry demanded the attention of all. The mewling infant nation, threshing about in its crib, was reaching westward. So the troops went home to their families and their affairs. It took some little time, this demobilization, but Congress finished its destructive work at last. On June 2, 1784, it brought forth the final legislation:

"And whereas, standing armies in time of peace are inconsistent with the principle of republican governments, dangerous to the liberties of a free people, and generally converted into destructive engines for establishing despotism;

"It is therefore resolved, That recommendations in lieu of requisitions shall be sent to the several States for raising the troops which may be immediately necessary for garrisoning the Western posts and guarding the magazines of the United States . . . [and] that the commanding officer be and he is hereby directed to discharge the troops now in the service of the United States, except twenty-five privates to guard the stores at Fort Pitt and fifty-five to guard the stores at West Point and other magazines, with a proportionable number of officers, no officers to remain in service above the rank of captain."

Thus was the old fear, the old hatred, of men and things military reiterated. The record of the War of the Revolution could count for nothing against such emotionalism. And yet, as that record showed, from the moment that Washington had accepted the behest of the Continental Congress to take command, he had remained true to the idea that he was merely an instrument of the Congress, and not an independent executive. And that, too, was another foundation stone of American military tradition.

For Washington had built an Army complete with the combat elements of horse, foot and guns; and the supporting elements of supply and general maintenance without which an Army cannot exist. There were the departments of the Adjutant General; the Inspector General (von Steuben, who had put the muscle and the coordination into the military body); the Judge Advocate General; the Quartermaster General; the Commissary General; a Medical Corps; a Pay Department; and, of course, the ubiquitous Corps of Engineers, in which for a time French influence prevailed.

All these things Washington had accomplished while leading his troops in war as their commander-in-chief—not in the role of dictator, but acting for the Congress. The task completed, he put away his sword.

The action of Congress deserves some consideration, for it was not just something decided on the spur of the moment, nor was it done without competent advice available to the lawmakers. In 1783, Alexander Hamilton, then heading a Congressional committee, had asked Washington's recommendations on the formulation of a military policy for the new nation.

George Washington's reply, contained in his *Sentiments on a Peace Establishment,* was available to Congress, its essence well worth the reading now:

"*First*: A regular and standing force . . . as . . . necessary to awe the Indians, protect our Trade, prevent [foreign] encroachments . . . guard us . . . from surprises; Also for security of our Magazines [arsenals and various types of supply depots] . . .

"*Secondly*: A well-organized Militia; upon a Plan that will pervade all the States, and introduce similarity in their Establishment, Manoeu᾽ vres, Exercises and Arms.

"*Thirdly*: Establishing Arsenals for all kinds of *Military Stores*.

"*Fourthly*: Academies, one or more for the Instruction of the Art Military . . .

"[Fifthly:] Also Manufactories of some kinds of Military Stores."

This is a blue-print for national defense the principles of which stand four-square today. Washington also pointed out that the development of the regular forces he recommended should include, as rapidly as the national budget would permit, "building and equipping a Navy, without which in case of War we could neither protect our Commerce nor yield that Assistance to each other, which, on such an extent of Seacoast, our mutual safety would require."

The Congress flouted his suggestions.

So now, at Congress' dictum, they were disbanded—the officers and men who had been hammered and forged into soldiers and into capable fighting units to win, under Washington's indefatigable spirit of leadership, the national freedom. With few exceptions, their names alone—on dusty muster rolls and records—perpetuate these units. But these exceptions we should note as a hall-mark of tradition and *esprit de corps* in proud units of today's National Guard. Some, whose origin reaches back to the seventeenth century, we have already mentioned in Chapter 1. Let us look now at the others.

The Light Horse of the City of Philadelphia, later the First Troop Philadelphia City Cavalry, organized November 17, 1774, escorted George Washington to Kingsbridge, New York, as he rode north to take command at Boston in 1775. It still exists today as the 28th Reconnaissance Company, 28th Infantry Division, Pennsylvania National Guard.

The 24th Regiment Connecticut Militia—organized, of all places, in the Wyoming Valley of northern Pennsylvania—is now the 109th Field Artillery Battalion of the Pennsylvania National Guard. It dates from 1775, when settlers from Connecticut, claiming their colony's territory extended "from sea to sea," clashed with Pennsylvanians in the area and organized a local militia company for defense.

The 175th Infantry, Maryland National Guard, better known as the old 5th Maryland, springs from the Baltimore Independent Cadets, formed December 3, 1774, and absorbed into William Small-

wood's Maryland Regiment, nucleus of the Maryland contingent of
the Continental Line.

The Groton Artillery, organized in 1775, exists today in the lineage of the 181st Infantry of the Massachusetts National Guard, late
the 6th Massachusetts. And the 150th Infantry of the West Virginia
National Guard, formerly the 2nd West Virginia, remains as physical
link with the Greenbrier County Militia of Virginia, which was constituted March 1, 1778, and furnished drafts to various Virginia
regiments of the Continental Line.

So goes the roll of honor in the militia record.

But as for the "twenty-five privates to guard the stores at Fort Pitt,
and fifty-five to guard the stores at West Point," theirs is another story
and a most important one, too. It is the story of the birth of the
Regular Army.

*   *   *   *   *

• • • •

3

WE HAD TO FIGHT THE INDIANS

There is a battalion of artillery in our Army today, whose unique characteristics set it apart from all others. It is the 1st Battalion, 5th Artillery; once Battery D, 5th F. A.

To all old-timers, this battalion is still "Battery D," as it was until the pentamic divisional reorganization of 1959 shuffled units up. So let's look at the one and only "Battery D."

In the first place, the guidon staff of this battery, which bears the swallow-tail flag fluttering proudly at the head of the column, is, as one can plainly see, literally plated with the little silver rings that mark participation in battle. To read the names on these rings, plus the battle streamers on the battalion colors, is to read a list of most of the important battles in every one of the wars in which the nation has engaged, beginning with Long Island.

Only when we come to World War II is there any real hiatus in the battle honors, the one reason being that, after all, this battery belongs to the First Infantry Division and even the famous "Big Red One" could not fight in both the Atlantic and Pacific theaters at the same time.

Look now at the guidon itself. It, too, is something out of the ordinary—the oblong red and white flag is bigger than the other guidons. It has to be, for on it, in addition to the prosaic regulation identification—"D" and "5" between crossed cannons—are more bold letters spelling the words, "Alexander Hamilton's Battery," and the motto, "Faithful and True."

Mark it well, this "Battery D," 5th United States Field Artillery Battalion, for it is the personification of the tradition of the Regular Army, the sacramental, so to speak, which represents the soul of our Army—its one living, full-time link with George Washington's Continental Army. This battery, which has borne a number of different names and numberings, came into being as Captain Alexander Hamilton's Company of New York Artillery on March 1, 1776, when Hamilton, then a hot-headed nineteen-year-old King's College (now Columbia University) student, recruited it in New York City, uniformed and equipped its members out of his own pocket, and led it into action.

Transferred into the Continental Line, this battery fought in every major engagement of the Revolutionary War—save Saratoga— from Long Island to Yorktown. When the struggle ended, the fortunes of war found it, as Captain John Doughty's Company of Colonel John Lamb's Continental Artillery Regiment, at West Point when the Act of June 2, 1784, was passed.

There was no particular reason why this organization should have been picked to become the entire United States Army, except that it was at West Point when the Congress officially rubbed the rest of the Continental Army off the books. There it was, and in that status it was to remain for nearly a year.

The Congress, of course, well knew that a new nation, its frontiers ablaze from Indian depredations and still threatened by British garrisons not yet evacuated, needed something more for its protection than eighty caretakers guarding military equipment salvaged from the Revolution. So the day after it had swept the last of the Continental Army—except Hamilton's old battery—into the discard, another act was passed resolving to raise from the militia, for a twelve-month enlistment period, a regiment of seven hundred men, "to consist of eight companies of infantry and two of artillery . . ." The Secretary of War was specifically directed to procure one hundred and sixty-five men each from Connecticut and New York, one hundred and ten from New Jersey and two hundred and sixty from Pennsylvania, "arming and equipping them in a soldier-like manner."

This hybrid outfit, to which from West Point came Hamilton's old battery as one of its two artillery companies—the other being a Pennsylvania militia levy—was entitled the First American Regiment. It was commanded by Lieutenant Colonel Josiah Harmar, of Pennsylvania, a veteran of the Revolutionary War.

History's moving finger has a way of establishing tradition, putting people, places and institutions on its records, no matter how impermanent their original status or design. So it is that the First American

Regiment, specifically established by Act of Congress of June 3, 1784, for a one-year period only and deliberately recruited from the militia lest any Federal force resembling a standing Army come into being, was never disbanded. It became the senior infantry regiment of the Regular Army, today's 3rd Infantry.

When Harmar's First American Regiment, slowly gathered at Fort Pitt and never recruited to full strength, moved westward in .1785, a pattern was established which was to last for slightly more than one hundred years in a particularly ugly portion of what was otherwise a magnificent tapestry—the pageant of a nation's growth. It was a pattern which was to be stained by blood and by tears, with embossings of treachery and broken promises on the part of both white man and red, but relieved by the thin blue thread with which the shuttle of Fate wove the destiny of the Army on our frontiers.

It was a simple pattern. First came a troop movement beyond the then established frontier of civilization. Then followed the building of a succession of army posts—little forts—scattered throughout an area selected by the instinct of an expanding nation. These were manned by detachments of Regulars charged with pacification of the region and with establishment of law and order—the preservation of peace in a no-man's land, where the Indian and the frontier desperado preyed on one another and on the peaceful settler.

The particular area in this initial case was the Ohio Valley and the territory from the Great Lakes to the Mississippi, which in 1787 was to be lumped into a provisional Northwest Territory under the governorship of Revolutionary War leader General Arthur St. Clair.

Into this region was pouring an ever-increasing flux of settlement, coming down the rivers in great flat-boats, or trekking across country from the Allegheny ridges then marking civilization's western fringe. Settlements were popping up; more were to bloom beside the scattered line of log forts which Harmer's men were to hew slowly and painfully out of the forests.

There is in this something reminiscent of feudal days in Europe when settlements rose in clusters about the protective walls of castle-keeps. For here, too, there was no other law and order. The Indians, their lands invaded by this always-increasing tide of settlement, were hostile. In the river settlements, such as Louisville, cutthroats and bullies gathered. Harmar's force, charged with the protection of the settler, was the only bulwark—but it was so small and so scattered that it was in many cases ineffective.

It lived a life of dreary isolation. Let us look at Fort Harmar, headquarters of the frontier force, built by the troops in 1785 on the west side of the mouth of the Muskingum emptying into the Ohio River. Across from the fort, on the flatlands, within two years was to grow Marietta, original settlement of the Ohio Company which was exploiting the region.

A pentagonal log fort, large enough to house a thousand men, Fort Harmar's bastions—corner towers—were two stories high with small cannon mounted to sweep the sides. The lower floors of the bastions, each divided into two rooms twenty feet square, were used as officers' quarters. The stockade walls connecting the bastions were the outside walls of barracks and storehouses, their roofs sloping inward to catch rainwater. The arsenal, surmounted by its flagstaff, sat in the center of the enclosure. High above one wall rose a watch-tower in which stood a sentinel night and day, scanning the surrounding country for approaching enemies.

The main gate opened on the river side, and a sally port on the land side looked out on a cleared stretch of ground used for drill and parades. With the coming of spring ground was turned both behind and close to the wall, and soldiers and their women—those few bold souls who had followed their men—started to become gardeners. Precious packets of seeds, jealously hoarded on the long trip out, were planted to blossom into flowers and vegetables. And Captain Doughty of the artillery, who still commanded Hamilton's battery, developed an orchard—his carefully tended trees within a few years producing what was to become the once well-known "Doughty Peach."

Fort Harmar was, relatively speaking, a large post. The others dotting the region were much smaller; but all followed the same general pattern of a bastioned stockade with living quarters inside. Open fireplaces furnished the only warmth in winter. In barracks the soldiers huddled together against the cold. Officers were in no better plight, of course.

The pay tables of this little Army are interesting, indeed. Colonel Harmar drew fifty dollars a month as lieutenant colonel commandant.

Majors drew forty-five dollars, captains thirty-five, lieutenants twenty-six, ensigns twenty. The surgeon was paid forty-five dollars and his mate thirty. Sergeants got six dollars, corporals five, and privates four (Congress was to cut this to three dollars within a year). The actual payments were usually made not more than twice a year and then in depreciated Continental currency. Rations, clothing and, in fact, all supplies were received on a contract basis, the Quartermaster's Department having been abolished with the rest of the old Army. Contractors skimped and cheated. Frequently the meat was bad; sometimes it never arrived. Usually the uniform cloth was sleazy, the garments badly cut.

A dreary routine governed this garrison life. In the daytime hours there was wood to be cut, water to be drawn, sinks to fill. There were drills, with von Steuben's regulations as the bible. So the troops turned out smartly in their blue coats faced with red, wearing cocked hats, clean white waistcoats and belts, with their faces shaven and hair powdered, and their weapons clean and polished. There was daily guard mounting and parade.

As for recreation, that was another thing. Men might hunt—and liked to, for it meant good food—provided that at the moment the Indians did not make it dangerous. But entertainment was nil, except what whisky could furnish and whisky was cheap—one dollar would buy a barrel. Books were a rarity, and indeed few of the men could read or write. Always there was guard duty—the sentinels in winter muffled in fur coats of their own skinning and cutting, in summer tormented by mosquitos. And there were occasional detachments guarding groups of settlers moving on, quelling sporadic Indian raids, or protecting supplies coming down-river.

This detached duty was no pleasant chore, either. Not only might there be fighting, but there were also accidents from natural causes aggravated by lack of medical attention. One such case was that of the unfortunate soldier who fell overboard on a winter ration trip. His legs and feet frozen, he was carried to Fort McIntosh where the only hospital quarters available was a room already occupied by three persons—Sergeant Major Duffy, his wife, and a corporal! In the next room were Colonel and Mrs. Harmar—the commander was always circulating about his area. Mrs. Harmar and Mrs. Duffy assisted in the nursing.

The high point of this story is not that the patient survived, but that here we have, perhaps, the first recorded appearance of the American Regular Army woman. And that was to become part of the pattern, too. "The Colonel's lady and Judy O'Grady, sisters under their skins," made their bow, prototypes of thousands of American women who were later to share the vicissitudes of the lives of their soldier men in war and in peace.

Social activities, it can be imagined, were few. Yet there were some festive occasions. One learns of a dinner given by the officials of the Ohio Company to the officers and ladies of Fort Harmar on July 4, 1788. The booming of guns from the fort opened the occasion in salute to Independence Day. Fish and game in profusion were washed down by grog and wine, with toast following toast until midnight, when a rousing dedication to "The Amiable Partners of our Lives" broke up what had been evidently a very wet party in more ways than one. Two drenching rainstorms had doused the area. With one last maudlin toast to "All Mankind," the party broke up. One may believe that the whisky flowed in barracks also that day; one doesn't know.

The officers of this embryo army were mostly veterans of Continental service—men who found it hard, for one cause or another, to adjust themselves to a civilian life. The men varied from the farmer boys of the militia originally enlisted—most of whom wanted nothing better than to return home when Congress in 1786 approved a three-year enlistment—to the dregs of the towns back home. Ne'er-do-wells, vagabonds, and tavern hangers-on seemed to predominate, though there was also a proportion, as always, of adventurers. These last, their eyes open to their own betterment, were frequently ready to desert to join some civilian project in the wilderness.

In fact, desertions continued to be one of the principal difficulties of the Army. The timorous, the disgusted, and the vagabonds, frequently slipped away. Bounties for their return were offered, and one hundred lashes was the official punishment were the culprits caught. But the ranks were never full.

However, the men who stayed were soldiers—hard, disciplined soldiers, as befitted the survival of the fittest. They were to have the opportunity to show their mettle in 1790 when the Indian outrages in the Ohio country became insupportable.

WE HAD TO FIGHT THE INDIANS

A page in national history had been turned—we had a Constitution and a Federal government. George Washington, idol of the people, was President. And dependable Henry Knox, his wartime chief of artillery who had been struggling along as Secretary of War, had been reappointed to a task now more clearly defined.

The War Department, as re-established, was responsible for military commissions, land grants, and naval and Indian affairs, in addition to army affairs. An oath of allegiance was now required from all "in the service of the United States," and the officers served under new commissions, by Presidential appointment. The kind, quality and amounts of rations and of clothing had become stabilized—at least on paper. The skeleton of a permanent organization was being articulated.

Furthermore, the President's position with regard to the armed forces had been defined by the Congress. He was "the Commander-in-Chief of the Army and Navy of the United States, and of the militia of the several states when called into the actual service of the United States."

According to Knox's report of August 10, 1789, presented by President Washington to the new Congress, the authorized strength of the United States Army consisted, on paper, of the one regiment of eight companies—now titled the Regiment of Infantry—totalling five hundred and sixty men. Besides Harmer, the lieutenant colonel commandant, there were two majors, seven captains, seven lieutenants, eight ensigns, one surgeon and four surgeon's mates. The artillery had grown to a battalion of four companies, two hundred and eighty strong; its officers were a major, four captains, eight lieutenants and one surgeon's mate. This was the entire United States Army, eight hundred and forty officers and men, as Congress had dictated.

Actually, Knox reported, it wasn't even up to its paper strength, there being one hundred and sixty-eight "wanting to complete the establishment." There were, he pointed out, seventy-six men on duty at West Point and Springfield, Mass., which left a net of five hundred and ninety-six "at various posts northwest of the Ohio." They were to be badly needed within a year.

The situation in the Northwest was indeed serious. Not only did the British still maintain garrisons and forts well within our national boundaries, despite the agreement to withdraw made when peace was concluded in 1783, but there was on foot a calculated British effort to remain. In collusion with the Indians, who were being coaxed to form a strong confederacy against American settlers, a sort of no-man's land was to be established as protection for British interests, particularly the fur trade. The Indians, naturally, their lands and hunting grounds menaced by the flow of immigration, needed little incentive to raise trouble. Something had to be done to counter this program.

An expedition against the Indian towns along the Maumee River was undertaken. Governor St. Clair after much difficulty gathered at Fort Washington, on the site of Cincinnati, three so-called battalions of militia from Kentucky, another from Pennsylvania, and a volunteer troop of light horse. The militiamen were short of training, arms and camp equipment; their pot-valiant officers were ignorant. General Harmar, placed in command of this force by the War Department, added what he could of the First Regiment—two small battalions and three guns, some three hundred and twenty men in all.

Burdened by a huge pack train hired from the settlements, and a herd of beef cattle, Harmar moved his motley array forward in a square of sorts. It was no way to march through the wilderness, against Indians, but it was the only way in which he could control his command. Several abortive raids were attempted by detachments; in each case they were ambushed by the Indians. The militia elements of these detachments deserted en masse, while the small Regular elements accompanying them stood and were slaughtered.

After a month of futile fumbling of this sort Harmar returned to Fort Washington with the loss of one third of his pack train and nearly a quarter of his Regulars. The first expedition of the new Army had been a complete failure.

Worse was yet to come. On March 3, 1791, the Congress authorized another regiment of infantry—the 2nd, which through subsequent Alice-in-Wonderland juggling of War Department paper-work has come down to us today as the 1st Infantry. The regiment was slated to go down to disastrous defeat and massacre in its initial campaign, exactly eight months after its organization.

The Miami Indians, emboldened by their success over Harmer, were ravaging the frontier, supported by British connivance and British supply from the garrisons still illegally established in United States territory. The white man, so announced the Indians, must be driven from the country. So, during the summer of 1791, Governor

St. Clair, commissioned Major General, began gathering forces for an intensive campaign against the Indians. Fort Washington was the mobilization point. The two Regular regiments, plus their artillery, were shifted from their garrisons. Levies of volunteers—the usual short-term militia enlistments with a bounty to boot—were called from Maryland, Massachusetts and Pennsylvania. Kentucky furnished a militia force.

A makeshift arsenal was set up to repair old gear and attempt to make up the appalling shortages in arms and equipment of the militiamen drifting in. Not until early autumn did the little force—some seven hundred regulars and fifteen hundred volunteers and militia—move out, searching for the Indian village.

By November 4, St. Clair—a very sick old man now, who had to be carried in a litter most of the time—had reached a spot on the upper Wabash some fifty miles from today's Fort Wayne, Ind. A part of the militia had already deserted in a body and were threatening to loot St. Clair's unwieldy baggage train. So one regiment of Regulars—the old First—was sent back to guard the train. The remainder of the army made camp, amid snow, ice and rain; the Kentucky militia on the north bank of the river, the rest on the south.

Here the Indians attacked. The Kentucky militia and the other levies fled at once through the ranks of the Regulars, throwing everything into confusion. For a while the Regulars stood, the artillerymen serving their guns until overrun by the savages. Then the entire force collapsed in blind rout, leaving more than nine hundred dead and wounded on the field. The Indians, among them Simon Girty, the bloodthirsty white renegade, butchered all who came into their hands in indescribable slaughter.

Among the lost were nearly all the thirty women accompanying the Regulars. They were there legitimately, these women, and they fought beside their men. Three of them survived. "Red-headed Nance" is the only one whose name has come down to us; a big-boned Amazon, she was now berserk for she had seen her child butchered. A wounded lieutenant, a civilian packer, a corporal and Nance—an odd quartet—fought their way back to Fort Jefferson, now Greenville, O., where the First Regiment, up from its task of pack-train guard but too late to join battle, offered refuge.

At the time of St. Clair's defeat four women were allowed to each Regular company as washerwomen, but the militia took with them as

many as they pleased. So, along with the wives—and mistresses, too—
of officers and men, it is quite probable that as many as two hundred
were among the unfortunate group of camp followers massacred along
the Wabash.

Perhaps it would be well at this time to examine the status of
women in the United States Army in its early days. Women, of course,
have always followed men to war. Trollops, baggages and ladies fair—
honest married women and light o' loves both—have played the role
of camp followers since time immemorial. It was no different during
the Revolution. Martha Washington accompanied her husband at
Valley Forge; Lieut. Colonel George Baylor's 3rd Continental
Dragoons was known as Lady Washington's Horse. Molly Pitcher—
her real name was Hays—beside her sergeant husband at the Battle
of Monmouth, handled rammer and shot to serve his cannon when
he was wounded. "Captain Molly" Corbin at Fort Washington, earlier,
also served her disabled husband's gun until she was severely wounded.
"Captain Molly," who was granted by Congress a soldier's pay and
allowances for life as reward, lies today in an honored grave at
West Point.

We have already noted Mrs. Harmar and Sergeant Major Duffy's
wife at Fort McIntosh. One difference there was between the officer's
and the soldier's wife—the former was her husband's charge; the
latter, if she went to war, was probably on the rolls of the establishment as one of the washerwomen allotted to each outfit, and drew
rations but no pay. By 1798, the regulations permitted thirty women
to a regiment of infantry, twenty-two to a light dragoon regiment, and
fifty-nine to a regiment of artillery. In 1813, the regulations prescribed
one ration in kind for "women (in the proportion of one to every
seventeen men) . . . also to matrons and nurses allowed in hospitals."

"The enlisted women," remarks James Ripley Jacobs, historian of
the early Army, "recognized that life was hard and they made what
they could of it, gratefully accepting the government's rations . . .
and whatever else the soldiers might spare them. In return they washed
for the living, nursed the sick and bound up the wounded . . . They
suffered stoically and when necessary they would, and did, fight
bravely . . . when one of their men went down, they seized a musket
and levelled it . . . well knowing that, if captured, roasting or cruci-
fixion might be their fate."

Slowly the survivors of St. Clair's disaster retreated all the way to Fort Washington, the First Regiment covering the move. The disaster was shocking in its scope. Every officer in the Regulars had either been killed or wounded. The guns, the stores, the pack train itself, all were gone. And when they reached the fort the militia survivors, all danger past, became valiant again in their own interest, clamoring and rioting for their pay and discharge.

President Washington, aroused by such repetition of Braddock's blunders in the Indian country, called St. Clair "worse than a murderer," but retained his sense of justice and fairness. Like Harmar before him, St. Clair underwent a Congressional investigation. Both commanders were cleared, responsibility being placed on the "lack of discipline and experience of the troops." Thus in effect a Congressional committee rightly accused itself of dereliction of duty in its responsibility for raising and maintaining an Army.

One thing was sure: a larger Army was needed. So Congress took action, although it still disregarded Washington's sage recommendations. First, following the ratification of the Bill of Rights, with its Article II stipulating that "a well regulated Militia, being necessary to the security of a free State, the right of the people to keep and bear Arms shall not be infringed," a Militia Act was passed, providing for the enrollment of every free white citizen of the United States between the ages of eighteen and forty-five. But this would be no Federal force; enrollment and organization was separate in each State. And no machinery for a national organization was provided. This act, by the way, was to remain upon the statute books for a century to come.

Then Congress evolved a legionary system for the Regulars. The Legion, in which the entire Regular Army—slightly larger now—was embodied, comprised four sub-legions, each of which had two battalions of infantry, one battalion of rifles, a troop of dragoons and a company of artillery. It was all very pretty and precise on paper, this forerunner of the task-force of today. To organize and lead the Legion, General Wayne—"Mad Anthony" of Revolutionary War days—was chosen. In June, 1792, his mobilization began at Pittsburgh, later moving on to Cincinnati, a fit birth-place for a reborn Army of the people.

It was about time. The British efforts to arouse the Indians were succeeding all too well. Lord Dorchester, Governor General of Canada, told the delegates of the Six Nations on February 10, 1794, that the British might be at war with the United States before the year ended, and in that case the Indians would probably regain the lands they had lost. As a result of this prodding the Indians took the war path, well provided by the British with arms.

Wayne was a disciplinarian, a tactician and a strategist. He refused to move his ill-trained, undisciplined mob of recruits into the wilderness. Instead he set up a grinding training system, integrating the remnants of the old Regulars in the mass. He drilled them and marched them and hardened them; he taught them the use of the bayonet. It was von Steuben all over again. And he raged—with effect—at the shyster contractors who delayed and dissembled and tried to short-change the Army in food, clothing and equipment.

He was plagued with dissension among his officers, a good deal of it caused by the reshuffling of the troops with consequent wrangles over rank. And a certain slick, ambitious officer named James Wilkinson—we'll hear more of him later—was fomenting discontent. Wayne was getting old; he was crotchety, and gouty, too, said his detractors. Perhaps he was. But he took out his ill-temper only on the unfit and the unregenerate, and he made an Army—a striking-force of disciplined men. It took him nearly a year to do it, but when he at last moved into the wilderness his Legion was a legion—comparable to the legions of Rome. It could march and it could fight. Its camps each night were entrenched and fortified; no Indian raid could surprise or disturb them. This Army was built for the objective—to fight Indians in the wilderness.

Wayne marched irresistibly back over St. Clair's ill-fated route, establishing posts and driving the Indians before him. On August 20, 1794, at Fallen Timbers near the present Toledo—a slashing of trees uprooted by some long-past tornado to form an almost impenetrable thicket—the climax came. The Indians, egged on by British influence, were there in force. Wayne's infantry fired one blasting volley into the underbrush, then charged, forcing the enemy from his refuge with its bayonets. At the same time the dragoons and Kentucky mounted riflemen came circling around both flanks. The remnants of the Indians were driven back and their villages put to flame under the eyes of a British garrison in a post impudently maintained on our soil.

For some time to come the Indians lost interest in Britain's plan to organize them into a buffer nation within United States boundaries. The Northwest Territory was safe—for a while.

✳   ✳   ✳   ✳   ✳

• • • •

4

THE BRITISH COME AGAIN

The United States, craving above all else peace which would permit prosperity, and yet not quite knowing what to do about it, was in ferment from 1794 until the outbreak of the War of 1812. The South's role of cotton production had been set when Eli Whitney invented the cotton gin in 1793. In 1798, an Army contract for ten thousand muskets set the same inventor's brain to production of machinery for interchangeable gun-lock parts—the first element of a mass production which was to launch New England and later the entire North on its colossal industrial expansion.

Industrial prosperity, however, was still in the future. The more highly populated Eastern seaboard was predominantly poverty-ridden. But across the Alleghenies a rosy dream of abundant land and freedom from taxation beckoned. So westward poured a tide of immigration in an irresistible torrent—a people's migration instinctively dictated by geography and by social economics.

These growing pains of an empire, the future of which as yet very few Americans could realize, permitted neither time nor money to be expended upon the Army, real as was the need.

In the Northwest these waves of migration, created by the trappers and hunters of the rapidly-growing fur trade, lapped and clashed with England's rival domain across a still-moot boundary line. In the Southwest, commercial interests waxing large in the Ohio Valley were debouching into the Mississippi. The Father of Waters was becoming a great artery of American trade—choked by the Spanish bottleneck of New Orleans. The Spaniards, their garrisons extending northward as far as Natchez and across to the Atlantic along the northern edge of Florida, constituted another menace to the new nation.

This shifting of scenes on the national stage brought with it a change in national character. The new West was coalescing into a social as well as a geographical entity rivalling those two already existing, though mutually quite different, social and geographical entities—the North and South. The trio bucked and galled one another in a Constitutional harness as yet new and poorly fitted. A new breed was in the making, putting more than ever before a premium upon individuality. At times this became a false value, in that through ignorance it flouted cohesion and discipline.

The Army, an uneasy cork in this cross-chop of internal unrest and international tensions, bobbed about—its meager personnel scattered in thin patches from the Ohio Valley to the wildernesses of Tennessee and Georgia. It had been shuffled and reshuffled. General Washington was brought back in 1798 as commanding general for a while when it seemed that full-scale war with France was imminent. On his death Alexander Hamilton succeeded him. And Congress puttered about, changing the Army's strength and formations.

The Legion concept was discarded shortly after the Battle of Fallen Timbers. In 1802, the Army was reduced to two regiments of infantry, a regiment of artillery and the newly-formed corps of engineers (actually only a handful of officers and men). In 1806, Congress authorized the addition of five regiments of infantry, one regiment of riflemen, a regiment of light artillery (its horses were sold a few years later as a measure of economy!) and a regiment of light dragoons, soon to be distributed as foot soldiers among the infantry garrisons. These new formations, however, were never recruited to full strength. It is interesting to note, too, that the officers needed for the increased strength did not come by promotion from the existing Regulars, but were nearly all appointees from civil life.

Some effort had been made toward putting this little force upon a self-sustaining basis. Staff departments were once again provided— Judge Advocate, Quartermaster, Paymaster, Medical and Ordnance. But, from 1806 to 1811, the Army stagnated in its garrisons under the command of General James Wilkinson. Along the Atlantic coast a great number of fortifications were built; twenty-four forts and thirty-two batteries and works mounting 750 guns. However, to man this Chinese Wall would have taken at least twelve thousand men and, by 1811, the entire Army numbered less than three thousand officers and men.

During this period the number of volunteer militia units chartered as independent companies in our larger cities was on the increase. One of the most colorful of these was the Richmond Light Infantry Blues, formed in 1789, and later incorporated in our famous old 1st Virginia, the 176th Infantry of the National Guard. But nothing had been done toward formalizing and training the militia in general. So, in fact, the nation had practically no troops available—Regular or militia—for any major mobilization.

In 1802, our little Regular officer corps was still a haphazardly gathered aggregation of individuals, many of them lacking in broad education and all racked by dissension, political jealousy and uncertainty as to their future. Nor was there much temptation for men of such diverse type, immured in the solitude of frontier garrisons, to mellow or improve themselves.

Here was something that had been worrying America's few military minds since George Washington first assumed command of the Continental Army. Thoughtful men among the Founding Fathers had long realized that the attributes essential to a good officer went far beyond those sufficient for a counting-house clerk, a merchant, or a trader. Henry Knox had said as much in 1776; John Adams, too. Alexander Hamilton had stirred the matter up in 1783, by requesting an opinion from General Washington on the military establishment necessary for the new nation. In response, as we know, Washington's now famous *Sentiments on a Peace Establishment* contained recommendation for one or more military academies, with specific provision "for instructing a certain number of young gentlemen in the theory of the art of war."

A feeble first step was taken by the Congress in this direction in 1794, upon the organization of the Corps of Artillerists and Engineers, to whom a maximum of thirty-two cadets was authorized, and a school of application of sorts was established at West Point.

Toward the end of 1799, Alexander Hamilton presented to the Secretary of War a plan for an academy embodying the basic theory of West Point today, in that it was to build officers for all arms of the services and would embrace the sciences. He sent a copy of his plan to General Washington and the latter, in the last letter he ever penned, on December 12, 1799, wrote that the establishment of such an institution "has ever been considered by me as an object of primary importance to this country." Washington concluded with the hope that Hamilton's reasoning "will prevail upon the Legislature to place it upon a permanent and respectable footing."

Thomas Jefferson, for once in agreement with Hamilton, took the matter up as soon as he was inaugurated. At his insistence Congress a year later passed the Act of March 16, 1802, providing for a Corps of Engineers, which "when so organized, shall be stationed at West Point, in the State of New York, and shall constitute a Military Academy."

It is remarkable that Jefferson, an opponent of a standing army, should have been responsible for establishing the Military Academy which was to play such vital part not only in the fabric of the United States Army but also—as we shall see later—in the building of the nation itself. Not only did he do so, however, but he was also responsible for the creation of a new role for the Army—a pertinent role in this national configuration. For in 1803, he started putting into effect his long-cherished plan for exploring the vast unknown region west of the Mississippi.

In May, 1804, Captain Merriwether Lewis and Lieutenant William Clark—brother to George Rogers Clark—moved westward from St. Louis, heading some thirty non-commissioned officers and privates and a dozen guides and interpreters on an epoch-making expedition. With Jefferson's warmest sanction and assistance they had been training all the previous winter for their trip. Two years were to elapse before their return, with the loss of only two of their original party, during which time they pushed through country never before visited by white men, crossing and recrossing the Rockies to the Pacific coast on an eight-thousand-mile survey.

Jeffersonian diplomacy had—with the able assistance of James Monroe and Robert Livingston—doubled the land area of the United States by the Louisiana Purchase, and obtained the Mississippi. Jeffersonian acumen hit upon the Army as the most logical agency to explore the land and pave the way for further national expansion.

In 1805, James Wilkinson, in his dual role of commander-in-chief of the Army and also Governor of newly acquired Louisiana, started Lieutenant Zebulon Pike to make further explorations up the Mississippi and later in the Southwest. On these trips Pike discovered the peak now bearing his name. Wilkinson's motives may not have been as altruistic as Jefferson's, for this self-seeking soldier was acting as a spy for Spain, and at the same time was involved in Aaron Burr's notorious, and still mysterious, Mississippi Valley "conspiracy." Burr was indicted and tried for treason in 1807. The charges didn't hold, but Burr later fled the country. Wilkinson, who wriggled out of the affair by testifying against his former associate, won the dubious cachet of "Tarnished Warrior," which his future career was to support.

However, Pike's explorations, supplementing those of Lewis and Clark, were the first steps in what was to be for a century or more a most important part of the Army's chores—the exploration of our Western empire.

Meanwhile our relations with Great Britain had been gradually worsening. That nation's high-handed actions on the high seas, as well as inside our Northwestern frontier, enraged the United States. Jefferson's Embargo Act, freezing all American shipping in home ports—an economic measure to restain both warring Britain and France—alienated New England and the shipping interests because of its immediate adverse reaction upon our own trade. Thus our country—divided in opinion against both the "traditional enemy," England, and our own administration—teetered in political turmoil.

In 1811, the uneasy Northwest frontier flamed. Tecumseh, great chief of the Shawnees, supported by the British governor of Canada and the British fur traders, succeeded in organizing the long-sought-for Indian confederacy to halt American westward settlement. General William Henry Harrison, governor of the Indiana Territory, mobilized his militia to destroy the Indian villages clustered in "Prophet's Town" on the Wabash, at the mouth of Tippecanoe Creek.

The Federal government furnished him the 4th Infantry (since become the 5th), and they came marching into Vincennes some three hundred strong, their uniforms and discipline in sharp contrast to the nondescript militia.

Here Harrison trained the entire force assiduously for nearly a month before moving. On the site of Terre Haute he constructed an advanced base—Fort Harrison. But serious trouble broke out. The militia resented the discipline and hard work imposed upon them by the Regular regimental commander, Colonel John P. Boyd, a Massachusetts soldier of fortune who had been commissioned in our Army, in 1808, after a dozen years' service with the Moguls of India.

Harrison proved his qualities of leadership, although his previous military service had been but a few years as a captain shortly after the Revolution. Gauging, like von Steuben, the character of his mixed command, he assembled the entire force and harangued them. He explained the task and the trouble facing them. The weaklings, he told them, should go home to claim from their loved ones the rewards of desertion; the strong men must carry on. The resulting roars of applause were further stimulated by issuance of an extra ration of whisky. There was no further trouble.

Attacked by the Indians as they lay under arms in a well-organized bivouac on November 7, 1811, Harrison's troops threw back the enemy, then counter-attacked and routed them. Thus was the Indian confederacy broken at Tippecanoe, and the foundation laid, as well, for a future Presidential campaign slogan—"Tippecanoe and Tyler, too!"

We drifted then to the very brink of war with Britain, while the "war-hawks" of the administration and the Congress—there were many of them, fat in the valor of ignorance—dreamed of immediate invasion and conquest of Canada once the conflict started. All the nation had available to carry out such a fantastic plan was a little Regular Army already scattered over the land. Of the seven infantry regiments, three were in the Northwest, one was in Kentucky and the three remaining in the South and Southwest. The artillery was dotted in little packets in the fortifications along the coast. None of the frontier garrisons could be depleted for any offensive move, lest immediate disaster follow at the hands of hostile Indians. Some slight idea of this situation did finally penetrate the mind of Congress in January, 1812, as it waved its paper wand to authorize ten more regiments of infantry, three of artillery and one of light dragoons.

Recruiting this force was another matter; the men wouldn't come in. So the existing five-year enlistment period was cut down to thirteen months; a sixteen-dollar bounty was offered the new recruit, together with a bonus of three months' pay and one hundred and sixty acres of land on discharge. Still the men didn't come in. So Congress authorized the President to call up one hundred thousand militia. Actually President Monroe called for eighty thousand. As a result the states, to fill their respective quotas, also offered bonus and bounty and once again the Federal government and the several states were bidding for bodies against one another. We were right back where we had started in 1775.

The President's call for militia received scant recognition from some of the states. Massachusetts and Connecticut in particular refused to order any men out, their governors denying the right of the President to issue such call or to assign Regular Army officers to command militia units when in Federal service.

War against Britain was declared June 18, 1812. On August 16, came the first of several disasters characterizing our hot-headed attempts to invade Canada. General William Hull, a Regular, with a well-armed and equipped force, surrendered—abjectly and without a fight—at Detroit to a much weaker Canadian force.

Dry rot and inefficiency characterized the high command. General Henry Dearborn, first directing Northern operations, was old and infirm. Wilkinson, who succeeded him, gained the reputation of being a man "who never won a battle or lost a court of inquiry." The one oldster of determination and leadership qualifications—Harrison—was relegated to a defensive role in the Northwest. In addition, John Armstrong, the Secretary of War, complicated matters by meddling in person, moving himself and the War Department to the front. Between them all they managed to fritter away any chance for American success.

The small Regular Army, the successor to the Continental Line, had by this time existed for twenty-five years, during which time a species of dedication, or at least a tradition of service, was coming into being. Then, too, the still-few graduates of the new Military Academy had begun to take their places in the professional ranks; a mere handful, these, but the beginnings of what would become a potent leaven. The younger men of the Regulars, whatever their military origin, began to forge ahead even in this atmosphere of inefficiency. Among them a new star began to twinkle, that of a young lieutenant colonel of artillery, Winfield Scott, who, in 1807, had come direct from civil life—commissioned by virtue of having raised a volunteer company.

The additional officer corps was also a mixed bag, with state-appointed officers in the new levies, and Congressional appointees also, rushed into uniform as political plums. Most of these men lacked previous military experience of any sort, but fortunately for the nation a few natural leaders bobbed up—among them such men as Jacob Brown in the North and fiery Andrew Jackson in the South.

It is not a pretty page in our Army's history, this War of 1812, but it furnishes an object-lesson in the value of military preparedness and leadership. Its effect on the Army itself and on the Army's future is of even more importance to us, for from this conflict stemmed in great measure the long-continued rift between the Regular and the militiaman.

In the past the Regular had noted on several occasions, and sometimes had paid for in his own flesh and blood, the shortcomings of the raw levies of citizen-soldiers and political commanders foisted on him by the Congress in emergency. In this war he saw the militia system fall flat on its face, bringing not only disaster to our arms but also disgrace to the nation.

Shocking example was that of Queenstown Heights, on October 13, 1812. New York's aged General Stephen Van Rensselear, with some thirty-five hundred militia, stiffened by four hundred and fifty Regulars, assaulted across the Niagara River into Canadian territory. About half the Regulars—all who could be carried in the few boats available —gained the Canadian bank and gallantly took the heights.

But when the Canadians rallied and counter-attacked in overwhelming strength, Van Rensselaer's part-time warriors on the American side—far outnumbering all the Canadian command could put in the field—became acutely conscious of their constitutional rights. They had, they asserted, been enlisted simply to repel invasions and not to fight outside their own country. Orders, cajoling, threats, moved them not at all, these militiamen who until that moment had been vociferous in their demands to be led to battle. So they stood, interested spectators, watching their comrades across the river melt away, either killed or captured. Among the latter was young Winfield Scott.

All along the border, defeat and disaster followed each American attempt to invade. By year's end the militia had either been discharged —their short enlistments terminated—or had taken French leave, all taste for war departed. So the few remaining Regulars went into winter quarters while Congress set about getting more men. The enlistment bounty was increased, and the recruiting officer now received four dollars for each man he delivered. Incidentally, "healthy, active boys," between fourteen and eighteen, could be enlisted "for musicians."

Minors, however, had to have consent of parent, guardian or "master."

The goal was twenty additional regiments, enlisted for one year, to bring the Army's paper strength to forty-four regiments of infantry, four regiments of artillery, two of dragoons and one of rifles, in addition to the corps of engineers and the staff. But of this fictional strength of fifty-eight thousand not more than ten thousand were ever recruited.

Among the minor vexations of Army life at this time the ogre of "paper work" first raised its horrendous head. The regulations of 1813 specified stationery allowances for officers, ranging from twenty-four quires a year to a Major General or a district commander, to two quires for "every other commissioned officer." A proportion of fifty quills, as many wafers and one "paper of ink powder" was allowed for each six quires of paper issued.

The victories of our Navy on the Lakes, in 1813, led to the only bright spots in Army activities of that year. Commodore Isaac Chauncey's flotilla on Lake Ontario ferried over the force that took York (now Toronto) on April 27 and moved our troops in the next offensive—against Fort George on the Canadian side of the Niagara River mouth. A real amphibious operation this was, planned and executed by two rising figures—the Navy's Oliver Hazard Perry and the Army's Winfield Scott, exchanged now from captivity. Both operations were nullified by later mistakes of other men.

But on Lake Erie, Perry's victory of September 10, 1813, brought about one of our two real Army victories in the North. "Old Tippecanoe" Harrison, who had been on the defensive against the British and Indians along the Maumee—and meanwhile assiduously training his Ohio and Kentucky militia—seized the initiative to invade Canada on receiving Perry's famous message, "We have met the enemy and they are ours." His cavalry pushed north overland, the rest of his army was transported on Perry's ships. On the Thames River in Ontario, Harrison caught up with the British and their Indian allies who had retreated and evacuated Detroit. The Battle of the Thames, October 5, was a decisive victory. Here Tecumseh, the great Indian chief, now a brigadier in the British Army, was killed.

Indian participation in the war was ended by this bright action, but once again the War Department's bungling nullified long-range results. Harrison's militia was ordered discharged, and the Regulars sent back to Sacket's Harbor and winter quarters. Harrison, in disgust, resigned.

Dark indeed was this winter of 1813-1814 for the United States Army. Wilkinson's futile invasion down the St. Lawrence ended in defeat at Chrysler's Farm, and General Wade Hampton bumbled fruitlessly about Lake Champlain and the Richelieu Valley.

In Vermont, Governor Martin Chittenden, a bitter opponent of the war, did his best to help the enemy. On November 10, 1813, he issued a proclamation to a brigade of Vermont militia in Federal service, then fighting on the front, commanding it to return home! All honor to this Green Mountain State outfit, who repudiated their Governor's craven gesture by retorting that . . . "An invitation or order to desert the standards of our country will never be obeyed by us, although it proceeds from the captain-general and governor of Vermont."

But in the Buffalo area where the Regulars were in winter quarters a leader was emerging. Jacob Brown, New York militiaman, now commissioned in the Regular Army—and soon to relieve the inefficient Wilkinson—was learning war. Training was needed, he had found out, and he had the man to carry out the job—twenty-seven-year-old Winfield Scott, now brigadier general.

In the spirit of von Steuben, Scott leaped into the task, beginning his instruction with the officers, including those of field grade. He found one copy of French regulations issued by Napoleon, the sole textbook in the Army. From it he taught the sweating officers to march and wheel, to handle their muskets and to use the bayonet. He instructed in military deportment and courtesy, in the basic rules of field hygiene and camp police. Then the officers, their schooling completed, instructed their men. It was a three-month grind of ten hours a day, and when it was over Scott had what in his own words he termed "a handsome little army . . . the 9th, 11th, 21st and 25th regiments and two companies of artillery . . . If, of such materials I do not make the best army now in service, by the 1st of June, I will agree to be dismissed the service."

The pay-off came that summer. Brown, with two well-trained brigades of Regulars and six hundred Indians—four thousand, one hundred men in all—invaded Canada across the Niagara and started north. At Chippewa, July 5, 1814, Brown met the enemy—four thousand strong, mostly British regulars. Major General Phineas Riall. hurrying to drive back the impudent invaders, saw before him clumps of soldiery clad in gray instead of the usual American Army blue; more militia nonsense, doubtless, more popinjays in gaudy trapping to make sport for their betters.

But the gray clumps topped by glinting bayonets were deploying now into serried ranks as precise as those of Riall's red-coat regulars. Furthermore, they kept coming under fire.

"These, by gad!" said the startled Riall, "these are regulars!"

They were. It was Scott's brigade, and it wasn't going to be stopped. The British broke, crumbling into rout across Chippewa Creek.

"The battle of Chippewa," wrote Henry Adams, "was the only occasion during the war when equal bodies of regular troops met face to face, in extended lines on an open plain in broad daylight, without advantage of position; and never again after that combat was an army of American regulars beaten by British troops."

A tradition was born at Chippewa, a tradition living today in the dress uniforms of the West Point cadets, copied from those worn by Scott's brigade. For Scott's efforts to replace the tattered clothing of his men had resulted in production of gray uniforms—the only shade of cloth in stock in Philadelphia. In 1815, the War Department ordered that the Military Academy uniform should thereafter be of the gray worn at Chippewa.

Three weeks later Riall and Brown met again, at Lundy's Lane, proportionately one of the bloodiest battles of history. Scott's brigade again took the brunt of a struggle in which both sides, from late afternoon until far into the night of July 25, fought themselves to a standstill. Brown and Scott were both severely wounded. Riall was captured.

The storming of the British main battery at Lundy's Lane by the 21st Infantry (one of several regiments to be absorbed later by the present 5th), was occasion for another addition to the Regular Army's mosaic of tradition. Brown, pointing to the objective as the regiment moved out from reserve, asked Colonel James Miller if his regiment could take it. His reply is today emblazoned as the proud motto of the 5th Infantry, "I'll try, sir!"

Leadership and training proved their worth again at Fort Erie, opposite Buffalo, where Brown's army had retired because it was not strong enough to continue invasion. Fresh British troops besieged it.

The Americans stormed out in a successful three-pronged assault, the leaders each dying at the head of their respective columns—two of them West Pointers, the third a New York militiaman.

This was, according to Sir William F. C. Napier, the British historian, "The only instance in history where a besieging army was entirely broken up and routed by a single sortie."

For the rest of the Northern front it was another dreary year, marked only by Commodore Thomas McDonough's naval victory on Lake Champlain, which ended Britain's second attempt to split the Eastern states down the Hudson Valley. The first, we will recall, was Burgoyne's ill-fated move during the Revolution.

But overshadowing all, the crowning disgrace to American arms had occurred just outside the capital city of Washington. Nearly six thousand militia and a handful of equally raw Regular recruits commanded by General William H. Winder, a well-meaning but unmilitary lawyer, scampered in panic from a force of British regulars less than one-third its strength at Bladensburg, August 24, 1814.

The fugitives, who had started on their ill-starred military venture in a Falstaffian county-fair atmosphere, never stopped running until sixteen miles beyond Washington, while the British troops marched into the city to burn the Capitol, the White House and other public buildings. "From the distant hills of Maryland and Virginia," wrote Adams, "the flying President and Cabinet caught glimpses of the ruin their incompetence had caused."

The fact was that for two years the administration and the Congress had given no thought to the protection of the capital; even the presence of a British squadron harrying the Chesapeake Bay area seemed no cause for alarm. Only when the squadron was reinforced by some fifty-four hundred British troops—veterans of the Napoleonic wars—did they wake up. There were no Regular troops available; so frantic calls for militia went out. The only resistance put up when the British landed was that of Commodore Joshua Barney, USN, and his little force of about four hundred sailors and marines who stood at Bladensburg until overwhelmed.

British Admiral George Cockburn and General Robert Ross, their mission of sacking Washington accomplished, next turned attention to Baltimore. However, the defense of Fort McHenry, immortalized by "The Star Spangled Banner," held up the squadron. Ross, landing south of the city, was checked by militia fighting behind entrench-ments. He was killed and the invaders withdrew.

On returning to the sacked capital the frenzied Congress now set about providing more armies—on paper. The recruiting laws were revised to coax men into uniform; the bounties increased from one hundred sixty to three hundred and twenty acres of land; substitutes could be hired for enlistment; and masters could share in the bounties of their apprentices. Two new arsenals were established, at Watervliet, N. Y., and Pittsburgh, Pa.

However, war-weary Britain now paused on the eve of final vic-tory. Peace came officially with the signing of the Treaty of Ghent, December 24, 1814. But the fighting was not yet over. An English expedition—six thousand regulars, the cream of Wellington's Penin-sula War veterans—landed on the Mississippi delta, ten miles south of New Orleans, December 23, 1814. General Andrew Jackson, hur-riedly summoned, opposed them.

Jackson's previous war experience had been against the Creek Indians in Alabama and Tennessee in 1813. Leading a force of militia and volunteers, Jackson, at that time a major general of Tennessee militia, inflicted two decisive defeats on the red men. Then his force evaporated. Commissioned in the Regular Army now, Jackson recalled this lesson as he prepared the city's defense.

With iron hand, Old Hickory enforced martial rule with an energy which brought results but immediately embroiled him with civilian judicial authority. He had a crazy-quilt of soldiery. Two small regi-ments of Regulars were there—the 7th and the 44th Infantry (now incorporated in the present 1st). He had Creole Louisiana militia, Tennessee riflemen, free Negroes, Lafitte's pirates under Dominique You, some sailors, and some New Orleans city volunteers.

Realizing that most of these men would break and run if they met British regulars in the field, Jackson improvised an almost impregnable defensive position between the Mississippi and a cypress swamp. Part of the works consisted of cotton-bales, whence comes the "Cotton-baler" nickname of the 7th Infantry to this day.

Sir Edward Pakenham, the British leader, distinguished brother-in-law of the Duke of Wellington, chose to assault Jackson's works, January 8, 1815. His impetuous, gallant, but foolhardy attack, as we know, was repelled with tremendous losses; Sir Edward himself fell.

The enemy retreated sullenly to their ships; Jackson, knowing well what would happen to his motley force were they to issue from their breastworks, was content to let the British go.

One might ask why, with this position facing them, did the British make any attempt to storm? Why not send naval vessels up-river to New Orleans, as Farragut was to do a half-century later? The answer is that they did try—and thereby hangs another and little-known tale of Army tenacity.

Down at Fort St. Philip, sixty-five miles south of New Orleans, a small force—of which Alexander Hamilton's Battery, at that time Captain Charles Wollstonecraft's company of artillery, was a major element—successfully fought off a British naval contingent consisting of a sloop of war, a brig, a schooner and two bomb-ketches which bombarded the fort incessantly for ten days. Then the Royal Navy gave up.

On this high note of victory at New Orleans the dismal war ended, muting the dirge of inefficiency. But the Regular didn't forget. Above all, he didn't forget Queenstown Heights nor Bladensburg; he hasn't forgotten them today, for that matter. He didn't forget that the British practice in this war was to turn militia prisoners of war loose as not worth the keeping. It was hard to explain away those things; to reason them out cold-bloodedly and assess the basic causes.

The fleet-footed militiaman who couldn't stand up in the open had, of course, as much natural courage as any other American. What he lacked was military training and educated leaders. Newly enlisted Regulars, under newly appointed officers, ran as far and as fast. Only when discipline and leadership intervened to nurture the soul of the soldier did the Regular Army make good—as it did at Chippewa, at Lundy's Lane and at Fort St. Philip.

But, human nature being what it is, it is far easier to blame the man rather than the system. So the professional, the war over, contemptuous of all part-time soldiers, began to draw into a shell of isolationism. It was too bad, for the rift was to last long. In the meantime the Army was doing other things.

*   *   *   *   *

• • • •

5

WESTWARD, HO!

The period between the end of the War of 1812 and the onset of the Mexican War may be considered as the formative one for the Regular Army as well as for the nation. For this was the first great era of national growth. On the land, thin lines of rails were beginning to creep westward from tidewater where the tall ships plied the seas. On the Ohio and the Mississippi, steam paddles were churning, while canals linked the Great Lakes to the Atlantic. Textile mills and blast-furnaces in the East, King Cotton in the South, were making economic history. The new nation craved technical know-how to control the genii of Iron and Steam; craved communications to move its products to market. The Army furnished both.

When the United States Military Academy was reorganized under the able administration of Brevet Major Sylvanus Thayer in 1817, it became the first of the nation's technological schools. As Henry Adams pointed out, the government—perhaps we had best say Thomas Jefferson and James Monroe—through West Point, had projected "the first systematic study of science in the United States."

A. Riedler summed it up: "Engineering as a profession in the United States dates back no further than 1850. Its first beginning may have been as early as 1830 . . . Before 1840 real instruction in engineering was offered almost exclusively in the Military Academy at West Point. Up to 1840, even up to 1850, nearly all the civil engineers had received their preparation in this military school . . ."

Passage of the Rivers and Harbors Act of 1824, which placed the Corps of Engineers in control of the nation's seaports and inland waterways, was the first official Army share in nation-building. But the task went far beyond that, for the Army was not only to help build the nation's roads, railroads and canals, but was also to lay the foundation stones of all American scientific education as well as take part in the development of general education.

It was in 1827 that the founders of the Baltimore & Ohio Railroad, which was to become the first link in the nation's great rail communications chain, petitioned President John Quincy Adams to loan Army officers to initiate its construction. He did so, for, as the Secretary of War wrote, "the Chief Executive considers the proposed project of connecting Baltimore with the Ohio [River] as an enterprise of great importance . . . and is disposed to afford every facility in aid of the execution of it . . ."

That was but the curtain-raiser. Before the chore was finished the Regular Army had had a part in the construction of every railway system now existing in the United States. Commerce and industry, as well as the several states, watching the new trend, began asking the Army for help in other developments, too, and the Congress was not loath to give permission.

In 1837, the Topographical Bureau of the Corps of Engineers outlined the War Department's policy, authorizing "surveys of a national or highly interesting commercial character applied for by states or incorporated companies. In those cases, such officers as can be spared (with their instruments) are allowed to be assigned. All other expenses . . . are supplied by the parties interested in the survey . . ."

As machine industry and the technological demands of the Industrial Revolution clamored for education, the demand for teachers grew, and West Pointers in an ever-widening stream were diverted from the Army into civil life and civilian schools to satisfy the thirst for learning of the growing nation.

By 1832, we find the Board of Visitors of the Military Academy somewhat plaintively noting that "experience of the past shows that as soon as an officer, by dint of application, renders himself useful and respectable [at West Point] he is taken away by a higher inducement offered by some literary institution."

In 1834, the House Committee on Military Affairs remarked, "The Academy . . . has accomplished a nobler service by sending forth numbers annually competent to superintend the construction of those chains of internal improvement which are to be the eternal bonds of our national Union . . . Other testimonials and other rewards have been accorded it by the literary institutions of our land which have invited its graduates to fill important professorships . . ."

This sort of thing was but one part of the Army's responsibilities through the period. Its exploratory function was in full operation. The country west of the Mississippi was being probed and mapped; overland trails across prairie and over mountain were being blazed and guarded as prelude to the creaking rumble of emigrant trains westward bound.

Between 1817 and 1820, Major Stephen Long's extensive explorations on foot and by boat had brought knowledge of the Platte, the Arkansas, the Canadian and the mid-section of the Mississippi Rivers. Slender columns of Army men began pushing westward in extension of the frontier.

Fort Atkinson, at Council Bluffs, Iowa, in 1821, became the first stronghold west of the Missouri River—constructed by the 6th Infantry from the wilderness on the spot, with walls of logs, shingled roofs and planked floors. Soldiers' barracks had eighty-eight rooms, and officers' quarters had at least two rooms apiece for married men.

Ten miles south of St. Louis, Jefferson Barracks rose in 1826—destined to be a jump-off point for further westward movement. And, in 1827, Fort Leavenworth, Kan., which in later years was to become the seat of Army higher education, was constructed as another gateway to the West. Both these posts were built by elements of the 3rd and 6th Infantry. The stage was set for the next national surge of emigration.

The scope of movement of these infantry units opening the frontier was immense. Many of their marches were by river-boat; but foot-slogging, too, played a prominent part. The 1st Infantry, for instance, in 1828, made one movement from Baton Rouge, La., to the upper end of the Mississippi by boat. But in 1829, four companies of the 6th Infantry escorted a party of traders to blaze the way over the Santa Fé Trail, a two-year trip from Fort Leavenworth to Santa Fé and return.

By 1830, seven Army posts were staggered, far apart, on the western slopes of the Mississippi Valley—from Fort Snelling, Minn., near St. Paul, to Cantonment Gibson down on the Arkansas River. Captain Benjamin L. E. Bonneville's explorations, from 1832 to 1835, produced the first authentic reports and maps of the entire Northwest. In 1832 also, Lieutenant James Allen and his little detachment, accompanying the Schoolcraft expedition, discovered the sources of the Mississippi and revealed valuable data on Minnesota's mineral deposits. The most widely publicized explorations however were those of Lieutenant John Charles Frémont—the "Pathfinder." From 1842 until 1844, Frémont was elaborating the national knowledge of routes previously blazed. Through his efforts the Oregon Trail was opened wide to the settler. He surveyed a great part of the country between the Missouri River and the Rocky Mountains, then probed across to the Columbia River mouth. Striking down through Oregon and Northern California, the fortunes of war found Frémont at Monterey when American settlers there precipitated revolt; this was a prelude to the Mexican War.

It was this period, it must be remembered, that was euphemistically termed the "Thirty Years' Peace," a misnomer as far as the Regular Army was concerned, because it engaged in three separate wars against the Indians—the Seminole War of 1817, the Black Hawk War of 1832 and the Second Seminole, or Florida, War, which lasted from 1832 to 1841.

In fact, the period opened with Army participation in a naval engagement on the high seas on June 17, 1815—the very day before the Battle of Waterloo. Captain Samuel B. Archer's Company H of the Corps of Artillery, acting as marines on board Commodore Stephen Decatur's flagship *U.S.S. Guerriere* off Capo de Gata in sparkling Mediterranean waters, played its part in the capture of the Algerine frigate *Mashouda,* the engagement which ended our country's long-continued troubles with the Barbary pirates.

All in all, this "Thirty Years' Peace" was a very busy time for an Army that had been cut, immediately on conclusion of the War of 1812, to a force of ten thousand scattered about the country in little packets. This reduction brought about a telescoping of existing regiments that did little good to the growing spirit of tradition. So small was the force available when the Seminole War broke out in 1817 that General Andrew Jackson, commanding in the South, took matters into his own hands to obtain sufficient troops to put down the Indian depredations. He called out the Tennessee militia to supplement his little force of two regiments of infantry and a battalion of artillery. Actually both he and General Edmund P. Gaines flouted constitutional provisions by enlisting volunteer troops and appointing officers without Congressional or Presidential sanction—among them a brigade of Indians of the Creek tribe.

Jackson, invading Spain's Florida, defeated the hostiles and captured Spanish posts. Finding two British subjects inciting the Indians to further outrages, he hanged them out of hand. Old Hickory's actions gave the State Department a great deal of work to mend diplomatic fences after British and Spanish protests, and kept Congress busy for several years untangling the pay claims of the illegally enlisted and commissioned volunteers. On the other hand he had accomplished the job of pacification with minimum cost in American life and effort. And when Florida was ceded by Spain in 1819, to the Army fell the task of establishing new garrisons.

Momentarily, however, the Army's attention lay with the flow of immigration into the Mississippi Valley and beyond. Infringements upon the Indians' lands and hunting grounds brought about uprisings which culminated in the Black Hawk War of 1832 and the final defeat of the Sac and Fox Indians by detachments of the 1st and 6th Infantry and Illinois volunteers under Colonel Zachary Taylor, at the Battle of Bad Axe in Wisconsin.

Settlers and soldiers, too, were beginning to clash in the West with what was to them a new type of Indian warrior—the Plains Indian, the best irregular light horse soldier the world has ever produced. It was patent that slow-moving infantry could no longer cope with the situation. As a result, on May 23, 1833, the Regiment of Dragoons —today's 1st Cavalry—was born. We must pause a moment on this as the inception not only of a new tactical method of war in our Army but also of what was to become one of the most colorful facets of an epic pageant—the winning of the West.

From the disappearance of the Continental Army in 1784 until this time—some forty years—such mounted units as had popped into existence were either militia, volunteers, or had been raised in emergency and later discharged or disbanded. Most of these old organizations followed the old yeomanry concept of the English militia; that is, they furnished not only their arms but also their horses. As a matter of fact, the Congress took a dim view of the horse as an expensive luxury. It had gone so far, as we know, as to sell the horses of its light artillery, and up to the time of the Mexican War all artillery—light and heavy—were foot-soldiers. Except for some exercise with the cannon of the coastal forts, they were drilled and used as infantry, thereby acquiring the Army nick-name of "red-legged infantrymen," from the fact that their blue trousers had a red stripe.

But now, it seemed, with the organization of the Dragoons, the

horse was back in American warfare. Three years later—in 1836—
the 2nd Dragoons made their bow, and the United States Cavalry was
really in business.

They got about, did the dragoons; at times treaty-making with the
Indians, at others screening and scouting while the plains country
began to fill up with settlers. One dragoon, who found time to take
notes while the long column of twos plodded through the Ozarks,
noted that at Springfield, Mo., just settled, "the inhabitants are idle
& Lazy depending upon their negroes for support which is the custom
of all slavestates (*sic*)." He snorted at the high prices extant; whisky
sold for twenty-five cents a pint and milk cost twelve and one-half
cents a quart. The Leavenworth country, he related, "is remarkable
for insects such as snakes, Ticks and Cattipillars."

Meanwhile, in the deep South, the Seminoles and Creeks of
Georgia, Alabama and Florida rebelled against the white man's efforts
to move them west of the Mississippi. The white settlements and little
garrisons of troops in the area were harried and menaced. The uprisings culminated in the massacre of a column of troops surprised
while on a peaceful march—the so-called Dade Massacre of December 28, 1835, near the present site of Dade City, Fla. Three men only,
of a force of one hundred and fifty, survived.

Seven years of desultory warfare followed while Eastern artillery
garrisons were denuded in effort to provide sufficient troops. The
highlight was the Battle of Okeechobee Swamp, Christmas Day, 1837,
when Colonel Taylor, with Regular infantry and artillery decisively
defeated the enemy. Though some Missouri volunteers fled during
the engagement, Taylor's men fought waist-deep in stinking quagmire
and through five-foot-high swamp grass. After this the war degenerated
into a guerrilla campaign for four more years, during which jungle
heat and disease carried off more men than enemy fire, until the
Seminoles finally yielded.

The task of nation-building which of necessity took officers from
their normal stations—whether it was to survey a railroad or to map
unexplored areas—threw an unequal load on actual troop-leaders, for
Congress had made no provision for additional officers. In 1836, one
hundred and eighty-three officers were on detached service, practically
one-third of the total corps of six hundred and forty-seven.

The situation was really serious. In one force of eleven companies in campaign that year only six officers of a total of fifty-five were available for company duty. In the 1st Artillery seven companies had a total of nine officers; three companies no officers at all. And this was in wartime, under combat conditions.

Such a situation, added to the slowness of regimental promotion (a lieutenant had but little hope of becoming a captain), the poor pay, no prospect of retirement, and the inequalities produced by brevet rank, was certainly not conductive to good morale. So it is not surprising that in this same year of 1836, one hundred and seventeen officers resigned the service. Most of these were young West Pointers, whose scientific talents were now in great demand in civil life.

Yet the Army as a whole carried on. And a way of life—the so-called "Customs of the Service"—was coalescing. Two definite personalities were combining in this formation of a military code of ethics: Winfield Scott in the Army itself, and Sylvanus Thayer at the Military Academy now pumping a continuous flow of graduates into the Army's life-stream. Both were gentlemen in the Chesterfieldian sense of the word. They were not alone in this quality, far from it. But these two men of outstandingly vigorous personality and high concept of honor were in positions whereby they were able to shape the character, the thought and the conduct of the Army officer, and through him, the Army itself.

The impact of Thayer's West Point upon the Army was that of a stone cast into a pool, its concentric ripples spreading wide. Thayer was one of those rare individuals with both an ideal and the capacity to make that image fact. Pedagogically, he was a century ahead of his time. His grouping of cadets in small sections—usually not more than ten or twelve men; the continuous application—every man reciting in each of his subjects every day; and the elastic progression which enabled the brighter mind to advance in knowledge beyond the rigid minimum; all were revolutionary.

It was a concept of a foot race in which each individual strove to the fullest extent of his capacity, rather than that of a mental convoy moving at the speed of the slowest unit. With the approbation of President James Monroe, who had picked him, Thayer reached wide to develop his academic staff, including among others Claude Crozet, the brilliant French *Polytechnicien*.

But above all else, Thayer was establishing a code of probity.

Thayer's character-building, epitomized in the basic premise that a cadet does not lie, cheat or steal, was already producing a sense of rigid personal rectitude in the young officer. He had established a military novitiate whose graduates would in turn permeate the Army with their doctrine—a situation which, of course, still continues as West Point moves along the lines laid down by Thayer.

Scott's influence was something different. A rare character, too, was this great soldier whose tempestuous career—for he was always at loggerheads, it seemed, with some of his superiors and his peers on some nice point of honor—was to affect the Army by example until the opening days of the Civil War.

Scott was a military leader; he had already proved it and was to prove it again. He was a diplomat, twice quelling the hot international flames of border disputes. He was magnificent in personal appearance, meticulous in language. He was to gain the nickname of "Old Fuss and Feathers," true; but that was given more in affection than derision. For this spick-and-span disciplinarian could do more than face bullets and parade-ground formalities. He could—and did, in 1832—brave for days on end the stinking confines of a cholera-ridden transport on Lake Michigan, tending personally to his sick and dying soldiers.

Such was the man and the leader the professional soldier saw during this formative period of the Army; a shining example along the path of a service which led on the one hand into the wide spaces of the expanding frontier, on the other into the quickening niceties of life in an Eastern garrison. It was an example to all the officer corps.

Early in the period—1820-21—General Scott, by War Department directive, revised the Army Regulations. This was in reality a monumental compendium of how the Army should drill, fight, eat, live, and be clothed in war and in peace. It included the first U. S. Army manual of military law, governing the dispensing of military justice and court-martial procedure. In these regulations was an express prohibition against duelling, under penalty of dismissal. Ironic this, perhaps, in view of Scott's own proclivity for issuing challenges when his pyrotechnic sense of honor was touched off.

This subject of personal honor was part and parcel of the times. Carried as it was sometimes to an absurd degree in the Army, nevertheless it held within it a sense of *noblesse oblige* which was slowly to be tempered within the ranks of the officer corps to a more reasonable if equally rigid code of personal behavior.

This tempering took time. Sparks were flying all through the period under discussion. The majority of such clashes came as a result of brevet rank, which, until its abolition in 1869-70, constituted one of the most irritating and frequently heart-breaking sources of jealousy and turmoil in the officer corps.

Brevet rank consisted of temporary higher rank conferred on an individual for outstanding service—usually gallantry in action. The Duke of Wellington characterized it as "the greatest stimulus which the [British] army received." Scott himself wrote that "brevets are the cheap and peculiar rewards of military prowess or genius. But it does not follow that they are to be cheaply won."

A brevetted officer within his own regiment or corps held only his normal relative, or as the British put it, substantive rank and seniority. But when two different units served together, or "on other occasions," the officer "highest in the rank of the line" took command. Thus a junior captain holding brevet major rank might leap momentarily above other captains much senior and naturally resentful. Furthermore, the regulations were so vague about those "other occasions" that clashes occurred constantly, sometimes shivering a life-long friendship. Pecuniary elements entered into the argument, too, because on assuming brevet rank the higher pay was drawn—something not to be sneezed at.

Actually the controversy over brevets was to continue through the Civil War. One finds General James A. Garfield at that time complaining that "it is now impossible to judge from an officer's title or uniform what his actual position and command may be . . . Captains command majors and colonels, and a colonel not infrequently finds two or three brevet colonels among the company and field officers of his regiment."

Such a match, dangled above the powder-keg of exaggerated personal honor of the period, brought explosion after explosion. In 1817-18, it caused West Point's one and only mutiny. Captain Alden Partridge, the acting superintendent, with whom President Monroe was not satisfied, was officially relieved by Brevet Major Sylvanus Thayer. But both were officers of the Corps of Engineers. West Point was an Engineer post, and Partridge was much senior to Thayer as a captain. So the deposed superintendent, after brooding over his removal, returned and forcibly seized command by virtue of his seniority. The affair and its repercussions in the corps of cadets became a *cause celebre* that rocked the halls of Congress for several years. Partridge, ordered dismissed as result of court-martial, was permitted to resign.

From 1821 until the late '40s, Regular officers were to note the continuous bitter and public conflict between the Army's two senior officers, Generals Scott and Gaines, over their respective ranks by brevet. Both held the same date of rank as colonels and as brigadier generals. Scott's brevet of major general dated from July 25 and Gaines' from August 15, both in 1814. But Gaines' name, for some reason, had always let Scott's on the Army Register. The dispute could not be composed. It went on first in letters between them, then in protests to higher authority. Gaines became so vituperative that Scott challenged him to a duel, which Gaines declined—quoting Scott's own regulation prohibiting dueling.

When Major General Jacob Brown, commanding the Army, died in 1828, both men loudly claimed their right to succession, with individual Congressmen taking sides in the dispute. President Adams finally cut the knot—or so he thought—by reaching out and appointing Colonel (and Brevet Major General) Alexander Macomb, after giving serious consideration to recommending abolition by Congress of the rank of major general itself. Scott, in a tempest of rage, at first refused to take orders from Macomb, hoping for a court martial which would either dismiss him from the service or find in his favor. Upon election of Andrew Jackson to the Presidency Scott was suspended from his command. He memorialized Congress, stating his case and asking for a law to definitely fix the rights and privileges of brevet rank. Congress held that the President was within his right in appointing Macomb and that no further determination of the rights of brevet rank was needed. Then and only then did Scott acquiesce. However his bitter feud with Gaines persisted until the latter died in 1849.

By and large, it would seem that the Regular officer of the period had sufficient troubles of his own during this period to keep his mind as well as his body busy. The fluctuations of politics and international affairs troubled him little, except when drawn into their aftermaths.

The rest of the nation was little worried over the Army; it was too busy. Two financial panics, in 1819 and 1837, the Missouri Compromise, the Monroe Doctrine, abolitionism, the political rumblings of "Manifest Destiny," and the saber-rattling slogan—"Fifty-four forty or fight!"—in turn stirred the politicians, the mercantile East, and the cotton-growing South, but they were mere whispers in the Army's isolated islands of existence, whether in the picturesque but damp casemates of a Boston harbor post or log hutments in a Florida cypress swamp.

One of the intriguing points about this existence is how the amenities of life persisted under such circumstances. The Army wife in the East, at such posts as Watertown Arsenal, Mass., for instance, where decent quarters were already built, might entertain foreign dignitaries formally. But her sister in a one- or two-room log or adobe hut on the frontier was in different circumstances. There tin cups served for crockery; trunks and packing boxes for furniture. A rustic chair hammered together by a soldier carpenter was luxury; the regimental colors were the principal decoration of the commanding officer's quarters.

But even the mustachioed dragoons now picking their way through the plains country and establishing outposts to guard the long emigrant trains beginning to roll westward, had their visitors. It was in 1834 that George Catlin, the painter, writing from Jefferson Barracks, noted, "I start this morning with the dragoons for the Pawnee country, but God only knows where that is."

The Army made do, somehow. Everyone was on the same footing as far as pay went—ranging from the 2nd lieutenant's $63.91 to the colonel's $172.66 a month; major generals and brigadiers received $401.50 and $257.75 respectively. And on such pay, with the sliding additions of brevet rank, and of such additional crumbs as ten dollars a month for company commanders and staff jobs, they survived. Uniforms had to come out of this, of course, and the Army was sprucing up now, too, which stretched the slender purses still further.

In a way, if one wished to philosophize, the comforts and discomforts cancelled out. The cost of living was high in the East; but in the West there was game of all sorts and buffalo steaks to lay on the table. Out there, too, hunting-shirts and buckskin overalls could be substituted for expensive uniforms on campaign.

Hospitality quickened in the frontier posts. The newcomers arriving in the stockade from long and frequently dangerous journeys were welcomed; blankets, bedding and other meager comforts proffered; comrades' quarters shared until they could set up their own establishment. From this hospitality grew the Army's gracious custom of an immediate call upon the new arrival on post.

Army life on the frontier was grim. Danger lurked always, and vigilance was the keynote. The good commander was one who kept his post on its toes by frequent tests to prove its alertness and readiness for action. Once in a while this was carried to excess, especially if the commander toyed with John Barleycorn.

Such was the case with the commanding officer of the 1st Infantry at Camp Morgan, near Pensacola, Fla., during the winter of 1825-26. This officer, a strict disciplinarian, brevetted for gallantry in action during the War of 1812, kept things humming by constant night test alarms. Unfortunately, these alarms usually came after the good colonel had befuddled himself.

He had the habit, it was brought out in his court martial, when the drums' long roll had sounded and the troops were assembled, of ordering that a volley be fired; the fact that the ranks were drawn up facing the barracks made no difference, except to such unfortunates as might come scurrying out late to the formation.

On Christmas night, 1825, the post surgeon bustled out just in time to receive a blast. Perhaps he was coming out backward—the record is uncertain on this point—or maybe the bullets just ricocheted. Anyway, as he testified, "several balls did penetrate deponent's coat-tails." Another witness, asked if the colonel appeared to be "deranged" on this occasion, responded: "In no other respect than that he spoke of Indians being about his quarters, when there were none." Convicted of drunkenness on several counts, the colonel was cashiered.

Not all officers took to the bottle for diversion and recreation, however. Zachary Taylor, when commanding the 8th Infantry in Florida was reading and rereading David Hume's *History of England*. He would frequently discuss it with his young teetotaler adjutant, Lieutenant Ethan Allen Hitchcock, who was himself—when not fighting Indians—poring over such literature as Immanuel Kant's *Critique of Pure Reason*.

Some of the peculiarities of other senior officers deserve mention.

One learns of two colonels who, evidently distrusting their memory of drill regulations, pasted selected orders into their cocked hats, and on parade—after surreptitious glances therein—rattled off commands. One of these flustered elderly gentlemen on one occasion electrified the troops by his order, "Brewster's patent waterproof cocked hats—March!"

In the East, regimental and post officers' messes came into existence as permanent institutions towards the end of the period. The 1st Artillery Mess was organized in 1840 at Houlton, Me., and the West Point Army Mess the next year. It is true that the artillerymen had had a mess of sorts as far back as 1821, at Fort Independence in Boston harbor, where for a time officers dined each night in full dress uniform, each with a soldier, also in full dress, behind his chair. But it took the upheaval and uncertainty of a war threat along the Canadian border to bring about the institution of the permanent mess, which, incidentally, was to continue in the Coast Artillery long years after the 1st Artillery itself ceased to exist.

The occasion of the founding of the 1st Artillery Mess is notable, because it took place in the midst of an episode wherein professional soldiers averted possible war. Canada was in the throes of a rebellion; American sympathizers were aiding the rebels, and at the same time dispute over the Canadian-American boundary line was bitter. In Maine the militia was being mobilized by the Governor to forcibly assert the state's boundary rights. The 1st Artillery, just returned from the Florida War, was strung along the border from New York eastward, while across the line British regulars—including battalions of the Grenadiers, the Coldstreams, the 7th Hussars and other famous regiments—were posted.

But while the civilians on both sides were taking pot-shots at one another, and Maine's Governor was huffing and puffing fire and brimstone at the British Lion, the regulars began fraternizing. Scott, who had acted as peacemaker in a Niagara River border clash three years previously, had been sent up posthaste by President Van Buren to pour oil on the troubled waters. He found Sir John Harvey governing New Brunswick. Sir John had been a fast friend since 1813 when his personal baggage, including a miniature painting of his wife—looted by Americans in the taking of York—had been chivalrously returned to him by Scott. In command of British troops on the border was

Sir John Colborne, another old acquaintance. The trio of professional soldiers talked the same language—peace. So the 1st Artillery's invitation to conviviality found response in the British ranks.

Dances and parties were thrown by both sides; American and British uniforms intermingled without regard to international boundaries. Evening sleigh-rides were frequent—the feminine portions of both sides turning out in force. The climax was a formal challenge by the American artillerymen to a two-day week-end of horse-drawn sleigh racing at Plattsburg. The country-side turned out; Plattsburg had never seen such goings on. It all ended with a grand banquet, after which the British went gaily home.

But the 1st Artillery had not reckoned either on New York State laws nor the sanctimonious attitude of some New Yorkers. For each individual officer was indicted by the local grand jury for horse-racing on Sunday! It apparently took some doing to have the indictments quashed, but it was finally accomplished. More to the point, this sane relationship between the two regular forces did much to throttle civilian war-spirit, and that is what really counted.

As for the enlisted men, life during all this time was still one of drab dullness intermingled with periods of fighting, and enlivened—or perhaps embittered—by long marches, counter-marches and trips by riverboat or coastal transport. They were blotched and bloated by scurvy; they died by the hundred in cholera outbreaks. The artillerymen were pulled occasionally from their coastal forts to hike into battle as "red-legged infantrymen" in Florida swamps, and to go on border guard along the Canadian frontier. The infantrymen varied their existence from the cantonments west of the Mississippi and long hikes into the prairie country, to interminable stretches of existence along malaria-ridden southern bayous.

This soldier was changing in character. Although native-born recruits were still obtainable, there were not enough of them. Irish and German immigrants, driven from their homes by starvation and by political upheavals, now arrived here in increasing numbers and began to trickle into the Army. Were one to look hard enough, one could find almost anything from a Donnybrook plug-ugly to a Dublin University graduate, from a Bavarian peasant to a cashiered Prussian officer or an English ex-school teacher.

It was not high pay and prospects that beckoned to such men.

The private's pay had been raised, it is true, to eight dollars a month before the period ended, with corresponding raises in the non-commissioned ranks. But a bricklayer in the United States was getting one dollar a day now, although he had to house, feed and clothe himself out of that. These new soldiers were men seeking other things —most of them desiring above all to shirk responsibility. That many of them were later to assume responsibility when chevrons were pinned on their arms alters not the basic fact. If the officer was changing professionally, so, too, was the private soldier. He had become a tough mercenary—asking only three square meals a day and found.

These men had no recreation other than the saloons and bawdy houses which sprang up in the new settlements and about the Eastern posts. They had their legal whisky ration in barrack and camp, also. The government in 1830 alone issued 72,537 gallons, at a cost of $22,132. Whisky and desertion went hand in hand, the principal banes of the service. To cope with them, iron discipline and severe punishment were necessary. Sometimes—as old court-martial records show—sadism crept into this, such as illegal brandings, excessive floggings and even—in Florida during the Seminole Wars—hunting down deserters and shooting them off-hand like so many mad dogs.

To Winfield Scott the Army owes a debt for bettering the enlisted man's condition. Through his efforts the whisky ration was abolished in 1832; coffee and a sugar component became an issue item instead.

Scott had written into his regulations many things of importance to the enlisted man. One of these provisions had to do with the sutler— the civilian camp follower who had obtained permission to sell to the troops food, liquor, tobacco and such trifles and items as might otherwise be impossible to obtain, particularly on the frontiers. Such military peddlers—a necessary evil—have always followed armies in the field; we had ours since the days of the train bands. But until Scott took the matter in hand no one had attempted to lay down a general rule of conduct. Some of these traders were good men; many others were rapscallions who gouged and cheated.

Scott's regulations put the sutler in his place. The approved trader was considered to have the courtesy rank of a cadet. For the privilege of service the sutler had to pay, whether in the field or in garrison, from ten to fifteen cents a man monthly. This fund was to be used for the benefit of the troops, under control of a council of administration comprising three officers next in rank to the commander. If sufficient commissioned officers were not available, senior non-commissioned officers served.

The council prescribed what articles the sutler should carry in stock—a very common-sense provision, because the needs of the men varied with the hardships of the campaign, the locale and the climate. In garrison the sutler could be allotted a house, if available; if not, he was permitted to erect one.

Definite provisions governed the expenditure of the funds received from sutlers. The council of administration could give immediate relief to widows and orphans of officers and enlisted men; to "deranged or decayed" officers and to infirm or disabled soldiers "discharged under circumstances such that they are not pensioned." The education of soldiers' children in post schools; books for the post library, "part of which shall be adapted to the wants of the enlisted men;" and finally the maintenance of the post or unit band were the only other objects for which the funds could be spent.

The sutler was enjoined not to sell "even the smallest quantity" of liquor—an injunction more honored in the breach, as it turned out, for if he erected his store outside the military reservation or camp site he was technically free of military law.

The sutler was also authorized to grant credit to soldiers of up to a half-month's pay, and stoppages from pay were authorized to cover this, although, of course, the government was under no compulsion to act as a collection agency.

This forerunner of the company fund and the post exchange was a big step forward in providing for the needs and comfort of the enlisted man.

On the technical side, the Army saw the period end with the production of a percussion-cap rifle firing a spherical bullet which the Springfield and Harper's Ferry arsenals began to turn out. However, a number of years were to pass before the flintlock musket was wholly replaced. A new and really light field gun carriage was put in production. And the bugle was substituted for the fife and drum as company field music.

At Fortress Monroe, Va., a School of Instruction for artillery was established—the first of the Army's graduate schools for officers. And, in 1843, a school for infantry brigade drill was set up at Jefferson

Barracks. Here it was that the 3rd Infantry, then commanded by erudite Ethan Allen Hitchcock—nephew of the Green Mountain hero —won its nickname of the "Buffsticks." The gleam, glitter and precision of Hitchcock's regiment on parade became famous throughout the Army, which, perhaps in envy, bestowed the appelation—taken from the name of the little slotted contraption used to protect uniform cloth while buttons are being shined.

By the time the thunderheads of war gathered along the Rio Grande, the Regular Army had come of age—a taut, tough little aggregation of trained soldiers led by trained officers. It would be needed.

*   *   *   *   *

6

DOWN BY THE RIO GRANDE

Expansionist James K. Polk, who was in the White House in the spring of 1845, mistrusted all Whigs and particularly those of potential Presidential timber. Winfield Scott, national hero and major general in command of the Army, who had made an unsuccessful bid for the Whig nomination in 1839, was one of those mistrusted. So, to a lesser extent, was Zachary Taylor, brevet major general commanding in Florida, whose exploits in the Black Hawk and Seminole Wars were still fresh in the public mind.

That was too bad; for Polk, balancing a hot teacup of potential war on his thin knees, was going to need these two men, as well as the rest of the little Regular Army. He was going to need them badly and nothing had been done to put the Army on a war footing.

This thing had been brewing for ten long years—since American settlers, overflowing the boundaries of New Spain, had rebelled against Mexico and established the Republic of Texas. The blood-baths of the Alamo and Goliad, Sam Houston's victory at San Jacinto over Santa Anna, all were now part of American history; "Remember the Alamo" was a household phrase.

Furthermore, the trans-continental spread of Mexico, alien to us in custom and religious tradition, reached from the Caribbean to the Pacific and lapped northward enticingly. Texas, carving herself from it, had just been accepted as another State in the Union to prevent the dabbling of France and Britain in that area, despite Mexico's ultimatum that annexation would mean war.

Why should not New Mexico and California follow and, with the Oregon territory we already claimed from Britain, establish "the fulfillment of our manifest destiny to overspread the continent allotted by Providence for the free development of our yearly multiplying millions"?

Thus reasoned Polk and his administration, and Taylor was sent to Corpus Christi, Tex., to mobilize a so-called "Army of Occupation" to check further moves of Mexican troops now massing south of the Rio Grande. Aside from that gesture—which drained the rest of the country of more than three-quarters of its Regular Army—he did nothing more in way of preparation. Scott's long-continued efforts to make the Army strong enough to carry out national policy were still flouted.

Taylor's force at Corpus Christi consisted of the 2nd Dragoons, the 3rd, 4th, 5th, 7th and 8th Infantry and the 1st, 2nd, 3rd and 4th Artillery ("red-legged infantry" these, for the most part; there were but three field batteries). They had been gathered from all over the United States and all except the cavalry, which marched into southern Texas, had been funneled through New Orleans and thence by water. Not until March, 1846, when the Mexican strength built up below the Rio Grande, was Taylor ordered to the north bank, opposite Matamoras, to prevent invasion. Taylor's orders also admitted the possibility that he might have to invade Mexico, yet he was categorically denied any increase in strength unless the Mexicans should first invade.

This six-month delay at Corpus Christi Taylor utilized in incessant drill and training of troops already seasoned. As result, as James E. Edmonds remarked, "what slackly-clad 'Old Rough and Ready' held in his well-schooled commander's hand was a thin, rightly tempered, Damascus blade."

It was Mexican General Mariano Arista who started hostilities, crossing the river April 24, 1846, and ambushing a scouting party of Dragoons. Six days later he brought his entire force over. Taylor, outnumbered two to one, accepted the challenge. He met Arista at Palo Alto May 8, defeated him, and completely routed the Mexicans next day at Resaca de la Palma. The American field artillery dominated the action in both battles.

The American people exploded in war fever. President Polk, on May 11, delivered a robustious message, declaring that "Mexico has . . . shed American blood upon the American soil." This was a moot point, because Mexico with at least equal legality held that the fighting had occurred on her soil.

The Congress, declaring war on May 13, went into its usual tizzy of preparation after the fact. The size of the Army was increased to fifteen thousand, including a regiment of mounted riflemen, and the President was authorized to call for fifty thousand volunteers. The usual error of short-term enlistments followed. Half the volunteers were enlisted to serve only for six months, the remainder for one year. This not only made it all the harder to recruit men for a five-year hitch in the Army, but when the six-month men—as well as a horde of militia illegally raised in the southern states by old General Edmund P. Gaines—descended on Taylor's base at Point Isabel, their time was so short that they were all discharged before they ever smelled powder.

On the other hand, Polk's call on the states was for volunteers, not for militia units as such, although many men did respond from existing militia organizations. Hence the vexing question of Constitutional rights was never to rise in this war. We were spared repetition of the shameful militia refusals to cross national borders which occurred in the War of 1812. And the new officers, although the vast majority of them were ignorant of war, received Federal commissions. So the volunteers held no allegiance to the several states and their training was in Regular Army hands, thus insuring uniformity. A number of West Pointers who had resigned the service came back with these volunteer units, too, a welcome leaven.

In the high command, however, Polk played parlor politics in no mean fashion. His former law partner, Gideon Johnson Pillow, made first a brigadier and later a major general, not only was to show his costly ineptness to handle men in battle, but was to become a thorn in Scott's side. Robert Patterson, also blessed with general's stars through political pull, was as inept as Pillow, though lacking the latter's jealous venom. But John Anthony Quitman, a third individual to come in the back door as a brigadier general, proved himself an able field commander who was well to merit the testimonial sword later bestowed by Congress for his gallantry at Monterrey. And that, too, was in the American tradition. Franklin Pierce, who was later to become our fourteenth President, chose brigadier's stars in preference to the attorney generalship which Polk had originally offered him in return for his political support. He comported himself reasonably well, winning Scott's regard, and gave him in turn loyal support in after years. James Shields, fifth to be tendered general's rank from civil life, also became a good soldier; he was brevetted for gallantry in action at Cerro Gordo.

Taylor, short of supply and transportation, made no move to invade across the Rio Grande until July, 1846, his requisitions for wagons and pontoon bridges being unfilled. The wagons, as it turned out, were not to reach him until his campaign was ended, because, forsooth, according to the Quartermaster General, "there was no information at Washington . . . to enable me or the War Department to determine whether wagons could be used in Mexico." Already, it appears, the dead hand of bureaucracy lay heavy on the War Department.

But Taylor was not wasting his time. Emory Upton quoted an unidentified contemporary writer:

"Since . . . General Taylor compels the volunteers with him to receive six hours drilling per day and relieves them of all other duties, to make soldiers out of them, we venture to predict that they, too, when they meet the enemy, will add to the reputation of our arms. 'Rough and Ready' will make them soldiers and then win victories with them."

Regular and volunteer did not mix well at first. Lieutenant George B. McClellan, just out of West Point, kept a diary in which he several times noted his detestation of the volunteer. Of General Patterson he remarked he had "that air of dignity and importance so peculiarly characteristic of Mustangs." "Little Mac" is here using the Army slang term for volunteer officers, first appearing in this campaign because so many volunteers, lacking horses, were riding jackasses. In later years the term was to become peculiarly Naval, to denote an officer commissioned without benefit of Annapolis training.

McClellan also wrote scornfully of General Pillow, who, he said, when one of his officers pulled a revolver on him in an altercation, first put him under guard but, when the culprit's regiment mutinied as a result, freed him. The Mexicans, McClellan noted, didn't mind the Regulars, who were polite to them—but the volunteers robbed and killed them. One gathers that Taylor had his troubles in pulling this heterogeneous mass together and shaking it down into an efficient force.

Women went to this war, too, at least the enlisted women. Captain Ephraim Kirby Smith, writing home to his family, told of giving up his transport stateroom—this in September, 1845—in emergency to a Mrs. Roth, "a camp woman of my company," who by morning had given birth to a son. It was, Kirby Smith related, the second birth on board; "the mothers are now doing well and doing their regular washing for the men."

Later, in campaign, Kirby Smith wrote that "Corporal Riley of my company lost his youngest child this morning, about a year old . . . [I saw] the mother, an excellent little woman whom he married at Dearborn Arsenal, sitting with her dead baby on her lap, the tears quietly dropping on its face." This was in camp, shortly after the battle of Palo Alto.

"Your old friend Ryan," Kirby Smith wrote his son, "who once saved your life (Private Ryan, it seems, had rescued the four-year-old boy from drowning) has been wounded." He also thought it important that he tell his family of his pride that two of his sergeants had been commissioned.

What better illustration of the patriarchial Regular Army of the time could one want than these terse comments on life, death and long-lasting officer-enlisted relationship?

While Taylor was whipping his troops into shape, the administration in Washington was making medicine. It must be remembered that strategy as well as policy was made by Polk and his politicos in this war. Scott, although Army commander, had no hand in the over-all direction.

Colonel Stephen Watts Kearny, commanding the 1st Dragoons at Fort Leavenworth, was ordered to take possession of all northwestern Mexico to the shores of the Pacific—peaceably or by force. And Brigadier General John Ellis Wool, at Louisville, Ky., was ordered to concentrate a force at San Antonio, Tex., then move south to Chihuahua in central Mexico where he was to come under command of Taylor when the latter made his invasion.

Preposterous in concept as was this plan, it was accomplished by grace of leadership, inflexible determination, and devotion to duty.

Kearny was joined at Fort Leavenworth by a force of Missouri volunteers, who much to the amazement of the Regulars, held a mass-meeting to choose their colonel. Candidate after candidate harangued his "constituents," each promising inducements and improvements in the soldiers' lot should he be elected. Alexander William Doniphan,

St. Louis lawyer and evidently a man of parts, was elected—to the later regret of some of his men, for Doniphan, as it turned out, was a hard-driving leader.

With his dragoons in the van—crooning their favorite song, "The Hunters of Kentucky"—Kearny's command moved out June 6, 1846. Forty-five days later they were in Santa Fé, and New Mexico was formally annexed. Leaving Doniphan to drive for Chihuahua and join Wool, Kearny, with two companies, now rode on across the Rockies to, as one of his officers wrote, "conquer or annex a Pacific empire; to take a leap in the dark of a thousand miles of wild plain and mountains . . . Our success—we never doubt it, and the very desperation of any alternative must ensure it." Worn, ragged and weatherbeaten, they successfully ended their march at San Diego, December 12, 1846, linking with U. S. naval forces occupying the port.

Kearny's wagon train, escorted by a battalion of Mormon volunteers—all under command of Captain Philip St. George Cooke of the dragoons—took a more circuitous route over country where never wagon-wheel had turned before, blazing what was later to become the broad highway to the Pacific. They came hiking in to San Diego January 29, 1847.

Thus was one part of Polk's problem of "manifest destiny" solved by a handful of determined soldiers well led. Doniphan's Missourians were to play a role almost as fantastic. After pacifying New Mexico, his little force of some twelve hundred drove to El Paso where it was learned that General Wool, with whom they were to rendezvous at Chihuahua, was not going there at all!

That did not deter Doniphan; he had his orders. By March 1, he had crossed the desert wastes to Chihuahua—his move culminating in a defeat of local Mexican forces in which he lost but one man killed to some three hundred of the defenders.

Doniphan's exploits are perpetuated today in the battle-streamers of the 138th Infantry of the Missouri National Guard, which originated in 1832 as the St. Louis Grays and volunteered in 1846 as the St. Louis Legion.

General Wool's expedition, too, had a flavor all its own. His force of Regulars and volunteers gathered from all over the United States started for Chihuahua from San Antonio September 23, 1846. The only reason he never got there was because at Parras he was diverted by Taylor's command. His men had covered nine hundred miles of strenuous marching through enemy territory, and on the way had been welded into the toughest sort of professional soldiers. It was well they had. Taylor was going to need them badly.

Taylor, on the Rio Grande in June, 1846, had been instructed to move on Monterrey in the interior of Mexico. Reinforced by new quotas of volunteers, he now had a total strength of twelve thousand. But he well knew that neither his supplies nor his transport (he had only what wagons he could scrounge in the area) could support such force. Nor, indeed, had he any intention of dragging a mass of untrained men along.

So, with all his Regulars, about three thousand, and as many volunteers already trained by him, Taylor moved out, leaving the remainder behind for further seasoning. At Monterrey, in a three-day battle, Taylor drove the Mexicans back into the center of the city and General Pedro de Ampudia requested terms. Taylor, short of ammunition, permitted him to march out with the honors of war and agreed to an eight-week armistice subject to approval by both governments.

Back in Washington Polk frowned. Conclusion of hostilities at this time was to leave the question of "manifest destiny" still unsettled. Besides—so Polk and his political cronies held—it would place Taylor on a pedestal. He had already been mentioned as a Presidential possibility by the Whigs. So the armistice was disapproved and hostilities resumed. Taylor, suspicious that the administration was engaged in intrigues against him, pushed on to Saltillo, where he received War Department recommendations that he now strike for Mexico City, across several hundred miles of desert.

Taylor demurred, for sound military reasons, pointing out that such operation should best be launched from Vera Cruz, a maneuver long recommended by Scott. The idea was approved.

The Washington politicos were on the verge of appointing Patterson to command of this most important campaign. Patterson was a Pennsylvania militiaman and Polk needed Pennsylvania votes to combat Whig strength in the East. Fortunately for the Army—and for the United States—this shameful project fell through and Scott was put in command.

Scott's plan, in brief, was to assemble the largest force possible.

including all Taylor's trained men, take Vera Cruz and then strike directly up the highway to the Mexican capital; Taylor could go on the defensive. He so wrote Taylor, who complied. But a copy of Scott's letter fell into the hands of Mexican General A. L. de Santa Anna—called back from exile to lead his country's forces—who decided to fall at once on Taylor in his weakened condition and dispose of him before Scott's expedition could intervene. He arrived near Saltillo with sixteen thousand men.

Taylor, most of his battle-trained troops now on their way to Tampico to join Scott, had less than three thousand men to oppose the Mexicans, most of them volunteers just up from training at his base. Because of this he had already called in Wool's hardened, disciplined marchers from Parras. With them, he had now some five thousand effectives, all volunteers except for artillery and dragoons. Falling back from Saltillo he occupied a strong defensive hill-position near Buena Vista, burning behind him such supplies as he could not move. Santa Anna, taking this for sign of flight, pressed eagerly in for the kill.

The Mexican attacks, driven home with gallantry, February 23, 1847, nearly overran the position. But the American artillery, on at least one occasion firing until overrun, checked the enemy and the tide turned. Santa Anna was completely routed.

Tradition was made at Buena Vista. There was Zachary Taylor, sitting sideways on his horse, unperturbed under point-blank musketry fire, calmly ordering "A little more grape, Captain Bragg!" (That is the polite version; another is "Double-shot your guns and give 'em Hell!") There were Lieutenant John Paul Jones O'Brien's guns— two brass field pieces captured by the enemy and later recaptured— that stand today at West Point, with the inscription, "Lost without dishonor, recovered with glory!"

There was Lieutenant William H. Shover's one-gun pursuit of Piñon's Mexican cavalry after the action for three miles with a single field-piece of the 3rd Artillery, unescorted. This was a feat unparalleled before or since.

There were Colonel Jefferson Davis' red-coated, white-trousered 1st Mississippi Rifles, immovable in obedience to their leader's command—"Stand Fast!"—given as he fell severely wounded. Davis' Rifles were volunteers from the Legions of Mississippi Militia, organ-

ized in 1798, who had fought the Creeks and later stood with Jackson
at New Orleans. The 155th Infantry, National Guard, their present-
day successor, carries Davis' words as its motto.

At Buena Vista, too, were four other volunteer regiments which
later were to be incorporated in their respective state militias. The
2nd Kentucky Rifles (Theodore O'Hara, one of its officers, was inspired there to write "The Bivouac of the Dead") is today's 149th
Infantry. The 151st (2nd Indiana Volunteers), the 152nd (3rd Indiana Volunteers), and the 166th (2nd Ohio Volunteers) also all
proudly display "Buena Vista" on their battle-streamers.

There was glory enough for all at Buena Vista, the greatest American victory since Yorktown; glory that was to send Taylor to the
White House at the next election. It was the last of his victories; for
the remainder of the war his command was to remain the comparatively inactive pivot of Scott's great maneuver which ended the war.

Scott's own sparkling campaign started with our first relatively
large-scale amphibious operation, in which Army and Navy cooper-
ated in a workmanlike manner—the landing at Vera Cruz, March 9,
1847. Immediate advance was essential; on the coastal plain the
threat of yellow fever was imminent. At Cerro Gordo, the first Mexican attempt to check his progress inland, Scott wrote another brilliant
page in Army history. The shortcomings of our own wartime legislation brought him to a halt at Jalapa.

For, by this time, his volunteers had reached the end of their one-
year enlistments. Seven regiments—some thirty-seven hundred battle-
wise veterans of a force of less than twelve thousand—had to be
started back home for discharge. Scott was left sitting in the midst of
an enemy country with the remainder—approximately nine-tenths of
the Regular Army and four regiments of volunteers—while Santa Anna
was hastily rallying forces to defend the capital.

Scott pushed on to Puebla on the fertile central Mexican plateau,
where he could find subsistence. There, more than half way to his
goal, he went on the defensive momentarily, waiting reinforcements
promised by the War Department.

These were still mainly on paper, the result of more hasty Congressional action. The Regular Army was to be increased by eight
new regiments of infantry, one of voltigeurs (light infantry), and one
of dragoons. At the same time, volunteer recruiting was going on

apace. The officers for all the new formations came from civil life, fresh and untrained. This increase didn't help Scott much. Some new troops did come dribbling in, but most of the new units, as it turned out, did not reach him until long after the campaign had ended. Meanwhile, the Mexicans were getting stronger every day.

By early August, Scott made a decision that caused the world to gasp. Cutting himself loose from his line of communications he pushed on to his goal—with some eleven thousand men fit for duty. It was a definitely calculated risk; those of his troops not Regular in name— four half-filled volunteer regiments—were professionals in fact by this time.

The Duke of Wellington, learning of Scott's audacity, voiced world opinion: "Scott is lost. He cannot capture the city and he can not fall back on his base." The old soldier had something there, for barring the way Santa Anna had at least thirty-six thousand men and one hundred guns; but Wellington had not reckoned on Scott's leadership nor the quality of his troops.

The successive victories of Contreras, Churubusco, Molino del Rey and Chapultepec ended the war.

As the American flag broke out on the topmost pinnacle of Chapultepec, a gruesome scene took place at Scott's headquarters in the valley below. Twenty-nine American deserters, captured at Churubusco, went dangling simultaneously to death from a massive gallows. It was the end of the *Tercio San Patricio* (St. Patrick's Battalion) of Santa Anna's army.

This strange outfit had been composed entirely of American deserters, Regular Army soldiers, most of them Irish Catholics lured from their allegiance by continuous and cleverly-worded Mexican appeals to their religion. Some two hundred and sixty men in all had been recruited during the campaign, under the leadership of one Thomas Riley, a deserter from the 3rd Infantry.

Fully aware that were they captured they would probably be hanged, these unfortunate renegades fought with savage courage against their former comrades. At Churubusco, the San Patricios occupied a vital strong-point which resisted for several hours before being overwhelmed by artillery fire and bayonet charges.

Eighty survivors were captured. Scott, who declared he would rather be put to the sword with his whole army than do any injustice in the matter, resisted the vehement clamor of the Army that all be shot out of hand. A court martial acquitted a few as being merely catspaws or runaways. It sentenced fifty to be hanged. The remainder, convicted of desertion previous to the outbreak of the war, were branded on the face with the letter "D," flogged and held in chains until the Army left Mexico, when they were drummed out of the service.

But the Army was not thinking of the San Patricios when Scott, in full panoply, entered Mexico City, September 14, 1847, to the tune of "Yankee Doodle" played by the 1st Dragoon mounted band. Drawn up as honor guard were his beloved Mounted Rifles—who had fought, most of them, on foot—and who at Contreras had won his generous outburst: "Brave Rifles! You have been baptized in blood and are brought forth steel!" The regiment today—now the 3rd Cavalry—still carries Scott's encomium as its motto, "Brave Rifles!"

Until peace was signed in February, 1848, the troops remained in Mexico while the Army learned for the first time both the tribulations and the pleasures of occupation duty. The Mexican population was docile in general, even hospitable to the victors, who were kept in hand by Scott's iron discipline. Life was pleasant in Mexico City; although some soldiers seeking underworld pleasures, as soldiers do, found to their cost that knife and garrotte in the hands of riff-raff were deadly. A corps of military police to reinforce the Mexican police, established at once by Scott, kept matters under control.

But an indignant Army now boiled with rage at something else. For Scott, at the height of his triumph, was relieved of command by President Polk and ordered to face a court of inquiry! Gideon Pillow was the villain in the piece—with his poison pen writing anonymous articles for the American press in which Pillow was held up as the real leader and hero of the entire campaign, while Scott was a stupid nonentity jealous of the exploits of his subordinates.

Scott had for a long time put up with Pillow's ineptness, and his self-fostered claim that he was a personal representative of the President of the United States. But when the newspaper slanders now trickled in to Mexico City, to be reprinted in the *American Star,* and hooted at by the troops in general, Scott blew up.

He issued a general order blasting "certain officers" as authors of the slanders and calling their attention to regulations. The upshot of the rumpus was that Pillow was arrested to await court-martial charges.

Pillow screamed to Polk and Scott was relieved of command and a court of inquiry ordered. Since Taylor, the logical successor to Scott, was also a Whig, he was passed over and General William O. Butler, next senior officer with Scott, appointed.

In the midst of the hurly-burly, a glittering temptation was dangled before embittered Scott. From highly-placed Mexican sources came an invitation to become dictator of Mexico. An immediate payment of one and a quarter million dollars was promised, to which would be added the Presidential salary. Guaranteeing the offer was a small group of wealthy and influential Mexicans seeking prosperity for their country and looking forward to eventual annexation by the United States.

The offer was legitimate. It involved no breach of duty. Furthermore, it appeared feasible. Should Scott resign his commission other officers could be induced to follow. The enlistments of the volunteers and of quite a few of the Regular troops would expire on the date of the war's end; thousands of them would have embraced the chance to enter Mexican service with promise of better pay and advancement under their idol Scott.

But Scott was neither fortune-hunter nor potential Benedict Arnold who could toss aside his citizenship and country because of the action of an ungrateful administration. He rejected the offer mainly because, as he later wrote a close friend, "If I failed to return home & face my enemies—the Executive & executive branches of the government— I should have been condemned as guilty of all their foul charges, &c. . . ."

So he came home. He left Mexico City with the cheers of an impromptu farewell from his troops ringing in his ears (he had declined all official honors) and the praise of the Mexicans, one of whom wrote his amazement at "the moral force of the American government, which, by a single slip of paper, written at a distance of two thousand leagues, could humble a proud and victorious soldier and make him descend from his exalted position."

Scott came home to find himself a national hero. There was no doubt where public opinion stood. A joint resolution of Senate and House extended thanks to "Winfield Scott, major general, Commander-in-Chief in Mexico, and through him, to the officers and men of the regular and volunteer corps under him." Much to Polk's embarrassment, Congress formally requested him to have a gold medal struck and presented to Scott, which he did with what might be termed thin enthusiasm.

The court of inquiry thrashed around fruitlessly. All charges against Scott were dropped, but Pillow, Polk's pet lamb, was white-washed. Scott's name was put in nomination for the Presidency at the next Whig convention, but Taylor defeated him. Later, through mutual friends, the coolness between the two—Taylor felt he had been "strip-ped of his army" by Scott—was melted and Scott found himself again commanding the Army.

The Mexican War marked a real coming of age for both the nation and the Regular Army. Scott and Taylor—two vigorous gen-erals completely dissimilar in all characteristics save leadership—had brought an unbroken succession of victories to our arms. This they did despite every obstacle that politics and shortsightedness in both administration and the Congress, as well as bitter jealousies among their subordinates—and to some extent between themselves—could put in their way.

It was the Regular Army's war; an Army consisting on paper in 1845 of nearly nine thousand officers and men but actually only five thousand, three hundred strong, scattered in approximately one hun-dred posts and stations. It consisted of eight regiments of infantry, two of dragoons and four of artillery. But this little Army, under-officered though it was, had, as we have seen, become professional. Its junior troop-leaders were for the most part graduates of the Mili-tary Academy.

And yet the Mexican War was also a vindication of the prowess of the American citizen-soldier when well-led, for part-time soldiers—volunteers, not militia—in the end made up two-thirds of the total force employed. On one stricken field—Buena Vista, as we have seen —all the troops, except for four small batteries of field artillery and two tiny squadrons of dragoons, were volunteers.

Not only had the wartime Army proved itself in battle, but it had also proved its ability in what was our first taste of military government of occupied enemy terrain. Both at Santa Fé, where Doniphan's legal talents were impressed by Kearny to draw up a code of law which worked to the satisfaction of both parties, and also in Mexico City under Scott's able and forceful administration, the civil population found its rights respected and its normal activities unrestricted.

Up at West Point, in 1849, Professor Dennis Hart Mahan, Professor of Engineering and the Art of War, whose pupils had done so well, penned an interesting summary of the result of the campaigns, for the eyes of future generations of cadets:

". . . All our battlefields, up to the glorious feat at Buena Vista, have proved to the world that the American soldier was wanting in no military quality . . . It was reserved for the expedition to Vera Cruz, and its sequel, the victory of Cerro Gordo, to bring into strong relief the fact, that we were unostentatiously, and almost silently, becoming a powerful military nation. The lesson will not be lost upon our neighbors, however slowly we, in the end, may profit by it.

"A shout has gone forth, from the Rio Grande and the shores of the Gulf of Mexico, which, heard on the Thames and the Seine, has resounded along the far-off shores of the Baltic and Black Sea, and will reach the further Ind, bearing with a significance that no prudent statesman will hereafter affect to misunderstand. What are the military resources of this great Republic is no longer a question: a more thorough organization is alone wanting for their complete development."

The Army had come back victorious from a war which had doubled the nation's size. One of its heroes—Taylor—was in the White House; the other—Scott—although defeated for nomination at the convention, was firmly established in the public mind as one of the country's great. Hundreds of others who had worn the blue were making names for themselves in civil life. The profession of arms had become a career in a democratic nation and young men were knocking at West Point's gates.

Under-officered, and outnumbered by its enemies as it was, the Army's brilliant record in the Mexican War proved the value of training and leadership, not only in the high command but, equally important, in the lower grades. Here it was that the Military Academy showed its value to the nation. Its graduates were commanding units far above their rank. Colonels led brigades, captains and majors, regiments; and lieutenants, companies.

Both Scott and Taylor made use of West Pointers on their respective staffs. Each had a graduate as chief of staff; and the invaluable reconnaissance which led to victory over almost impassable obstacles was carried out by West Point engineer officers. Scott summed it up when he later made his famous statement:

"I give it as my fixed opinion that but for our graduated cadets the war between the United States and Mexico might, and probably would, have lasted some four or five years, with, in its first half, more defeats than victories falling to our share, whereas in less than two campaigns we conquered a great country and a peace without the loss of a single battle or skirmish."

The Mexican War over, the Congress in 1849 began to take the Army apart. The volunteers went first, of course; so, too, did all the new Regular regiments except the Mounted Rifles. The professional could realize that this was about where he had come in. Two regiments of dragoons, the mounted rifles, four regiments of artillery and eight of infantry composed the fighting forces, approximating ten thousand men, who were to guard a new frontier area of one million square miles.

But the professional, who had seen the code and the tradition by which he was governed vindicated, could calmly go back to his frontier garrisons and take up the grind of continued scouting, patrolling and Indian-fighting, his language forever after tinctured with an assortment of Spanish slang become part of the Army's folklore.

*   *   *   *   *

• • • •

7

FRUITS OF "MANIFEST DESTINY"

The discovery of gold in California in 1849 galvanized the country. Incidentally, it provided another strain on the Army itself, because the desertion rate jumped as eight-dollar-a-month soldiers slipped away to the siren lure of "gold in them thar hills." Hordes of settlers and prospectors hurrying over the long trails to the West coast moved by grace of the gaunt blue-uniformed riders shepherding them, guarding water-hole and outpost. Stockaded posts rose in the wilderness. Fort Kearny at Grand Island on the Platte River, Fort Laramie in Wyoming, Fort Bridger in Utah and Fort Hall in Idaho constituted the main chain of protection along the overland routes, with some seventy other smaller posts scattered through the prairie country and over to the Pacific slopes.

The same old pattern pervaded. Every item of supply, from a horseshoe nail to the largest piece of ordnance, had to be carried along. Reconnaissance found a likely spot; the troops marched in and went to work. The wagon train disgorged tools, the countryside was scoured for timber; saws buzzed, axe and hammer blows resounded, while alert pickets and herd-guards protected the workers. Barracks, quarters and office buildings rose, squared about a parade ground, a tall flagstaff with the flag fluttering over all. One more army post was in being—where routine drills and evening parades intermingled with the bugle blast of "Call to Arms" or "Boots and Saddles"—its only link with civilization the bi-monthly mail carried in by courier and occasional supply trains.

Soon came the feminine contingent, and rude log cabins blossomed with bits of drapery on the windows and touch of flowers or greenery—brave extemporizations that only Army wives could invent to keep up the semblance of civilization. Maybe, as at Fort Bliss, founded at El Paso in 1849, the quarters were built of adobe, with thatched roof, no ceilings, and floor of hard-packed earth. And, of course, only essentials of food could be had at the commissary. Wrote one Army wife of the period, from a West Texan outpost station: "Butter, eggs and chickens were brought in from the ranches sometimes, eighteen or twenty miles away, the owners running the risk of being murdered by the Indians, every trip they made." But the brave lady also comments that although her 1st lieutenant husband's pay was but ninety-three dollars a month, they were able to save money.

Fighting was incessant during the period. War Department records note twenty-two distinct "wars" in the '50s, and from 1849 to 1861 this scattered Army engaged in two hundred and eight conflicts. Seminoles in the South, Apaches and Navahoes in the southwest, Sioux and Cheyennes of the Great Plains, and the Pacific coast Indians in Oregon were in continual ferment. Gouged by commissioners sent out to pry him from his lands, resentful of the white influx, and covetous of the white man's possessions, the Indian was always on the war path.

But the Army had not only the Indian to contend with in preserving frontier peace. From 1855 to 1857 the Kansas-Missouri border flared in guerrilla warfare between slave-owners and abolitionists. Massacres and pillage at Lawrence, Potawatomie and Osawatomie in Kansas were followed by Federal troop movements which quelled the civil war. And, in 1857, the Mormons in their Great Salt Lake fastness of Utah refused to obey Federal laws. Furthermore, transcontinental immigrant trains traversing Mormon territory were either run out or, in several cases, massacred. The condition became so serious that a considerable force of troops was sent to establish a new Military Department in the territory and restore order.

Mormon guerrillas attacked and burned the trains, so harrassing this expedition that Brigadier General Albert Sydney Johnston, commanding, went into winter quarters at Fort Bridger while negotiations continued. To obtain supplies for his force, now on short rations, he sent Captain Randolph B. Marcy with forty enlisted men and twenty-five packers and guides across the Rockies into New Mexico.

Marcy struggled through deep snow and intolerable cold for fifty-one days to reach Fort Massachusetts, on Utah Creek, in what now is southern Colorado, then started back with a full pack train. A detachment of Mounted Rifles accompanied on the return trip, since word had been received that the Mormons intended to cut it off.

Not until spring of 1858, when reinforcements reached Johnston to bring his strength to fifty-five hundred men, did the Mormons see the light. Confronted with irresistible force they made peace. To ensure their continued compliance and free transit of immigration westward, Fort Douglas, overlooking the city, was later built and garrisoned.

Meanwhile, the country's cry was for better transportation between East and West. National expansion demanded the projection of rail lines from the Mississippi to the Pacific. Congress gave to the Army the chore of exploring, surveying and mapping potential routes, and transit and sketching case became equipment as important as carbine and Colt's revolver.

Specifically five separate parties worked westward, under Captains George B. McClellan, John W. Gunnison and John Pope and Lieutenants Amiel W. Whipple and John G. Parke, while from the Pacific a sixth party under Lieutenant Robert S. Williamson started—all in 1853. These were not only scientific expeditions, they were military operations carried out under warlike conditions, with frequent skirmishes against hostile Indians. Near Sevier Lake, Utah, Gunnison's entire party of Mounted Rifles was killed by Indians.

Realizing that the Army's strength was insufficient for the immense task now in hand—not only the pacification of the entire new empire but also the continuation of routine duties in the East—Congress in 1855 had authorized an increase of four more regiments; the 9th and 10th Infantry and 1st and 2nd Cavalry (now the 4th and 5th). Jefferson Davis, Secretary of War from 1853 to 1857, had pressed for this legislation, insisting that the railroad exploration include not only the originally proposed northern routes but also more southerly avenues branching westward from Atlanta, Ga.

The extremely high proportion of officers from Southern states detailed to the new cavalry regiments later gave rise to allegations that Davis was in fact preparing for an eventual break, but this is not borne out. However, so many Southerners were commissioned into the 2nd Cavalry (today's 5th), that it for a long time after the Civil War bore the nickname of "Jeff Davis' Own," appropriate indeed to a regiment that furnished Albert Sydney Johnston, Robert E. Lee, Edmund Kirby Smith, Earl Van Dorn, John B. Hood, Charles W. Field and Fitzhugh Lee to the Confederate cause.

Davis was responsible for another innovation—the introduction of the camel into the United States Army in an attempt to solve the transportation problem in the southwest. Some fifty or more of the animals were imported (with a number of Arab drovers) and used along the southern Texan frontier. However, the scheme proved impracticable and after several years was abandoned. A number of the animals were allowed to run wild and for years to come amazed occasional travelers and prospectors.

Garrisoning the West coast brought about troop movements both by land and by sea. Some of them were astounding. The Mounted Rifles, for instance, when the Mexican War ended, was ordered out to Oregon. Refitted and reconstituted at Fort Leavenworth, it started out May 10, 1849, overland, to reach its destination October 5, a hike of more than two thousand miles. Two years later the regiment marched back all the way to Texas where mounted troops were then urgently needed.

Another epic journey was that of a battalion of the 1st Artillery, also bound for Oregon. The outfit, from which all married officers had scrupulously been transferred prior to departure, left New York, November 10, 1848, to round the Horn. At Rio de Janeiro the expedition, the first U. S. troops to be seen in Brazil, received a royal welcome. At Valparaiso, on the Pacific coast, they heard news of the California gold discovery. Fearing wholesale desertions should they stop at any California port, the transport made for Honolulu. It was May, 1849, when they finally reached the mouth of the Columbia River and established camp at Fort Vancouver. Not a man had been lost, or officer put under charges, remarked a participant; there was little drinking and no gambling. Above all no quarrel or miff occurred, because, this narrator averred, there were no women aboard!

Not so fortunate was the 3rd Artillery in 1853. The vessel in which the greater part of the regiment was bound from New York around the Horn foundered in a storm off Cape Hatteras and two hundred officers and men were drowned. The four hundred survivors were rescued by passing vessels.

Eight companies of the 4th Infantry, transferred by water to the West coast via Panama about this time, had to hike across the Isthmus through miasmal jungle, overtaken by cholera and fever. Before the outfit reached San Francisco, one hundred and seven men had died.

In such fashion the Army passed the years from 1848 to 1860. It left its dead from the slopes of the Pacific coast to the churning waters off Hatteras, from the upper reaches of the Yellowstone and the Great Lakes to Panama, their monuments the nation's own development.

The new racial and religious stresses and strains brought about by the steady flow of migration from Europe, which racked the country during the period, were reflected to but little extent in the Army. "Americanism" and its anti-Catholic successor, "Know-Nothingism," which caused violence in so many civil communities, made little headway among the men in uniform. Some, remembering the San Patricio battalion of Irish deserters who fought for Mexico in the war, raised eyebrows, perhaps; but the Irish element in the Army was now being equalled by the German—and both were proving themselves loyal soldiers.

Agriculture, commerce and industry were booming throughout the land as the Machine Age made itself felt. Thin strands of steel crept westward, the Overland Mail and the Pony Express filling the still cavernous, but slowly closing, gap. But under all the pulsating energy of the young nation become a continental giant, volcanic fires were rumbling. The first hot spurt of lava came at Harper's Ferry in 1859.

Here was a problem long weighing heavy in men's minds, both in uniform and out of it. For this was a matter of conscience evolving from the very structure of the nation. Were we indeed one united republic, or were we but a collection of individual, independent states?

The solution was to come from the arbitrament of war, and by virtue of an Army divided against itself.

But, before taking that up, a note of comic relief during this disturbed period is interjected by War Department General Order No. 31, dated June 12, 1851. It specifically ordered the issue of "right and left foot shoes" to the troops. Our pedestrian Army had, it seemed, become shoe-conscious; no longer would the enlisted man have to torture his feet in rude brogans identical in shape!

*　　*　　*　　*　　*

• • • •

• • • •

8

THE BLUE AND THE GRAY

The Civil War, marking the rebirth of the United States, is as yet the most highly emotional experience of our country. Its imprint is stamped ineffaceably on the national soul, its saga told and retold in a spate of literature still unabated although more than ninety years have passed.

The division was on a matter of principle—the right of an independent state to secede from the Union. Not only was it the struggle of a nation divided, but of a military system divided, in which the leaders on both sides were indoctrinated with the same concept and the same principles of the art of war. That is the basic military reason why the war lasted as long as it did.

For the Civil War, by and large, was a West Pointers' war, and West Point concepts of training and leadership prevailed. If the fortunes of war swung to the South in the early days, it was because some of its graduates had been better utilized in the beginning by the Confederacy. When it started, not a single West Pointer held a general officer's commission in the Regular Army; when it ended, sixteen of the seventeen Regular Army general officers of the line were graduates.

When Sylvanus Thayer revitalized and reorganized the Military Academy in 1817 he established a curriculum designed towards a specific end—the production of officers for the Army.

Himself an ardent student of the history of war, and particularly of the military campaigns of Napoleon, Thayer went further. He ensured, as soon as he found the man fitted for the purpose, a solid teaching of the art of war, based on historical research. His man was Dennis Hart Mahan, a graduate of the Class of 1824, who was sent to Europe for four years of intensive military study and research and returned to become Professor of Civil and Military Engineering and of the Art of War, a position he filled until his death in 1871.

Mahan's influence upon the development of American engineering and technology has already been referred to in Chapter 5. His potent influence on military operations in the Civil War deserves some consideration here. Mahan was no innovator, no apostle of some get-rich-quick theory of war. This quiet, austere, shy little man who in his lectures resolved, as one of his pupils remarked, "what appeared to be a complex jumble of chance events into a striking illustration of the true principles of tactics and strategy," was an analyst who drew certain conclusions from the study of great captains of the past.

War, said Mahan, was fluid. Speed was his fetish; speed considered always in relation to the technological advance of the age. Anything which slowed up operations was to be shunned. "Against slow and over-prudent generals the very elements of Nature seem to array themselves." Mobility, surprise, boldness; clear thinking focused on the end to be gained; these were fundamental. "Celerity is the secret of success."

In a nut-shell, Mahan was preaching mobile warfare; the spirit of the offensive; a *blitzkrieg* geared, of course, to the horse-and-buggy age in which he lived, but *blitzkrieg* nevertheless.

Not only did this Mahan seed fall upon the graduates of the Military Academy, but it spread amongst others in the Army and in the militia, for his works on military tactics and strategy, first published in the late '40s, had wide reading. And, much to his rage—for Mahan was a staunch Union man—they were pirated in editions printed in Richmond and in New Orleans during the war. More than that; Mahan had been consulted and had taken a hand in the organization of Virginia Military Institute in 1839, and up until the war (V.M.I.'s annual summer encampment in 1860 had been named "Camp Mahan") was in frequent correspondence with its Superintendent, General Francis H. Smith, himself a West Point graduate and fond admirer of Sylvanus Thayer.

It is interesting to note, also, that as the war progressed, Mahan at West Point remained in correspondence with a number of his former pupils—in particular Grant and Sherman (he also corresponded with General Henry W. Halleck—"Old Brains," the Army nicknamed him—who coupled a vast store of military book-knowledge to an utter inability to command and direct. Here Mahan's advice fell on deaf ears).

Remember that all these men had been the captains and lieu-

tenants of the Mexican War; the men of whom Scott had given his
"fixed opinion." They were experienced, too, in Indian fighting.

In theory, collision between forces led by men all brought up in
the same concept of war and already practiced in it should have led
to stalemate. Actually, of course, these men were human. Few of them,
by 1861, had handled a unit larger than a company. The evolution of
brigades and divisions they knew only in the abstract. The problems
of leading mass armies were things only dreamed of, or touched on
in Mahan's lectures. So some of these men, when called upon, failed
miserably. Others, once given their heads, went on to victory, insofar
as the means available to them permitted.

Considering this background, one realizes why the Civil War
became the prototype of a *blitzkrieg* and total war of a later day; why
its operations became required study for military men throughout
Europe. One visualizes the foundation which brought about such
things as Grant's Vicksburg campaign, and his concept of a total war
splitting the South first longitudinally, then latitudinally; Sherman's
march to the sea; Sheridan's and James W. Wilson's utilization of
fire and movement in newborn cavalry tactics. One sees rhyme and
reason for Lee's brilliant strategy (no pupil of Mahan, Lee, when
Superintendent of West Point, had been in close personal touch with
him for three years), Jackson's lightning moves, and dozens of other
instances of brilliant troop-leading on both sides.

When war began, the problem facing President Lincoln was plain.
Eleven states had declared their independence of the Union, set up
a government of their own, and defied by armed force any attempt to
restrain them. To put down this rebellion the Union had to invade,
overthrow the recalcitrants, and occupy their territory.

The catch was that the United States did not possess the military
power in being to do anything of the sort. The potential was there;
the actuality lacked. When the guns first spoke at Sumter, and the
nation was faced with the fact that only by force of arms could it be
saved, Lincoln found himself powerless.

The Army in 1861 consisted of four regiments of cavalry (two of
them dragoons), one of mounted riflemen, four of artillery, ten of
infantry, the corps of engineers and the corps of topographical engineers, and the various staff and administrative departments. Its actual
strength was sixteen thousand, three hundred and sixty-seven officers

and men. The line companies, one hundred and ninety-eight of them, were so scattered as to prevent any immediate mobilization in force, with one hundred and eighty-three of them out on the wide frontier or on route to distant points and the fifteen remaining distributed along the Canadian border and on the Atlantic coast.

Actually the Confederacy was gathering some one hundred thousand volunteers, enlisted for a one-year period, and thirty-five thousand of them—more than twice the total Regular Army strength—were already under arms when Fort Sumter fell.

President Lincoln's first turn in this dilemma was towards that paper giant, the militia—three million men in nominal strength, but actually a huge, unorganized, untrained mob. Nothing had been done about the State militias since 1826, when James Barbour, then Secretary of War, had made a half-hearted and unsuccessful attempt to regularize and to standardize their training and to revise the ancient statute of February 28, 1795, which authorized the President to call out State militia into Federal service for not more than three months' service, subject always to the acquiescence of the governor concerned. Barbour's circular letter to all governors provoked much discussion. While most of them gave some lip service to the idea that three months' service was too short, nevertheless no agreement was reached on training or on expansion of the term, and the matter was dropped.

Now these chickens had come home to roost. Lincoln could get militia from states whose governors were willing to obey the request, but they would come for three months only.

Volunteer militia companies and regiments had become increasingly popular in some of the centers of population, although their variegated uniforms, allegedly snobbish attributes and the privileges granted them brought much resentment from the mass of the militia whose sole military duty was the annual one-day beer-and-skittles muster. A few of these newcomers are relatively noteworthy.

There was the "silk-stocking" 7th New York, uniformed like West Pointers, whose original name on organization—"National Guards"— was later to become the generic title for our citizen-soldiery. The 7th (now the 107th) Infantry dates from 1806. Then there was New York's "Fighting Irish" 69th (today's 165th) Infantry, whose lineage and wolf-hound cap badge date from 1846. But these and a handful of other outfits like them, with some semblance of training, were but exceptions to the general rule. As for the Southern volunteer militia units in existence, they, of course, were lost anyway, with all the Southern militia, insofar as the Union was concerned.

To all intents and purposes, then, when the call came, April 15, 1861, for seventy-five thousand militia, the heterogeneous mass that responded could only be compared in training and equipment to the armed rabble who rallied around Boston in 1775. So the President, with rebellion in his back yard as the Confederate forces gathering in nearby Virginia threatened the capital, by proclamation on May 3 increased the Regular Army by some twenty-two thousand men, the Navy by eighteen thousand men, and called for an additional force of about forty-two thousand volunteers.

His prompt action had added eleven new regiments to the Regular Army, one each of cavalry and artillery and nine of infantry. The cavalry became one generic group, the dragoons and the mounted rifles losing their distinctive names and being renumbered in order of seniority in the arm.

Lincoln's action was, of course, an arrant assumption of dictatorial power, since Congress alone has the power "to raise and support armies." But the Congress was not in session. When it did convene on July 4, 1861, it lost no time in legalizing the President's action. So for the third time in our national history—Congress twice had conferred dictatorial powers on General Washington—the commander-in-chief became in effect a dictator as a result of national military unpreparedness.

The growth of the new volunteer Army was fantastic, both in numbers and in its utter lack of proportion. The business of raising it having been turned over to the states, the Federal government had no voice in its composition, and necessarily accepted any and all sort of military organization. By the end of 1861 five hundred and sixty regiments of infantry, eighty-two of cavalry (of which some five hundred men only out of fifty-thousand-odd were actually mounted and serviceable), and an aggregation of artillery batteries equivalent to perhaps nine regiments, was in existence.

Some of these units were enlisted for three years; others were on the old, extravagant plan of a nine-month "hitch"—for Congress, exerting its prerogative to raise armies, was firmly set on its "too little and too late" policy. The three-month militia had come and gone by this time—although many of the units, on getting home, "re-upped" in the volunteers.

The volunteers came: farmer boys from the Northwest and the Corn Belt; city boys from the Eastern seaboard, Maine to Delaware; lanky mountaineers from the Alleghenies and the Green Mountains; as well as the Irish and the Germans who had found a new homeland for which to fight. They came in all the valor of ignorance, chanting "We are coming, Father Abraham, one hundred thousand strong."

From the East, too, came with them another song which a battalion of the old 2nd Infantry had been humming in garrison up Boston way. Why a tough Regular outfit should suddenly have latched on to a revival hymn tune is one of the many unsolved riddles of the soldier mind, but they had. It was, "Say, Brother, Will We Meet Again, Over on the Other Shore?" The professional soldiers had changed the words, and the 12th Massachusetts Volunteers, picking it up in their training days brought it down to war and to immortality as "John Brown's body lies a-mouldering in the grave . . . and we go marching on!"

They came in a multiplicity of uniforms, some already known in militia circles, some designed on the spur of the patriotic moment. The 7th and 8th New York (Washington Grays) and the 2nd Wisconsin wore West Point gray. The 39th New York (Garibaldi Guards) arrived all plumed in Italian *bersaglieri* uniform and complete with *vivandières* marching beside them—women probably no better than they should be. The 79th New York (Highlanders) sported kilt and sporran in dress uniform.

But the showiest of all were the zouaves. The odd fashion had hit the volunteer militia in the '50s, copied from the French units of that name who gained fame in the conquest of North Africa. The red fez, embroidered short blue jacket, baggy red trousers and white gaiters dazzled the amateur military eye, particularly when combined with the mincing little double-time step and fancy manual of arms of the zouaves.

Zouaves from New York, Brooklyn, Chicago and other places there were, complete, too, with *vivandières*. But the "Zou-zous" of them all, who made Army men's eyes pop and lips curl in derision, were Ellsworth's "pet Lambs"—the Fire Zouaves, plug-ugly Bowery-boy bullies recruited from New York City's volunteer fire fighters.

Their brawls and high-jinks kept Washington in a tizzy. In justice to them one should add that when the chips were down, the Fire Zouaves showed that they could die like soldiers.

Of different breed was a mid-west brigade commanded by West Pointer John Gibbon, who had been fortunate enough to transmute his captaincy in the 4th Artillery to a brigadier generalship of volunteers. They were the 2nd, 6th and 7th Wisconsin and 19th Indiana. They wore regulation blues, but Gibbon had dressed them up in black felt hats and white gaiters and whip-snapped them into the precision of regulars. Friend and foe alike promptly came to know and respect them, first as the "Black Hat Brigade" and later—a title well-earned—the "Iron Brigade." Their exploits and battle honors are blazoned today on the streamers of the 128th Infantry, National Guard.

All this fantastic array of citizen-soldiers had, of course, its counterpart south of the Potomac, where the militia which had so proudly marched to war in the Revolution, the War of 1812 and the Mexican War—together with a host of new-formed units—were now gathered to fight against the old flag. Of all of these, perhaps, the best-known won their first laurels at Bull Run—Jackson's "Stone-Wall Brigade." Its present-day successor, the 116th Infantry, National Guard, carries, together with the streamers of two World Wars, the battle honors of every major engagement of the Army of Northern Virginia.

They had their zouaves, too—the 1st (Tigers) and 7th (Pelicans) Louisiana. They had the Richmond German Rifles and Caledonian Guards, incorporated with the old 1st Virginia; as well as a bevy of other local aggregations such as the Rockridge Artillery of Virginia, trained by the Episcopal rector of Lexington, none other than one-time 2nd Lieutenant William N. Pendleton, who had resigned from the Army to take holy orders and who then became Lee's artillery chief.

But the Confederate soldiers had an initial edge on their Northern enemy, for their leadership was leavened by more than three hundred professional soldiers—Regulars who had just thrown up their commissions in the United States Army to join the Southland's cause. These men, together with Southern West Pointers out in civil life (ninety-nine joined up), Jefferson Davis, himself a soldier, carefully distributed as the hard core of the Confederate military command.

On the Union side, the Army's tiny force was almost completely submerged in the flood, and with it the majority of the professional officers, who found themselves forgotten in subordinate commands while—the lesson of the Mexican War forgotten—the horde of new officers was chosen by the Governors of the respective states in which the troops were raised.

Four of the first five major generals of volunteers commissioned by September, 1861, were civilians; twenty-four of the seventy-one brigadier generals had had no previous military experience, while perhaps one colonel out of each twenty appointed was qualified to lead men in battle.

The new armies were officered by individuals mainly picked, as Edmonds remarked, "on the good old rule of political patronage— he's a good fellow and he needs the job, and he's got backing!" All this because the Congress and the Secretary of the Treasury, Salmon P. Chase, refused to impregnate the mass by the trained Regular leaven. Chase had been appointed by Lincoln to the job because Simon Cameron, then Secretary of War, was too busy with the details of organizing the three-months' militiamen.

Actually, the situation was saved in the end through the fact that some Governors did try to procure good officers for their troops from former Regulars who had volunteered their services—something which the War Department itself refused to do. For instance, as of the writing of this book, the Adjutant General's Department has not answered the letter written by ex-Captain Ulysses S. Grant, early in 1861, proffering his services. But Governor Richard Yates of Illinois made the short, straw-hatted, shabby man in civilian clothing who had gratuitously drilled a company of Galena volunteers, a colonel.

The governor of Michigan succeeded in getting the War Department's permission to commission Captain Philip H. Sheridan, 13th Inf., as colonel of the 2nd Michigan Volunteer Cavalry, but dozens of similar requests for the services of other Regular officers were turned down flatly.

Ex-Brevet Captain William Tecumseh Sherman wished to return to the service, but it wasn't until political strings in Washington were pulled by his Senator brother, John, that Sherman was commissioned in the 13th Infantry.

Influential railroad president George B. McClellan, ex-Captain, 1st Cavalry, had but little trouble in obtaining a major generalship in the Ohio militia when the first call for three-month men went out.

Thus was produced an amazing contrast. Only one hundred and forty-two of the Regulars in uniform at the time ever donned general officers' stars; only two hundred and forty-eight became colonels or higher, and, of the West Pointers, three hundred and eight, including one hundred and sixty-one who were captains when the war started, ended the war in the grade of major or lower. Yet of the one hundred and two West Pointers who came back to the colors (only thirty-two per cent of the graduates then out in civil life), fifty-one became general officers and eighty in all reached the grade of colonel or higher.

Of sixty important battles, Military Academy graduates commanded on both sides in fifty-five; a West Pointer was in command of one of the two opposing forces in each of the other five. And yet, as far as the Union was concerned this came about, as we have seen, not through any foresight on the part of Congress or the administration but by grace of a few governors who rose above politics to obtain good leaders for their state's troops.

One of the amazing things about the Civil War was the manner in which the Regular Army (and the Navy, too, for that matter) divided. The enlisted men stood true to their salt; the records show that only twenty-six individuals out of some fifteen-thousand-odd men deserted to the Confederacy at the outbreak of war. There was, for them, of course, no question of resignation; they were professional soldiers, enlisted for a fixed period. Comparatively few of them were Southerners; many, as we have already noted, were recruited from newly arrived immigrants, others came mainly from the Northeastern seaboard with its large urban population.

With the officer, it was different. He had always had the privilege of resigning his commission, and no attempt was made in 1860-1861 to curb this privilege. But, considering the violence and bloodshed characterizing civilian differences at the time, and that this was nothing more or less than a conflict between two hostile nations divided by an undebatable difference of opinion, one might expect the war to open in a series of armed clashes on Army posts, with the Southern officers taking advantage of their position to seize arms and public property, and to lead their men in open mutiny. History tells us that such has almost invariably been the case when insurrection flares.

Nothing of the sort occurred. With but one shameful exception those officers who decided to throw in their lot with the forces of secession gave a most remarkable demonstration of adherence to the tenets of a code of honor built upon the tradition and the soul of an Army. First formally tendering their resignations, they then, with meticulous care, transferred to their successors all troops and public property—arms, stores and records—for which they were responsible. Then, and not until then, did they offer their swords to their respective states.

The one exception was septuagenarian Brevet Major General David E. Twiggs, from Georgia, commanding the Department of Texas. Without resigning, Twiggs turned over his entire command to Texas authorities; loyal subordinates, however, salvaged part of the troops. Immediate dismissal from the service ended ignominiously for Twiggs a career which had begun when he entered the Army from civil life in the War of 1812.

All the more remarkable is this orderly division of the officer corps when we recall the many overt efforts of civilians in high places of national trust to wreck the Union. Notorious in this respect was President Buchanan's Secretary of War, John B. Floyd, who, after deliberately hamstringing the pre-war operations of the War Department, slipped away to become a brigadier general in the Confederate service. Yet, with the one exception of Twiggs, there is no evidence of any Army or Navy officer having engaged in any treasonable plot, nor of having yielded to the rebels except because of overwhelming force and under honorable terms.

In active service at the time were one thousand and eighty officers, six hundred and twenty of whom came from Union territory, four hundred and sixty from the secession area. Yet the proportion of officers who went South was not based upon their geographical origin. Altogether only three hundred and thirteen Regular officers passed below the Mason-Dixon line. Standing true to the old flag were seven hundred and sixty-seven, including aged Winfield Scott, Virginian to his heart's core, but who had no doubt where duty called. So, too, with stern Virginian George H. Thomas. On the other hand, Pennsylvanian John C. Pemberton donned Confederate gray.

Curious also is the division amongst West Point graduates, of whom there were then eight hundred and twenty-one in active service. Southern West Pointers numbered three hundred and thirty, yet only one hundred and sixty-eight of them followed Pierre G. T. Beauregard and Robert E. Lee, as did also sixteen Northern graduates—all married, as was Pemberton, into Southern families.

Conversely, of the two hundred and fifty-nine officers originally appointed from civil life, one hundred and thirty came from the Southland. And every man of them, excepting Winfield Scott, threw up his commission to join the Confederacy.

At West Point for more than a year previous to the outbreak of war belligerent youngsters had turbulently milled on several occasions. The furlough class of 1860 came back to the Point charged with explosive differences of opinion. Sixty-five of eighty-six cadets of Southern origin later resigned in tempo with the officer corps. Yet when one of these young men, Charles P. Ball of Alabama, a cadet first sergeant, left the post, a group of his Northern classmates carried him on their shoulders down to the steamboat dock in token of goodwill.

And when popular Lieutenant Fitzhugh Lee threw up his commission at West Point, he was not only serenaded on his departure by the officers of the post, but the entire corps of cadets stood, hats in hand, in front of barracks as he rode past in the omnibus. Only two days previously the corps had joyously serenaded as a hero an officer just back from the tragedy of Fort Sumter.

By mid-summer of 1861, aged Winfield Scott—he was seventy-five now—had submitted his far-sighted and brilliant "Anaconda Plan." This proposed a complete naval blockade of the Southern coasts and the pressure of well-trained land forces to squeeze between them the forces of secession. But the policy of war was in civilian hands, and the unthinking pressure of an outraged North was breathing hot on their political necks. Immediate action, advance on Richmond—such was the popular demand. So Scott's idea was shelved (it came to fruition three years later, after millions of dollars and thousands of young lives had been squandered futilely). From his Massachusetts retirement old General Sylvanus Thayer, "Father of the Military Academy," in his wisdom barked prophetic protest:

"Whoever makes the first aggressive move will be beaten. The greater their numbers, the more certain their defeat. Let one division be driven to rout and the whole pack will run like children from an apple orchard when set upon by dogs. Of that whole army there will not be found 100 fit to form a forlorn hope, unless you take those officers who have received a military education . . .

"To make good soldiers out of good materials they must be drilled by competent men; to make a good army out of the best men will take three years. We should act on the defensive as much as possible until our army is better drilled. I pray the South makes the first move."

But no one then in high places cared what Thayer thought.

So young Major Irvin McDowell, raised to brigadier rank, was spurred to command and lead this Blue rabble in arms to victory while official Washington went picnicking out to Bull Run to watch the spectacle.

And Thayer's prediction came true. On that sad July 21, 1861, save for Major George Sykes' dogged little battalion of Regular infantry, McDowell's greenhorns, formed into brigades and divisions only one day before the battle, did panic and "run like children from an apple orchard." And as a dazed nation shook its groggy head, brash young George B. McClellan was raised to command along the Potomac line.

With the cry of "On to Richmond" still thundering from a public obsessed with the desire for immediate victory, Lincoln and his civilian coterie directing the strategy of the war had picked McClellan to supersede Scott. And McClellan, failure though he was to become as a great captain, was a master of organization. He forged the Army of the Potomac which better men finally led to victory. He brought order and cohesion and training to that Blue rabble in arms who so innocently in 1861 went singing to war in all their valor of ignorance.

He trained it, he led it to the Peninsula; and there he fumbled it away in a weird and heartbreaking campaign, from March 17 to July 2, 1862, in a succession of battles from Seven Pines to the Seven Days, while westward in the Shenandoah Valley Stonewall Jackson wrote a brilliant page in the history of war and set official Washington shaking in its Congress gaiters.

So Lincoln reached again to bring from the West boastful General John Pope, who sneered at his own soldiers of the newly formed Army of Virginia. Pope announced his headquarters were "in the saddle" (Lee to that dryly observing that Pope's headquarters seemed to be where his hindquarters ought to be), then permitted himself to be foxed by Lee's audacious pincers move which sent Jackson behind him in lightning stroke, while James Longstreet came through Thorough-fare Gap to close the nippers at Second Bull Run.

Before the North could recover from this, Lee was off for his first invasion and McClellan was called back to pursue with a rejuvenated Army of the Potomac.

On Antietam's bloody field Lee was stopped. But McClellan's indecision—"No one but McClellan would have hesitated to attack," Joe Johnston wrote to Lee—transformed what might have been a brilliant victory and death-knell for the South into a stalemate. And then McClellan was through. As footnote came the "black Republican" campaign against his Presidential ambitions and with it the disgraceful trial and conviction of Fitz-John Porter.

Pope, seeking a scapegoat to cover his defeat at the Second Battle of Bull Run, accused Porter of disobeying orders; this, he asserted, caused the disaster. Actually Porter's prompt action when Longstreet arrived on the field unexpectedly had delayed the Southern reinforce-ments for twenty hours and saved Pope's army from total rout.

But perjured testimony and the flames of political hatred, when linked to his own tactless criticism of his superior, destroyed Porter's brilliant reputation. Cashiered from the Army, he was not cleared until more than twenty years had passed.

Reluctant General Ambrose E. Burnside—his style of whiskers perpetuated in the popular nickname of "burnsides"—called up to relieve McClellan, was not sure what he should do, but felt that he ought to do something. So he divided his forces at Fredericksburg and made a series of uncoordinated frontal attacks against Lee's position. Doomed before it started, the Army of the Potomac then reeled back, leaving its waves of dead as monuments to its general's inefficiency. And the year closed in deepest gloom for the Union, while more sheaves of volunteers were added to the Federal armies.

Almost forgotten were the two bright spots of the early year—Grant's clever campaign against Forts Henry and Donelson in the West, which won him in February a major generalship and the fame of his immortal "unconditional surrender" dictum; and Admiral Far-ragut's victory at New Orleans in April.

Unforgotten, though, by both friend and foe, was the mulish pseudo-soldier Benjamin F. Butler's shaming of the uniform in the later occupation of New Orleans which did so much to harden Southern resistance—that infamous order that, should any woman "insult or show contempt for any officer or soldier of the United States, she shall be regarded and shall be held liable to be treated as a woman of the town plying her avocation."

Unforgotten, too, was Grant's later near-disaster at Shiloh, where surprised green Federal troops ran like sheep, and defeat might have followed had not Albert Sydney Johnston's equally green militia been just as fleetfooted in avoiding battle. So the North licked its wounds and added to its armies three hundred and forty-six new regiments of volunteer infantry, forty-four of cavalry, twelve of heavy artillery, and fifty-seven batteries of light artillery.

The basic fallacy in this lay in the fact that instead of utilizing this manpower to fill the depleted ranks of existing units, new and un- trained units were added, while war-wise outfits remained reduced in strength.

To add insult to injury, the Secretary of War circularized the governors of the loyal states, December 23, 1861, imploring them to commission in the volunteer forces the "large number of foreign offi- cers of military education and experience" who had tendered their services to the government! True it was that a horde of foreign adventurers had come clamoring for commissions, just as they had done during the War of the Revolution. And the Secretary of State had needled his Cabinet colleague to circularize the governors on their behalf lest these men "seek and probably obtain similar employ- ment in the forces of insurgents"—a pretty good estimate of the objectives and caliber of most of these gentry.

Such things our Army witnessed and pondered on, as 1863 came in, with Joseph (Fighting Joe) Hooker as Lincoln's New Year gift to. the Army of the Potomac, while imperturbable Grant, along the Mississippi, was feinting at Vicksburg's stronghold. But Hooker, pressing across the Rappahannock in what was to be the answer to the Union's prayer, was caught, May 2, in the web of Lee's strategy, at Chancellorsville, the "perfect battle." Jackson's thunderbolt came blazing in on the flank of the Army of the Potomac and once again it reeled back in defeat.

While political tom-toms thumped amid the throes of a nation entangled in war for survival and not yet sure of the result, initiation of a draft act, the first in United States history (the Confederacy had come to national conscription a year earlier), added fuel to Northern discontent.

Like most hasty legislation, this act was poorly drawn. Under its provisions any of the men called up by lottery—from among all citizens and foreigners who had declared their intention to become citizens, within the age brackets of twenty to forty-five—could purchase "commutation" (exemption) by simply paying the government three hundred dollars. Furthermore, one could produce a substitute to take one's place. In consequence a thriving market in human cattle rose; brokerage offices were set up in many large communities to arrange such barter.

There was, as George Fort Milton put it, "no bar to putting a cash price on patriotism . . . this helped make it the rich man's war but the poor man's fight."

Popular sentiment began to curdle as detachments of officers and men of the Provost Marshal General's Department started to put the law into effect throughout the loyal states. Disloyal elements made political capital out of the distressing situation.

Meanwhile, almost unnoted in the chagrin of Chancellorsville, something big had been happening along the Mississippi. Grant, stymied, it seemed, across the river from Vicksburg, made a surprise crossing of the river below, and cutting his communications, plunged into the heart of enemy land between his adversaries, Joe Johnston and Pemberton, pushing back the first, then turning and driving the second into Vicksburg. Grant's Big Black River campaign was to go down in history as one of our Army's most daring and most brilliant exploits.

And, in the East, Lee, driven by the economic and financial plight of a Confederacy choking under the U. S. Navy's blockade of all her ports, made his supreme gesture. He hurled his Army of Northern Virginia, hot in the glow of victory, across the Potomac to invade the North again.

Hooker followed with the Army of the Potomac, to be yanked out of the line-up and replaced by George G. Meade, able artisan of war who yet lacked the final spark of genius. To attempt retelling the story of Gettysburg, the greatest battle ever fought on American soil, would be redundant. Yet one must linger for a moment on the finale—Pickett's charge against that "clump of trees" still standing on Cemetery Ridge. Here indeed was West Pointer against West Pointer, leading citizen-soldiers, Americans all and by this time professionals, against one another in, to borrow Winston Churchill's language, their finest hour of devotion to their respective causes. But when the gray tide receded, Meade failed to pursue.

Simultaneously with announcement of victory at Gettysburg came the thrilling news of Pemberton's surrender to Grant at Vicksburg. Here were two successes bringing the nation confidence in its Army.

But a sour note followed when the hated draft law was put in operation in New York City. Riots and bloodshed there ceased only when troops of the Army of the Potomac were rushed up from Gettysburg.

For four days—July 13 to 16—mobs ravaged the city. Conscription offices were burned, stores ransacked. Police and firemen were powerless. The Colored Orphanage Asylum was attacked; a brutal mob's revenge for the slaves' role in bringing on the war. Several hundred children were saved as the police held the rioters back long enough for them to escape, but the building was destroyed.

The City Hall was threatened; Horace Greeley's *Tribune* building sabotaged. *The New York Times'* staff defended their offices with rifles and three Gatling guns spirited in. *The Daily News,* ardent anti-war sheet, applauded the outbreak. *The World,* at first acquiescent, later joined with James Gordon Bennett's *Herald* in demanding stern measures of repression. *The Herald,* however, played the story down on its inside pages; operations of the war itself came first.

Conservative estimates of the carnage in New York placed the deaths at seventy-five; others, including Theodore Roosevelt's later estimate in 1891, put them at twelve hundred. No one will ever know; no statistical record was kept. In any event those were four red days for the "Bowery Boys" and other hoodlums of the big city, who lynched Negroes and burned, raped and pillaged at will. Then the bayonets of tired men from Gettysburg brought halt.

A short time later the Army began to feel the personal impact of the draftee. It was not a good one; no poorer soldier had ever come into U.S. Army uniform. The appalling assortment of derelicts and criminals was gathered first into camps in New York and Boston, then shipped in batches—usually by water—to Virginia and the front. Some were bounty-jumpers—deserters who went back time and time again to reenlist and get their blood-money. Others were the fruit of the substitute-broker's business. The vast majority had but one objective: not to fight.

Kept under armed guard from the moment they entered their corrals until they were dumped ashore, they spent their time carousing, robbing one another and scheming to desert. The nightmarish conditions of this system nauseated the comparatively few men of honest intent who had either submitted to the draft or had been shanghaied. Attempts to escape were frequent; quite a few men were shot down by the trigger-happy guards, invalid veterans who despised their charges and had no compunction about killing those who tried to slip away.

Once assigned to troop organizations in the field, these "handcuffed volunteers," as the Army of the Potomac promptly dubbed them, immediately showed they could not be trusted in camp or in battle. If put on guard duty they would flit away to become campfollowers or *banditti,* or sneak back North to reenlist for another bounty. In battle they just simply ran away. So many deserted to the enemy that in the spring of 1864, instead of being received with open arms by the Confederacy, they were shipped off to the horrors of Andersonville.

The veterans of the Army of the Potomac, by this time an aggregation of professional soldiers, took a dim view of this swarm, and of the consequences of their behavior. Regulations tightened; the former comradeship existing between men who had fought and suffered together dimming to some extent as privileges were clipped, and the full disciplinary power of military law was poured on malingering draftees. Flogging had been abolished in 1861, but bucking and gagging, spreadeagling on an artillery limber wheel, the "sweat box"— a coffin-like contraption in which the offender stood for hours in semi-suffocation—and not infrequently the fists of their fellows, finally made soldiers out of those who stayed. As for the deserters, the Army thought itself well rid of them. Fortunately, not more than two per cent of our Army was recruited by conscription.

Meanwhile the haphazard raising of new volunteer regiments went gaily on, with state authorities offering ever-increasing bounties to men enlisting in them, while at the same time recruiting officers were scrabbling and contesting with one another for replacements for old regiments—volunteer and Regular. The terms of regiment, brigade and division became meaningless as yardstick of strength. Old outfits were shrinking to corporal's guards. For instance, the Iron Brigade, entering the fight at Gettysburg eighteen hundred strong, reeled out with six hundred men—and no replacements in sight. By the time war ended there were some seventeen hundred regiments of volunteer infantry alone in the Army of the United States.

No wonder that in 1863 a new song was heard about the camp-fires as old soldiers scoffed and sneered at johnny-come-lately regiments in spick-and-span uniforms. The pertinent words changed, of course, in accordance with circumstances:

> "I'm a raw recruit, with a bran'-new suit,
> Nine hundred dollars bounty.
> An' I've come down from Darbytown,
> To fight for Oxford County."

The veteran Union soldier who went into battle at Gettysburg and in the later portion of the war was a far different individual from the recruit who had gaily marched out of Washington in 1861. He travelled light. Gone were the bright trappings and variegated uniforms; gone most of the impedimenta which a well-meaning government handed him to clutter up his movements.

He wore a simple loose blouse of dark blue cloth and trousers of a lighter blue. The mounted man, cavalry or artillery, still kept the tight-fitting shell-jacket, and a scarf—usually red—was wound about his neck. On his head sat either the bell-crowned regulation kepi (forage cap), its leather visor crushed into a "vee" for better visibility; or a broad-brimmed black felt hat. Fashions in head-gear differed, with the Western regiments favoring the hat.

The badge of the soldier's corps was pinned or sewed on the head-gear, its color differing with the brigade to which he belonged. This fore-runner of the present shoulder-patch—the "flash" of our British friends—came into fashion in 1862 when General Phil Kearny ordered his 3rd Division, 3rd Corps, to wear a distinctive piece of scarlet cloth. The custom spread throughout the Army of the Potomac and the cavalry corps, in a wide variety of patterns and symbols.

Were this soldier an infantryman he walked with the long swinging step of the foot-slogger; the mile-eating pace the Army had learned the hard way—by example of Stonewall Jackson's "foot cavalry."

Our soldier usually scorned the heavy, regulation knapsack. In refitting for a new campaign a new one would be issued him. But on the first day's march and earliest opportunity the awkward leather shoulder-chafing contraption went into the ditch.

His hand-weapon, canteen and cartridge-box were essentials, of course. One blanket, or perhaps his overcoat instead (one or other was thrown away), wrapped in a rubber blanket, was in the roll slung over his shoulder. In that roll, or in his pockets or in the haversack he sometimes wore (or the mounted man's saddle bags), were a change of socks and underwear, with perhaps some letters, a pocket Testament, or even a curious little book, lying before me as I write this.

Something for the Knapsack is the title of this little three-by-four-inch cardboard-bound pamphlet of forty-eight pages, written by one J. B. Waterbury, D.D. It might be termed a religious tract, for it does enjoin piety and sobriety. Actually, it is probably the first attempt to psychologically fortify the American soldier.

"Something more is needed," it points out, "than mere animal courage, or brute force, or accurate drill to make a reliable soldier. He must know what he is fighting for; whether it is right or wrong; and he must feel the inspiring motive of patriotism." Then, in some eight hundred words, under "The Conflict—Is It Right?" it sums up the Union viewpoint.

"Duty," wrote the author in conclusion, "is the sublimest word in human language. Do your duty! You can't do *more;* you never should wish to do *less.*"

Our soldier, so accoutered, was wise in the little things that make for creature comfort on campaign; in foraging and in bivouac. He was wise, also, in the little ways of war; had he not been he would not be still alive. His eyes that stared from his wind-wrinkled, sunburned face could pick up the faraway movement of a bush or tall grass, his mind react instantaneously to what that meant on a windless day. He knew when and why—although he always hated the labor—to scratch out a shelter trench before the whining Minié balls sang too close.

In a nutshell, he had become the man who could—and did—lick the Army of Northern Virginia.

This Civil War soldier suffered a lot. He endured as a matter of course the fiery, crawling itch of the louse (as did his enemies). If he were captured he could expect to undergo such horrors as American soldiers had not met since the days of the British prison ships of the Revolutionary War—the "floating hells" of Wallabout Bay.

He would rot on the treeless, shelterless sixteen-acre charnel-ground of Andersonville, Ga., where ten thousand wretches died in one seven-month period. Were he a captive officer, he would probably end up in one of the bare barracks of Libby Prison's three-story gloom, beside the stinking little canal that carried off Richmond's filth.

The sufferings of these prisoners of war could not be traced necessarily to enemy vindictiveness or callousness. There was sadism, of course, at Andersonville. Henry Wirz, its superintendent, was to swing from a gallows later in payment for his crimes. But the Southern Confederacy, short of food and medicaments for its own people and its own army, had none to waste on enemy prisoners. And as the shortages waxed, so too did the number of prisoners, for before the war was over the North refused to make any more exchanges of prisoners.

One might call that an inhuman policy. But the North could write off its own manpower losses, and had no intention of letting good Confederate soldiers free to fight again. So the prisoners suffered; this was total war.

Nor was the inhumanity of camp administration one-sided. The Northern prison camp at Elmira, N. Y., for instance, at one time boasted two thousand cases of scurvy amongst its eight thousand prisoners.

Autumn of 1863 brought first another dash of disappointment and frustration to the nation as probings eastward from the Mississippi Valley met defeat at Chickamauga—relieved only by the stand of the "Rock of Chickamauga," stout-hearted General George Henry Thomas. But the beckoning finger of President Lincoln, beginning to feel that perhaps he had found his man, brought Grant down to relieve the situation.

The relief of Chattanooga, General Braxton Bragg's defeat at

Lookout Mountain and Missionary Ridge—the latter an example of well-led, well-trained and confident citizen-soldiers storming their way to a mountain-top—heartened the nation. It also confirmed Lincoln's appraisal of Grant and of the men he had pulled up to command under him—Sherman and Sheridan.

In consequence, Grant came to Washington, in March of 1864. He came to supreme command with Lincoln's *carte blanche*: "The particulars of your plan I neither know nor seek to know . . . I wish not to obtrude any constraints or restraints upon you."

And with Grant's coming came total war. To Sherman, poised now in Tennessee, Grant's directive had all the incisive grasp of the great captain: "It is my design . . . to work all parts of the army together and somewhat towards a common end . . . [General Nathaniel P.] Banks . . . to commence operations against Mobile as soon as he can . . . [General Quincy A.] Gillmore joins [General Benjamin F.] Butler and the two operate together against Richmond from the south . . . I will stay with the Army of the Potomac and operate directly against Lee's army wherever it may be found . . . [General Franz] Sigel . . . to move against the Virginia & Tennessee Railroad . . . You I propose to move against Johnston's army, to break it up and get into the interior of the enemy's country as far as you can, inflicting all the damage you can against their war resources . . ."

Interesting is Mahan's appraisal of his former pupil. Grant, he stated, "was always a first section man in his scientific studies . . . his mental machine was of the powerful low-pressure class, which condenses its own steam and consumes its own smoke, and which pushes steadily forward and drives all obstacles before it."

And that, of course, was just what Grant did, in the Wilderness, at Spotsylvania and Cold Harbor. Unrebuffed by Lee's able parries, unruffled by the mistakes of some of his lieutenants, he settled down before Petersburg while Sherman went marching through Georgia. The "big push" was on; the Army had found its leader.

Jubal Early's final fling to lift the pressure poked over the Potomac in the Confederacy's third and last attempt at invasion. It washed to Washington's walls July 11 and then receded. Sheridan, sent to the Shenandoah Valley by Grant to "eat Virginia clean and clear . . . so that crows flying over it for the balance of this season will have to carry their own provender," ended Early's forlorn hope at Cedar

Creek, October 19, when he came pounding from "Winchester, twenty miles away," to retrieve victory from defeat.

On November 15, Sherman abandoned his base and disappeared eastward, shearing a wide swathe of destruction, to pop up at Savannah December 10 and link with the Navy's sea blockade. The Confederacy, already shorn in two along the Mississippi, had been split again. And on March 28, 1865, Grant told Sheridan, back from the Valley, "I now feel like ending the matter."

Ten days later, the harried remnants of Lee's Army of Northern Virginia, breaking away from Petersburg, dragged down by General George G. Meade's Army of the Potomac and surrounded by Sheridan's swirling cavalry, met their end at Appomattox.

When the war closed the Army of the United States was the world's mightiest fighting machine; ground and polished by four years of strife into a professional force, led by professionals. It was an Army that had accomplished—with the resources of the nation girded behind it—tasks unprecedented in magnitude and fashion in the history of war. In the doing it had presented to the world not only a new technology of war, but also a prophecy of things to come: the military ability and national capacity which would twice later restore world balance in global upheavals.

The railroad as an agent of war was indeed something new. It was utilized by both sides. But the Military Railroad Construction Corps, wedding the technology of railroading to military strategy, was strictly an Army product. This was the outfit which organized and maintained, despite enemy fire and sabotage, the network of rails on which the Army of the Potomac depended throughout the war.

The corps not only ran existing railroads but built new ones. It threw bridges—constructed, as Lincoln whimsically remarked, "of corn stalks and beanpoles"—over ravines and rivers. It built and operated flatboats with tracks laid upon them, for ferrying trains— prototypes of the car-ferry of later commercial use. It got men and matériel and supply to the right places at the right time.

The creator of this logistical innovation was Herman Haupt, a Regular who had resigned and risen high in railroading. Called from civil life by Secretary of War Edwin M. Stanton—one must give him credit—Haupt applied his military background and knowledge to the already highly specialized business of railroading in amazing fashion.

Haupt's most astounding performance was a vital factor in the winning of the Battle of Gettysburg. He had rushed to Harrisburg when Lee started North. On June 30, 1863, out of the jumble of information and misinformation as to the activities of the Army of Northern Virginia, Haupt divined Lee's intention to concentrate in the Gettysburg area.

Warning both the War Department and General Meade, Haupt made haste to Baltimore and, entirely on his own volition, extemporized a railhead at Westminster to which by July 2 fifteen trains a day were heaping supply to Meade, and wounded men were being evacuated in the returning empties.

For the first time in the history of war an intelligent system of care and evacuation of the wounded had evolved; an amazing story, for with it is entwined the beginnings of concerted ministration by the home-folk to their men away at war. It is a story of trial and error, and also of devotion, in which three Massachusetts women were to play important parts.

Insofar as the Army itself was concerned, the Civil War found the Medical Department, like all other branches, inadequate in strength and methodology. From Bull Run to the Seven Days' Battles the condition of the wounded had been, as in all previous wars, one of horror. When they were haphazardly gathered from the field after fighting ceased, the few military medicos and their scanty staffs present hastily did what they could for them, and then they were rattled and bounced about in wagons to be dumped in hospitals, churches and barns in Washington.

Male attendants and teamsters were mostly interested in pilfering from their helpless charges, in whisky-guzzling, and in saving their own skins. Calls for volunteer civilians to assist in the task brought response mainly from Washington rapscallions equally bent on petty larceny.

Out in the field one man did something about all this. Army Surgeon Jonathan Letterman (he had been in uniform since 1849) devised a plan consisting, in essence, of a front-line regimental medical service from whose first-aid stations the wounded could be collected by ambulance companies and gathered in tented field hospitals. From there they were later to be transferred to base hospitals back of the war zone.

Bull-headed Stanton, War Secretary, would have none of such new-fangled ideas. But McClellan, who, as an observer, had had first-hand knowledge of the shocking handling of wounded in the Crimean War, gave Letterman free rein, and Grant in the West also adopted the idea at once. So the new system went into effect by extemporization, although not until March 11, 1864, did it receive official War Department and Congressional approval.

Meanwhile a shy, prim little forty-year-old Washington Patent Office clerk named Clara Barton had rushed, single-handed, into the mess, as had Florence Nightingale in the Crimea only five years before her. Overriding all opposition by her quiet insistence, she started an ambulance service of her own to bring to the overworked field hospitals supplies she begged from her Massachusetts friends.

A solitary woman handling a wagon filled with medical stores, Clara Barton lugged assistance from Washington to Fredericksburg's stricken field, to Second Bull Run, and again to Antietam. Letterman, in the red stress of Antietam, welcomed her as a miracle. So loud his praises rang that the fuddy-duddies in the War Department capitulated. Thereafter Clara Barton and her supply-train, grown now to four wagons and an ambulance, rolled by official permission with the Army of the Potomac.

How Clara Barton in later years was instrumental in organizing the American Red Cross to link with the international organization of that name is a story unfortunately not for this book. We must turn to the Washington scene, where the Army's human wreckage was overcrowding all available space.

How that situation was cared for is the story of the United States Sanitary Commission—the first national voluntary relief movement to help our Army. It was, in effect, an almost spontaneous explosion of the women of the United States—the combined strength of women's clubs and ladies' aid societies mushrooming to aid their soldiers. Its almost unlimited funds were coupled with a tremendous political influence, for prominent men in various professions also rushed to support it.

This was lucky for the Army, because the Commission was powerful enough to beat down all official opposition to a proposed shocking innovation—that female nurses, women of standards and character, should tend wounded soldiers in hospitals! The Commission selected fifty-nine-year-old Dorothea L. Dix, puritanical philanthropist already well known for her efforts to improve conditions in almshouses, prisons and insane asylums. She was the Federally appointed super-intendent of women nurses.

Miss Dix and her carefully gathered corps of volunteer women— no female younger than thirty was considered—went into action as the first shiploads of wounded men from the Peninsula campaign began to flood the hospitals. The soldiers in the crowded wards, at first shy and puzzled as the ladies buckled down to their extraordinary routine and service, welcomed their ministrations—dazed, homesick boys and grizzled, cynical professionals alike. Out of the chaos began to come order; humanity in concerted action.

And one of the most ardent of the rustling, crinoline-skirted sorority was thirty-year-old Louisa May Alcott. The author of "Little Women" broke down under the strain by the time the streams of wounded from Fredericksburg began to surge into the capital.

There were men, also, engaged in this merciful work. One of them was big, bushy-bearded poet Walt Whitman. He haunted the wards, distributing tobacco, fruit, and other delicacies; helping to write letters home; and in general radiating gentleness and good will.

All this was a new deal for the American soldier; the beginnings of departure from the old-time callousness of "a wooden leg or a gold chain." But innovations do not always last when immediate need ceases. The Sanitary Commission dissolved at the end of the war. And, although the desirability and the necessity for women nurses had been plainly written in Civil War history, the Army Nurse Corps did not come into being until 1901.

Other women went to this war, too. Not alone those Amazons whose espionage activities have come down the years in glamorized fashion, but also the Army women. Some followed their men into the battle zone. On the Confederate side there was the wife of General John B. Gordon, who shared her husband's campaigns. Testy Jubal Early, irritated by the sight of the sprightly Mrs. Gordon's light travel-ling wagon in her husband's headquarters train, once exploded: "I wish the Yankees would capture Mrs. Gordon and hold her until the war is over." They never did. But on the Union side, Mrs. James B.

Ricketts, learning that her captain husband, wounded, had been captured at Bull Run, entered the enemy lines and and shared the miseries of captivity with him in Libby Prison until he was exchanged.

The spiritual needs of the soldier had been recognized during the war in a big way. Each regiment, it seemed, had at least one chaplain, and they thronged in camps and hospitals. It is, perhaps indicative of the spirit of the era that, in most of the personal reminiscences of that time, the chaplain—regimental, camp or hospital—is treated in jocose and frequently ribald terms. It was evidently far different from the spirit and the record of the self-sacrificing Army chaplains of later years.

Chaplains were not new to the Army. In 1775, the Continental Congress authorized pay for them. The Regular Army's first chaplain, the Rev. John Hurt, Episcopal clergyman who had been chaplain of the 6th Virginia of the Continental Line, was commissioned in 1791. By 1808, chaplains were authorized for each brigade. The first Roman Catholic priests to be so commissioned were two chaplains-at-large, who served in Taylor's army during the Mexican War. Rabbis were first authorized as chaplains in 1862.

But all this while places of religious worship had been haphazard—a tent, a barn or a field—depending upon the whim of the commander and the energy of the chaplain. In 1861, General McClellan wired Simon Cameron, then Secretary of War: "Will you please authorize me to use boards to put up places of worship at Camp Denison. Parties furnish nails and labor."

Cameron's reply inaugurated the erection of chapels in our Army. It was classic: "The Lord's will be done."

To return to the technological side, in complete accord with Mahan's precept that in war the spade went hand in hand with the musket, the Corps of Engineers had done fantastic things. Its greatest achievement was the bridging of the James River in June, 1864, for Grant's surprise side-shift to Petersburg after the battle of Cold Harbor. General Edward P. Alexander, the Confederate commentator, calls this, with reason: "the greatest bridge the world has seen since the days of Xerxes. At the point selected the river was two thousand, one hundred feet wide, ninety feet deep, and had a rise and fall of tide of four feet, giving very strong currents. A draw was necessary for the passage of vessels."

It took the engineers just eight hours to link one hundred pontoons and three schooners, to fell and hew the timbers, lay the planking, and to dig and smooth the causeways over which men and guns and horses streamed. It was a feat indeed unparalleled. Not even the stupendous Rhine bridge laid by Army engineers of the VII Corps in 1945 was equal to this; it took twelve hours, the material was Treadway links, the span one thousand feet.

But the most significant change, which fitted into the revolutionary development of mobile warfare, was in the cavalry. It began when James H. Wilson, efficient young Regular who had been made chief of the Cavalry Bureau, rearmed our cavalry with the Spencer repeating carbine. In this President Lincoln took personal interest.

The Regular Army had entered the war equipped with the Springfield muzzle-loading rifle, firing the Minié ball. There were not enough of them at first to supply the mass armies (enormous purchases of foreign weapons, many of defective type, were made), but by late 1862 the Springfield Arsenal was turning out Springfields at the rate of two hundred thousand a year.

This weapon was to remain as the basic type of infantry arm. The war was over before the copper cartridge was fully developed and the breech-loading, repeating rifle eliminated the muzzle-loader. But already several types of repeating arms were coming out of the experimental stage, and one of them, the Spencer seven-shot carbine (its rimfire cartridges fed through a tube in the butt), caught Wilson's attention.

Wilson was trying to make something more than an ornamental nuisance out of the Federal cavalry. Its futility had developed an irritating habit in the infantry during the first two years of the war, of greeting our horsemen with the crack: "Who ever saw a dead cavalryman?" Wilson's use of the Spencer turned the cavalry from the saber-brandishing arm of shock-action into a supple combination of fire and movement in which the horse became a vehicle transporting the rifleman to the proper place to exert overwhelming fire-power at the proper time. It was indeed a signpost to *blitzkrieg*.

About this time Grant had assumed command. Well-knowing the value of mobility and surprise, as he had demonstrated by initiating Grierson's cavalry raid in 1863 through Mississippi to distract Confederate attention from his own river-crossing below Vicksburg, Grant demanded a complete reorganization of his own cavalry. He wanted for it, he told the War Department, "a thorough leader . . . the best man in the army." He got Phil Sheridan, who proceeded to show the world a new cavalry arm and a lesson in cavalry-infantry team work. Sheridan's operations at Five Forks, Sayler's Creek and Appomattox Court House were in principle those of armor and armored infantry of today.

It is interesting to note that engineer Wilson and infantryman Sheridan between them revolutionized the tactical employment of cavalry.

That was the sort of thing the soldier had seen in this new Army. He had also seen an amazing array of other technological developments harnessed to the war machine: the Parrott gun, a three-inch cast-iron rifle, supplanting the bronze smooth-bores he had started with; the telegraph; visual signalling; aerial reconnaissance; mines and booby-traps. He had seen such topsy-turvy happenings as the organization of Confederate prisoners of war into six regiments of volunteer infantry to fight under the old flag—not against their brethren but against Indian and desperado racking the Southwest now that the troops were away to war.

Our soldier, too, had seen the Negro organized in racial units for the first time; not only the Corps d'Afrique, whose duties were mainly those of guard and ceremony, but also such outfits as Robert Gould Shaw's 54th Massachusetts Volunteers, who blazoned on history's page the warrior qualities of the Negro citizen-soldier.

He had learned that the interplay of politics and military matters was unavoidable in a democracy; that political patronage would have its way, no matter how costly in human life; that star-chamber proceedings of a Joint Congressional Committee on the Conduct of the War could override justice and decency, and tarnish with fetid breath the career of honorable men in uniform.

In 1862, shortly after the close of the Peninsula campaign, Congress instituted our most cherished military decoration, the Medal of Honor. It was to be awarded "to such officers and privates as shall most distinguish themselves by their gallantry in action, and other soldier-like qualities, during the present insurrection." Two years later reference to the "present insurrection" was dropped, widening eligibility to all deeds of gallantry in action.

Not until 1918, however, was the medal to rise to its present superlative standard, comparable to Britain's Victoria Cross (the institution of which in 1856, during the Crimean War, spurred origin of the Medal of Honor). "Hereafter," the medal was to be bestowed only upon an officer or man who, in action against an enemy, should "distinguish himself conspicuously by gallantry and intrepidity at the risk of his life above and beyond the call of duty."

A change in Army Regulations of 1918 stresses that such a deed must be one "the omission of which would not justly subject him to censure as for shortcoming or failure in the performance of his duty," and provides that at least two eyewitnesses should testify in the recommendations for the award.

The Regular during those Civil War years had seen some recognition of his own dedication to the defense of his nation. The first retirement law had been enacted August 3, 1861. No longer were officers to be held on the active list until death, blocking promotions and stifling the initiative of the men following them.

But best of all the things our Army witnessed was the scene in that farmhouse parlor at Appomattox, April 9, 1865. Forever after American soldiers could pridefully recall the actions there of two men of their breed; two gentlemen engaging, after a simple hand-clasp, in courteous small-talk hiding their own emotions upon the death of an army and of a cause.

Grant, matter-of-fact in his dusty field blues spattered with red Virginia mud, apologizes for his lack of a saber as he eyes Lee's immaculate, sashed full-dress. His weapon, he explains, has been packed in his baggage.

These two, Grant recalls, have met once before, in Mexico. Lee, Scott's dashing engineer staff captain, had come trotting up to the brigade in which Grant served, and Grant had never forgotten; he would have recognized Lee anywhere. And courtly Lee, although remembering the incident, regrets he was unable to recollect the infantry subaltern's features.

And then, the terms of surrender.

Grant, scribbling in his note-book, jots them down. In substance, all officers and men of the Army of Northern Virginia were to give parole, then return unmolested to their homes. Arms, artillery and public property were to be surrendered. Grant pauses in his writing as his eyes rest momentarily on his opponent's elaborately hilted saber. The pencil moves again, deliberately.

"This will not embrace the side arms of the officers, nor their private horses and baggage."

Added oral concession was that all enlisted men could take with them their horses or mules, "to work their little farms." And that, like the twenty-five thousand rations rushed at once to the starving men in gray, was something which soldiers could appreciate.

Next day, the Army of Northern Virginia, its battle flags still flying above the thinned ranks, marching to lay down its arms, passed the Army of the Potomac drawn up in silent, frozen tribute, "as if," wrote General Joshua L. Chamberlain, commanding the Federal honor guard, "it were the passing of the dead."

Such things, expressions of the soul of the Army, softened the bitterness of defeat. As far as the soldiers were concerned, the nation was reunited. No one dreamed that four days later an assassin's bullet would undo it all.

*   *   *   *   *

9

· · · ·

• • • •

TOMAHAWK AND BRICKBAT

Hostilities ended, the wartime Army was, of course, dissolved. The volunteers went home to civilian life and perennial Grand Army of the Republic reunions; the Regulars returned to Indian-fighting and to take up the repulsive task of military occupation of the Southern States.

But before the national armed strength faded, the world was to see one of our infrequent demonstrations of military might used correctly as instrument of diplomacy and deterrent to future bloodshed. The mobilization along the Rio Grande of fifty thousand bayonets, under General Sheridan's command, brought quick end to the designs of France's Napoleon III upon the Western hemisphere.

Napoleon III had seized the opportunity, while the Civil War was on, to establish an alien rule over Mexico and thus gain foothold. Backed by the potential of a powerful veteran Army, the United States' demand in early 1866 that France get out was quickly acceded to. The French troops supporting the unfortunate Maximilian upon his throne were withdrawn, leaving him to his doom.

The Regular Army now went through a series of reorganizations and diminutions. In 1866 its line strength—fifty-four thousand, six hundred or so enlisted and three thousand and thirty-six officers—was set at ten regiments of cavalry, five of artillery and forty-five of infantry (including four of a Veterans Reserve Corps: invalids doing light duty). Six of the new regiments comprised Negro enlisted personnel; the 9th and 10th Cavalry and the 38th, 39th, 40th and 41st (all later consolidated into the 24th and 25th) Infantry. These Negro regiments had long and valued existence until desegregation in 1950 terminated their life. Another racial element, too, was entered on the Army list; a detachment of one thousand Indian Scouts.

Three years later the Congress drastically reduced the Army again. The Act of March 3, 1869, cut enlisted strength to thirty-seven thousand, reducing the infantry to twenty-five regiments; and the officer corps was pruned down to two thousand, two hundred and twenty-seven. The enlistment term, formerly three years for infantry and five for cavalry, was set at five years for all.

One lingers on these things, because here was not just a shuffling of statistical figures, nor was it painful to the enlisted men—the attrition of expired enlistments took care of their reduction. But it was the partial disruption of a profession as far as the officer was concerned. Following the war, in what had now become part of the American tradition, a large number of volunteer officers had been taken into the Regular Army in the course of its expansion. While some of these men were misfits, the majority, as they proved after their assimilation, became warp and woof of the profession.

All these men, in order to remain in their new-found vocation, had accepted permanent commissions far below their wartime rank. Commanders of corps, divisions and brigades were now leading regiments and battalions, while most of the new group was in subaltern rank.

To mention but a few of those who were to burgeon as leaders, there were, for instance, such men as Nelson A. Miles, Alfred H. Terry and Henry W. Lawton. And, last but far from least, there was Colonel Arthur MacArthur, 25th Wisconsin Volunteer Infantry, who had won the Medal of Honor on the crest of Missionary Ridge. MacArthur, senior member of the Army's most remarkable father-and-son team, his eagles doffed, began his distinguished professional career as a lieutenant of infantry.

All these men, as well as the rest of the Regular officer corps, were jolted by this drastic reduction. Boards of officers—promptly nicknamed "Benzine Boards"—began an immediate sifting in Washington and in the various departments. More than seven hundred and fifty officers, men just settling into their profession, were dropped with a year's pay; promotions froze. Once again a feeling of uncertainty—a feeling that careers were dependent more upon the whim of party politics than upon national need—beset the Regular officer at the very time he was immersed in what was perhaps the most arduous and thankless service he had ever experienced.

For two years the Army had been ruling the states of the late Southern Confederacy, under Congressional directive stemming from Lincoln's assassination. The resulting Northern hatred had crystallized under the "black Republican cabal" in three arbitrary Acts—of March 2, March 23 and July 19, 1867. No longer were the Southern states recognized as "the States lately in rebellion." They were prohibited from reconstituting themselves. The military governors of the five districts into which Congress had grouped these states were charged with registering voters and supervising all the process of forming new state governments, which might then apply to Congress for readmission to the Union.

"Carpet-baggers"—the carrion crows who always come winging in for rich pickings during a military occupation—and the Negro population milling in perplexity of new-won and barely understood liberty, were superimposed on the resentful white population, itself split into a number of bitterly discordant factions. Not even Grant's fervent "Let us have peace," uttered in his nomination speech of 1868, and sturdily adhered to during his administrations, could compose these differences.

In the midst of cross-currents of consequent disorder stood the Regulars, charged with keeping order; damned on the one hand by greedy politicians from the North, double-damned on the other by the white Southerners.

The soldier witnessed one of the most astounding and revolting spectacles in the entire history of the nation. For, by grace of his presence, Northern politicians and rabble-rousers were able to organize the ignorant Negroes politically, elect legislatures and bleed the already prostrate Southern states. James Truslow Adams noted, for instance, that in four years of Republican rule in Louisiana the state tax rose four hundred per cent and its debt from fourteen million to fifty million dollars.

State legislative halls were filled with swaggering Negroes and greasy carpet-baggers. Under guise of liberty, license reigned. A legitimate fear arose in areas where the population was predominantly Negro.

In consequence, out of Tennessee came a weird and monstrous thing—the Ku Klux Klan—to spread throughout the Southern states. White-sheeted, hooded, and masked, raiders in the night burned, flogged and murdered; their prey was the Negro and the carpet-bagger. The pendulum swung the other way. As the voluminous testimony of Congressional investigations shows, in Louisiana alone some two thousand persons were killed, wounded and otherwise injured just prior to the elections of 1868.

With the passage of the years an aura of romance has grown about this first Klan, and it is true that many Southerners of character and standing did join—in gesture of despair—the "Invisible Empire" that attempted to right the injustices of that drab era of Reconstruction by terrorism.

But there was no aura of romance about it to the officers and·men of the Regular Army who painstakingly rooted it out. Their duty was plain, and they performed it to the best of their ability. It should be noted, too, that many of the former leaders of the Confederate forces were trying earnestly to bring about reconciliation in those unhappy days, and restore the nation. Among them were such soldiers as Lee, Beauregard, Longstreet and Wade Hampton—the last three libelled by one southern writer as "burglars, because they counseled submission to military acts."

All in all, it was an era trying not only to the South but to the Army. It continued until 1877, when the last troops were withdrawn from South Carolina and Louisiana, the last of the "erring sisters" were restored on equal status to the national fold, and the reign of the carpetbagger was ended.

Meanwhile the Army was also engaged elsewhere, as the catalysing element in the greatest of our national expansions that knitted together and settled a United States reaching from Atlantic to Pacific, from Canada to Mexico, with Alaska—"Seward's Folly," purchased from Russia in 1867—thrown in for good measure. In the midst of the task, 1873, the Army was cut again to twenty-five thousand officers and men.

It was drama at its highest, this phase of the Army's life: the Wild West, the Indian and the cowboy, thundering buffalo herds, Idaho and Montana gold-rushes, cow-towns and cattle kings, bad men and sheriffs. One can see it, hear it, read it in Bowdlerized versions in all entertainment media today, from comic book to TV. But in digesting all this, and in hearing that best-known and most-worn of clichés to come out of it—"U. S. Cavalry to the rescue!"—one should remember something else:

The United States Army from 1865 to 1898 fought no less than nine hundred and forty-three engagements against the Indians—running the gamut from skirmishes to pitched battles—in twelve separate campaigns, to say nothing of a score of other disconnected bickerings, to insure that this national expansion should become fact. During that time hardly a three-month period passed without some expedition west of the Mississippi and between the Canadian and Mexican borders.

The dry official record sums it up in listing eligibility for the Indian Campaign Medal, awarded for services in (1) Southern Oregon, Idaho, northern California and Nevada, 1865-1868; (2) against the Comanches and confederate tribes in Kansas, Colorado, Texas, New Mexico and Indian Territory, 1867-1875; (3) the Modoc War, 1872-1873; (4) against the Apaches in Arizona, 1873; (5) the Northern Cheyennes and Sioux, 1876-1877; (6) the Nez Percé War in 1877; (7) the Bannock War, 1878; (8) against the Northern Cheyennes, 1878-1879; (9) the Sheep-Eaters, Piutes and Bannocks, June-October, 1879; (10) the Utes in Colorado and Utah, 1879-1880; (11) the Apaches in Arizona and New Mexico, 1885-1886; (12) the Sioux in South Dakota, 1890-1891; and (13) as sort of catch-all, any other action against hostile Indians between 1865 and 1891, in which U. S. troops were killed or wounded.

A long listing this, its scope unnoticed for the most part during the period, for war correspondents were few and far between. Congress itself—and this calls to mind another "police action" of ninety years later—did not recognize this Indian-fighting as war until March, 1890; the campaign medal was not authorized until 1907. Parenthetically, the same Act providing for the Indian Campaign Medal also instituted—long years after many of those eligible had died—our senior service decoration, the Civil War Campaign Medal.

The elimination of the North American Indian constituted a drab page in our national history. From the very beginning, as we have seen, he had been a stumbling-block to progress. His was the land; so the white man took it away from him. Resenting the encroachment of civilization, which deprived him of his hunting grounds, his reactions were violent. So, too, were the equally violent and frequently both provocative and inexcusable acts of the white man. If the Indian neither knew nor recognized the so-called rules of war, neither did the land-grabber, the politician, or many of the agents set up allegedly to assist the Indian, know or recognize any rule of probity.

The Army, charged with the mission, first protected the construction of the Union Pacific westward to meet the oncoming Central
Pacific line from California. In the doing—despite a continuous skir-
mishing with hostile Indians—once more the old story of an extended
screen of frontier posts took place.

The tide of settlement came surging behind the thin lines of steel
and the singing telegraph wires above them, linking East and West.
The cattle industry; the opening of the mineral resources of Colorado,
Nevada, Idaho and Montana; the destruction of the buffalo herds; all
these meant, as far as the Plains Indian was concerned, the invasion
of his domain and the loss of his means of subsistence. To make matters worse the United States, which had heretofore treated the Indian—
in theory at least—as an equal and attempted to deal with him by
treaty, now changed its policy.

The Indian became a ward of the government, to be concentrated
on reservations—always, it seemed, situated in some area considered
worthless by the white man (who, however, stubbed his toe on one
occasion when he turned the Oklahoma oil lands over to the red man).
The carpet-bagger and the "do-gooder," the Indian agent, the gangster
and the well-meaning Easterner who viewed "the noble red man"
through the eyes of James Fenimore Cooper, came surging in—Bible
in one hand and whisky bottle in the other. At least that is how the
soldier charged with subduing the Indian, gathering him and keeping
him in his pen, looked on it.

General Sheridan, commanding the Dept. of the Missouri in 1868,
summed up the situation:

"The present system of dealing with the Indians, I think, is an
error. There are too many fingers in the pie, too many ends to be
subserved, and too much money to be made; and it is in the interest
of the nation and of humanity to put an end to this inhuman farce.
The Peace Commission, the Indian Department, the military and the
Indian make a balky team. The public treasury is depleted and innocent people plundered in this quadrangular arrangement, in which the
Treasury and the unarmed settlers are the greatest sufferers. . . .

"The Army has nothing to gain by war with the Indians; on the
contrary it has everything to lose. In such a war it suffers all the hardships and privations, exposed as it is to the charge of assassination if
the Indians are killed, to the charge of inefficiency if they are not; to

misrepresentation by the agents who fatten on the plunder of the
Indians, and misunderstood by worthy people at home who are de-
ceived by those agents."

Not only was the Army thus handicapped in all its operations
against the Indian, but it also soon found its weapons to be inferior
to those of its opponents. Improvements in small-arms had jumped
by leaps and bounds. Perfection of the copper percussion cartridge,
developed at Frankford Arsenal, had brought the magazine repeating
rifle into mass production—the earlier Spencer, and the improved
Henry, Remington and Winchester were all available to anyone who
had the wherewithal to buy them. Unscrupulous traders enriched themselves by selling or bartering these arms to the Indians, while some
Indian agents shipped them in to the reservations on pretext that the
red man needed firearms for hunting! Quantities of these arms were
also stolen from frontiersmen and settlers.

The regulation shoulder arm now being issued to the troops was
a Springfield single-shot breech loader—a small improvement on the
weapon carried in the Civil War. For a short time the cavalry had
still clung to its Spencer repeating carbine but, Congressional economy
intervening, the cavalry was rearmed with a Springfield cut down to
carbine size. According to contemporary complaints, the ejector of
this arm frequently failed; the soldier in action was out of luck if he
did not have a knife to pry out the empty shell—while of course
during this time he was a sitting duck for an opponent.

As result, officers who could afford them purchased improved
civilian arms; the rare soldier who was fortunate enough to have ready
cash also discarded his issue weapon for another which would shoot
faster—a custom quite naturally winked at by officers under the circumstances. It might be noted in this regard that everyone carried
the rifle in the field; the saber which had brought the Indian appellation
of "Long Knives" to the cavalry remained in garrison.

By 1869, the Army's territorial organization was in three Military
Divisions—the Atlantic, the Missouri and the Pacific. There were in
all two hundred and fifty-five posts, of which fifty-seven clustered
under the Division of the Missouri, with headquarters at St. Louis.
Here was the nerve-center of a great part of the post-Civil War
Indian-fighting.

The Missouri River, from Fort Leavenworth to the head of steamboat navigation at Fort Benton, Mont., was the principal supply line. From it at a dozen or more points the Army penetrated the Northwest to the foothills of the Bitterroots, the Bighorns, the Bad Lands and the Black Hills. From the Platte and the North Platte, along the Yellowstone, and from the extending lines of the trans-continental Northern Pacific, the Army probed and fought. Scores of little posts, most of them now long-forgotten, rose by dint of soldier toil and sweat, each to become springboard for further active campaigning.

The women were there, too. The enlisted man's wife and the officer's wife—Mrs. O'Grady and the colonel's lady again—were part and parcel of that Indian-fighting Army. Some of them, bold spirits, arrived with the first troops; such women as Mrs. George A. Custer, who will always epitomize the Army wife of Indian-fighting days. Others followed close, in supply train, stage-coach, or ambulance (Army name for the light Dougherty wagon).

Sometimes our frontier fort—the same old pattern of stockade hewed out of standing timber—was assaulted before completion. There was Fort Phil Kearny, for instance, built on the Powder River in the Bighorn foothills of Wyoming, to protect the old Bozeman Trail. Troops were still constructing it during the winter of 1866, when Red Cloud's Sioux surprised a working party out cutting timber. A detachment which was rushed to their aid drove the Indians off, but in their exuberance—they were new at Indian-fighting—tried to pursue. Back to the post came the sound of heavy firing, then silence. The entire remaining garrison, some three hundred strong, was then turned out, but found only the stark bodies of the three officers, seventy-six enlisted men and two civilian volunteers who had rashly plunged into an ambush.

But some months later when Red Cloud tried the same trick there again, he found the fourteen wagons of the working party dismantled and their wooden bodies arranged in a rough square with the horse-herd inside it. The guard and the workers stood off incessant attacks of some fifteen hundred Sioux in this—the once-famous "Wagon-Box Fight"—until relief came.

Some of the main posts were slightly more pretentious. In 1870, Fort Laramie, on the North Platte in what is now southeastern Wyoming—where the temperature ranged from one hundred and two degrees in summer to twenty-one below zero in winter—had barracks for six companies, heated by stoves. Officers' quarters, of adobe construction, ranged in size from the four rooms of the commanding officer to cubicles in long huts. Plumbing was non-existent. The hospital boasted the post's sole bathroom, with a tin tub. All water was hauled from the river just below. The nearest supply depot was at Cheyenne, eighty-nine miles of wagon-haul. Six months' supply had to be kept at the post, except fresh meat (beef was kept on the hoof; buffalo was hunted).

But Laramie was just a suburban garrison compared with Fort Buford on the north bank of the Missouri, near the mouth of the Yellowstone. For half the year its supply came by water from St. Louis, more than two thousand miles away; navigation was closed from early fall to spring. Mail once a month was luxury; sometimes there was a three-month lag. And the water supply, hauled from the river, was drinkable though muddy—"six grains of alum to the gallon renders it perfectly clear and transparent after standing twelve hours!"

At Fort Yuma, Arizona, where the city of that name now lies, the garrison got a taste of something else; its dry atmosphere shrank foodstuffs. An official medical report notes among many other remarkable things that "eggs . . . on hand for a few weeks lose their watery contents by evaporation . . . this has probably led to the story that our hens lay hard-boiled eggs."

Thus ran the gamut of Army existence in garrison during the period; an isolated existence where officer and man were both thrown on their own resources for entertainment, where improvised minstrel shows and skits (impoverished Thespians were not uncommon in the ranks) were presented in crude halls erected by the soldiers; where Army wives made over gowns in accord with Paris fashions in six-month-old magazines; and where an Army way of life already established became moulded into rigid shape and social code.

It was a shirt-sleeve, informal, jaunty Army in the field—the Army which has been immortalized by the brushes of Frederick Remington and Rufus F. Zogbaum. It wore the comfortable wide-brimmed campaign hat of felt, adopted from the cowboy. But in garrison, whether in one-company post or larger station, it was spit-and-polish, too. Horse and foot turned out for drill in dress blues, while bands played at guard mounting and parade.

There emerges from this kaleidoscopic picture of incessant campaigning an impression of inner strength and vitality. This Army was self-sufficient, resourceful and, above all, confident. Leadership, discipline and training produced a fighting machine; forged the soul of the soldier.

Here was guerrilla-type, light-marching, fast-moving warfare against an enemy crafty, elusive, bold and savage. The Plains Indians —the Sioux, Cheyennes and Comanches—were the finest light cavalry in the world. The Apache was not a horseman in that sense; he used his animal as a means of transportation but preferred to fight on foot. All of these hostiles could cover ground at amazing rate.

The Army solved the problem by taking the war to the Indian— beating him at his own game. General George Crook—the "Gray Fox," the Indians called him—was perhaps the greatest Indian-fighter of them all. His Powder River campaign of early 1876 was as Spartan a bit of experience as ever American soldiers have undergone. Having decided that the Indian should be fought in wintertime—the worst time from the Indians' point of view—Crook's men rode to war in the lightest marching order organized soldiery have used since the days of Genghis Khan.

For officers and men alike, it meant the clothes they wore and no more. They messed together on half-rations from the pack-train, for there were no wagons. Capt. John G. Bourke, Crook's biographer, wrote that it challenged comparison with "anything seen among our officers outside of Libby or Andersonville prisons. General Crook did not allow us either knife, fork, spoon or plate." The headquarters mess gear comprised "one frying-pan, one carving-knife, one large coffee-pot, one large tin platter, one large and two small tin ladles, and the necessary bags for carrying sugar, coffee, bacon and hard bread . . . also one sheet-iron mess pan."

Crook adapted the uniform to the situation. Lambs-wool socks— two pair of them—protected feet stuffed into Indian moccasins with cork soles, while buffalo-hide boots, hair-side in, were outer covering. The individual soldier could wear such underwear as he saw fit, provided there were two layers. The flannel shirts were double-breasted, as were the blanket-blouses—the color of both these articles was immaterial, although blue predominated. Overcoats, color immaterial too, were of buffalo, bearskin, beaver or simple canvas, blanket-lined.

Fur caps and collars protected head and neck; wool gloves and over-gauntlets of beaver or muskrat, the hands.

Crook and his officers dressed like their men. The General's long bushy brown beard—neatly done up in two braids bound, the legend runs, with red tape!—protruded from his wolfskin collar. A heavy leather cartridge-belt hung by two straps from his shoulders and he was never separated from his rifle.

Such was the uniform worn by those who rode and fought in temperatures down to zero, when sometimes horses and men had to be kept moving at night to prevent freezing. Equally heterogeneous was their light garb in the summer campaigns when the plains baked in the sun and red dust caked on sweating faces.

That first campaign of Crook's up the Powder River ended in tragic failure. Crazy Horse and his Oglala Sioux were flushed from their winter hiding-place, a canyon on the Little Powder. Six troops of the 3rd Cavalry, under Colonel Joseph J. Reynolds, attacked at dawn March 17, 1876, to destroy the village, capture the pony-herd, and disperse the warriors.

They charged through, scattered the hostiles, and captured the pony-herd. But as they commenced a methodical destruction of the tepees with their stores of food and ammunition, Reynolds—no one to this day knows just why—ordered a withdrawal. The troopers fell back in disorder, leaving their dead and, it was alleged, some of their wounded. The rallying Indians recaptured their pony-herd.

Crook, infuriated at the failure of his plan, withdrew. Flushed in their triumph, the Indians were free to fight again. But no one at the time realized that Reynold's blunder was to make possible the thing that never should have happened—Custer's defeat.

This high tide of Indian-fighting came later in that same year, when the troops took the field again against Crazy Horse and his medicine man, Sitting Bull. Sheridan, commanding the area, was determined to clean the matter up. Three columns converged on the Yellowstone area—Alfred H. Terry, John Gibbon and Crook. Crook met Crazy Horse on the Rosebud, fought a drawn battle against odds of five to one on July 17. The Indians melted from the scene. Terry, who of course knew nothing of this fight, crossed Crazy Horse's broad trail and sent Custer to get south of this unidentified tribal movement, hoping that between them the three columns could box the hostiles in once and for all.

But Custer, following fast, flushed his foe and decided to go it alone. Impetuously and rashly he plunged with five troops of the 7th Cavalry into the midst of Crazy Horse's thousands on the Little Big Horn to be done to death with all his command on June 25.

It was late November before Custer was avenged. Crook discovered a huge Cheyenne encampment in an ice-bound gorge of Crazy Woman Fork. He sent Colonel Ranald Mackenzie and ten troops of cavalry on a stripped-saddle march in the dead of a frigid night to make a surprise attack, thoroughly ending that phase of the war. Dull Knife, Cheyenne leader, surrendered to Crook shortly after.

Up on the Tongue River a month later Colonel Nelson Miles—who won more fame later by the capture of Geronimo in the south—closed in on Crazy Horse's own village, high on a commanding bluff. The Sioux prepared to repel the infantrymen starting up the slopes, but Miles had a surprise for them. Out from under canvas wagon-covers came two light field guns whose shells began screaming over the hill-top. That was too much. The Indians fled, and soon after Crazy Horse surrendered. The Big Horn and Yellowstone expedition was ended.

It was during that year of 1876, when Regulars were fighting and dying in the apogee of Indian-fighting, that the Regular really tasted the full bitterness of national indifference.

For that was the year in which the Fifty-fourth Congress nonchalantly adjourned without passing an Appropriations Act for the coming fiscal year, and until November 21, 1877, when the next Congress cleaned up the mess, not an officer or man of Army or Navy was able to touch a penny of pay! The enlisted man could eat, for rations had been provided. But for the officer, dependent on his meager salary, the situation was tragic.

Some astute financiers, the firm of Drexel, Morgan & Co. leading, at once formed a syndicate which loaned commissioned officers up to ninety-five per cent on the face value of their pay vouchers, garnering six-per-cent interest in return. There were some notable exceptions to this turning of a quick buck. The Louisiana National Bank extended loans without interest. And the Occidental Hotel in San Francisco announced that no Army or Navy officer would be billed for accommodations "until Congress passed an appropriations act."

The memory of that incident lingered long in the Army, for the next Congress, while repairing its predecessor's omission, absolutely refused to consider reimbursement to officers for any interest mulcted from them. Interesting, too, is the fact that during that grim period the desertion rate among the enlisted men dropped!

Thus the Army kept on the job of fighting Indians. It endured blizzards, floods, financial catastrophe, prairie fires and sand storms. It concluded the job at Wounded Knee Creek, when the 7th Cavalry defeated Big Foot's Sioux December 29, 1890, and the last hostiles of importance surrendered to Miles fifteen days later. A postscript was written at Leech Lake, Minn. in September, 1898, when a detachment of the 3rd Infantry suppressed a minor disturbance. The sole interest to this episode is that the 3rd Infantry—Harmar's First American Regiment, which in 1790 was the first U. S. Army unit to fight the Indians—closed the book.

It is well to remember that in all this battling the Indian learned to respect the Regular not only as a fighter but also as a peacemaker. He had found that the soldier kept his word. Crook, in particular, throughout his career did much to alleviate the red man's sufferings. In Arizona, after outfighting the Apaches, he put them to work as civilized farmers. The Indian attitude towards him is best expressed by Red Cloud's words when he heard of the "Gray Fox's" death in 1890: "General Crook came; he, at least, had never lied to us. His words gave the people hope. He died. Their hopes died again."

And another Regular, Hugh Scott, who had painstakingly learned the Indian sign language and could converse fluently with them, also became a peacemaker of note. Following in Crook's pattern, he later turned Geronimo and his sullen band of Apache cutthroats into self-supporting, peaceful agriculturists at Fort Sill. He succeeded, as Miles remarked "in safely leading them in the pursuit of peace and civilization."

Looking over the record for this period, one finds several innovations improving the condition of the enlisted man. The first, and most important, had to do with the preparation of his food. It is amazing that, up until the Civil War, the military of all nations, it seemed, had considered that their responsibility for the soldier's food ended when the raw elements of this ration in proper quantity had been issued him. Our Army was no exception. Hunks of meat and bread, driblets of coffee (unground), salt and pepper were dumped helter-skelter from wagon-train or post commissary and divided among the men in each unit. What the men did with it was their own business.

In 1812, the Surgeon General noted that "the soldier is, in general, his own cook." Scott, beyond insisting upon the good quality of the ration and exhorting the men to prepare their food properly, didn't go much further. Bakeries had been long established in garrisons, of course. But the unit mess just didn't exist. Sometimes men grouped themselves in informal messes; sometimes the camp women earned a pittance by cooking. Otherwise the individual just scraped up a fire, pounded his coffee beans on a rock and with tin plate, cup and knife made himself a meal.

The militia influence in the opening days of the Civil War started a change. Posh regiments, like the 7th New York, with hired cooks and money to burn, startled the Regular into a "how long has this been going on?" attitude. Such folderol didn't last long in the stress of war, but a precedent had been set. "Contrabands"—Negroes on the loose—were frequently hired as cooks by outfits in the field, and the unit mess, the company cook, and the mess line came into existence.

By 1863, the War Department caught up with Bulwer Lytton's classic "civilized man cannot live without cooks" and authorized that "cooks shall be detailed in turn . . . at the rate of one for each company numbering less than thirty . . . and two cooks for each company numbering more than thirty men; and they shall serve as each detail ten days."

Through the post-war period the pattern settled, although not until 1894 was the cook to be given a sergeant's pay. But mess halls and kitchens were a part of garrison life and the folding sheet-iron Buzzacott field range rolled in the cook-wagon in the field. The era of "KP" had dawned; kitchen police, thoroughly detested and absolutely essential, with all its dishwashing, pot-walloping and potato-peeling. It was the irony of fate that just as the unit mess did come officially into existence, the guerrilla-type, fast-moving Indian campaigns of necessity brought back much of the hand-to-mouth catch-as-catch-can messing.

Equally important from the psychological viewpoint was the Presidential order in 1895, establishing the post exchange, "to supply the troops at reasonable prices with articles of ordinary use, wear and consumption not supplied by the Government, and to afford them means of rational recreation and amusement."

Gone was the sutler, abolished in 1866; gone was his successor, the post trader, who flourished from 1876 to 1893. A co-operative store, run by soldiers for soldiers, replaced them. Its slender profits, returned to each unit, furnished capital to purchase furniture for day rooms, books, and other recreations and comforts to relieve the stark drabness of garrison life.

Contact with the civilian population was, naturally, comparatively small during the period. At the posts along the Eastern seaboard, and at the Presidios of Monterey and San Francisco, civilians did rub shoulders to some extent with Army personnel. And in the West, communities growing to urban dimensions around the frontier garrisons learned to call upon the military for help from time to time.

The Army doctor had long found himself in role of general practitioner, far beyond the normal duties of attending to the needs of the male members of the garrison in this Army where family life had become part and parcel of the service. Now, in newly established communities where civilian physicians lacked, he was frequently in demand—a position finally recognized in regulations permitting him to engage in civilian practice.

But these links were thin, and the domestic unrest attendant upon labor's growing pains did nothing to cement relations between the civilian and the soldier. Between 1886 and 1895, the Army was called upon to maintain law and order and ensure the passage of the U. S. mail in no less than three hundred and twenty-eight different strikes and other upheavals. Of these the greatest was the Pullman strike that paralyzed the nation's railroads in 1894 and defied police and militia until Chicago's railway yards were turned into armed camps of Regulars.

On the technological side the Ordnance Department had accomplished much, particularly in developing heavy guns—for harbor defense—of the disappearing carriage type. Breech-loading field pieces, 3.2-inch caliber, had supplanted the Napoleons and Parrotts. And, although the Springfield rifle had been improved, the Army was glad to receive, in 1892, the new Krag-Jorgensen—our first high-velocity smokeless-powder shoulder-arm. However, the Gatling gun—familiarly called the "coffee-mill" because its many barrels revolved by hand-crank—remained our sole machine-gun from the end of the Civil War until 1898. A new-fangled weapon—a cannon hurling by compressed air a projectile filled with dynamite—was also tested, but never adopted; the Navy took it, though.

From the very beginning of this period, too, slowly—almost imperceptibly—was growing something most significant to the Army, although it is doubtful that either the Regular, or the nation at large, realized the boon it was later to become in time of national need. The so-called Land Grant Act of 1862 authorized grants of public land to such state-sponsored institutions as taught agriculture and the mechanical arts, "including military tactics." And after the war, as the nation turned to its further development and the demands for education increased, State universities and agricultural colleges began to spring up, each with its little islet of military training—to become in later years the Reserve Officers Training Corps. To Rep. Justin Morrill (Vt.), sponsor of the Land Grant Act, the nation justly owes a debt of gratitude.

Army bands came into their own during this period, although in a back-handed way. We had always had bands with us, as noted, but in the Regular Army they had been luxuries, with instruments and special instruction provided out of officers' pockets and from regimental or post funds (created by Scott, we will remember). And bandsmen up to now had been soldiers of the line playing in addition to their other duties.

There was a band at West Point in 1827, as noted in a cadet letter: "We have the best band of musick (*sic*) in the United States, which keeps a fellow's spirits up"—summing up the entire *raison d'être* for military music. In 1846, records of the 1st Artillery note that "the organization, equipment and instruction of [our] band had cost the officers of the regiment, during a series of years, much pains and expense, and it was regarded at this time with pride as not inferior to any in the service."

Tables of organization, true, carried provision for musicians—buglers in the cavalry—but these were company field musicians, although in fact these men might also be used in regimental bands.

The Civil War had changed this. Volunteer militia units had gone in for bands in a big way, and in the early days of the conflict their gaudy-uniformed wind-jammers attracted much attention. So, in August, 1861, regulations provided, for the first time, for regimental bands and band leaders.

In 1866, "fifteen brigade or post bands" appeared on the Army list, and in 1869, the Military Academy band was recognized with an authorized strength of twenty-four men. However, it does not appear that the regiments had any intention of parting with their own individual bands, even in the cavalry where we find by this time that all musicians had been stripped from the tables of organization and buglers replaced by "trumpeters."

So the bands went on playing, out on the dusty plains as well as on greensward in Atlantic coast garrisons. The 21st Infantry band played while the golden spike was driven, linking the trans-continental railroads at Promontory, Utah, May 9, 1869. Flamboyant Custer took his band along when the 7th Cavalry rode to war. They went, not as stretcher-bearers, which was how bandsmen were supposed to be used in combat, but to play his galloping troopers into action, as cavalry bands had several times done during the Civil War.

They did it when the 7th charged and destroyed Black Kettle's warriors on the Washita; the bandsmen's lips freezing to their mouth-pieces that bitter day of November 27, 1868, while "Garryowen" blared.

And in early summer, 1876, up at Fort Lincoln, N. D., where Bismarck city was beginning to huddle about the post, the 7th Cavalry band played Custer and his troops off to their rendezvous with death on the Little Big Horn. The column moved out to the strains of "The Girl I Left Behind Me," while children waved and Army wives held back their tears.

As might be expected, once the Indian-fighting had ended and the Army went to a garrison life, the Regular's life took on something of a stodgy aspect. He had nothing to worry about—except the always rising cost of living.

And yet it was during this time that certain Regular Army officers were taking thought upon creating a forum for professional "shop-talk" and mutual education in their profession. To realize what this meant one must cast back to the founding of the Corps of Engineers and the Military Academy in 1802. Colonel Jonathan Williams, first superintendent of the new school and also the first Chief of Engineers, was a nephew of Benjamin Franklin and, in his own fashion, as erudite a personage as his distinguished uncle. Franklin had founded the American Philosophical Society in Philadelphia. Why not, reasoned Williams, organize a parallel society to ponder on the art of war?

So, at West Point, the United States Military Philosophical Society came into being. Its mission was the promotion of military science and history; its meeting place to be "wherever the Military Academy may be established," and its membership open to "any gentleman, whether a military man or not."

It throve until 1824. Presidents Jefferson and Madison in turn were patrons. Prominent scientists, soldiers and sailors of the period among its members. But then it died on the vine; its funds and records were turned over to the New York Museum of Natural History.

Now, in 1878, fifty-two years later, a similar organization was proposed by General Winfield Scott Hancock, commanding the Department of the East, at Governors Island, N. Y. Hancock was considered one of the top-flight officers of the Army and his proposition received approbation. General Sheridan, then commander-in-chief of the Army, gave full approval. The Military Service Institution, with Hancock its first presiding officer, was organized at Governors Island as a recognized War Department project. Its membership was open to Regular and National Guard officers and to interested civilians.

A museum was established at its headquarters, and a bimonthly *Journal* published. Branches were formed on other Army posts, that at West Point being the most important, because faculty members assisted in the editing of the periodical. Officers were encouraged to write on military subjects and the society began sponsorship of publication of a number of books.

It was a good beginning, but there was much inertia still to be overcome as years went on.

In 1890, the old law of regimental promotion was superseded by seniority advancement within each arm and branch. No longer would one have to wait for dead men's shoes. This development had brewed since 1876, when youngsters just out of West Point assigned to the 7th Cavalry went flying instanter into captain's grades because most of its older officers had been killed on the Little Big Horn, while their classmates remained lieutenants for years. A man had to prove himself worthy of promotion, too, under this new regulation which prescribed that eligibles had to take a rigid examination before being stepped up in grade. None of this affected general officers, of course. Stars, awarded by the President to the officer of his choice—he could reach down into the captains if he saw fit—remained as potential political plums.

Elaborations to the laws affecting retirement by 1891 had stabilized the officer's career expectancy. Age sixty-four was the limit of active service. After that, the old war horse went out to grass, with a salary nominally based on seventy-five per cent of his pay and allowances— actually not much more than half-pay, but certainly sufficient to keep the wolf from the door.

Man for man, and company for company, there was probably not a better-trained, faster-shooting and more disciplined army in the world than ours as the century neared its turning. But the average officer, engaged in little wars as he had been, had had neither time nor inclination to study grand tactics or strategy, and those who had gained experience in handling large units during the Civil War had bowed out. True, at General Sherman's instance, when commanding the Army, a School of Application for Cavalry and Infantry had been established at Fort Leavenworth, Kan., in 1881. This forerunner to our great Army school system of today, one notes, contained in its curriculum the essence of Mahan's theories on war, but few officers could be spared to go there.

So, except for a handful of far-thinking soldiers such as Emory Upton and Arthur L. Wagner, and others of the "intelligentsia" of the Military Service Institution, the results of the Franco-Prussian War of 1870-71 and the growing military shadow the German Empire was casting on the world went unnoticed. The sea was still wide. President Cleveland's firm stand against Britain in the Venezuelan troubles of 1895 had aroused but a transient, chauvinistic "don't tread on me" attitude amongst the general public and even within the Army.

The trouble lay topside. Between the President—our commander-in-chief—and his Secretary of War, and the line of the Army lay a chasm bridged only by a War Department which had become ossified in bureaucracy. There was a General Commanding the Army, but he was hobbled by the paper restrictions and the mass of regulations and directions emanating without guidance from the various bureaus comprising the Department.

Actually, the Adjutant General of the Army and the Quartermaster General, who handled respectively the administration and the pay and subsistence of the Army, ran it.

Officers lucky—or unlucky enough—to be detailed to the various staff departments in the War Department remained indefinitely in their own little cubby-holes, for there was then no time-restriction on such service. There, out of touch with the line and completely unrealistic, untrammeled by any military policy or guidance, they played with paper work, a General Staff in name only. Implementation of national objectives did not concern them.

It was a vicious system grown, like Topsy, from the beginning of the nation. Scott, when commanding, had been hampered by it and took his own headquarters out of Washington. Grant, during the Civil War, kept severely away. So, too, did the nervous, high-strung Sherman.

It was a most unfortunate state of affairs. It was to culminate in near-tragedy when in 1898 the nation went suddenly singing into another war which found the War Department and the Army slumbering in a tangle of red tape and antiquated, inadequate practices throttling expansion.

* * * * *

• • • •

10

FIRST STRIDES OF THE GIANT

The explosion that sent the U.S.S. *Maine* to the bottom of Havana harbor on the fateful night of February 15, 1898, changed the course of national history and pointed the Army toward a new frontier. Two hundred and sixty-six officers and men of the U. S. Navy went to sudden death in the *Maine*'s twisted hull. Rocked by the shocking news, the American people exploded in frenzy which set the nation irrevocably on the path to world power.

Toward that path we had already, of course, taken the first tentative step by annexing Hawaii, thus throwing our outpost line one-third of the way across the Pacific. But few people had realized that fact. Nor were they, until long after, to grasp that by virtue of an *opera-bouffe* war against a decrepit European nation the United States had become ineluctably committed to the world of power politics and to a leadership necessitating the very thing so many Americans abhorred: adequate armed forces in being.

The *Maine* catastrophe struck a United States already steamed up to fever heat by Spain's long-continued colonial misrule in Cuba, where open revolution had now broken out. National sentiment, ever for the "under dog," was all with the Cuban insurrectionists; Spain was cordially disliked.

When a naval commission determined that the explosion had come from an outside underwater source (the *Maine*'s ruptured plates were bent inward), the pot boiled over. The American people clamored for revenge. While the slogan "Remember the Maine!" roared across the land, an ultimatum to Spain and a declaration of war followed fast. By April 25 we were at war.

The unfortunate fact was that neither the administration nor the Army knew what to do about it. The Navy did. Its ships put to sea to seek out and destroy Spanish naval power. From Hong Kong sped Admiral George Dewey and the Pacific squadron to Manila; from the

Atlantic seaboard Commodore Winfield S. Schley and Admiral William T. Sampson screened the seas in search of a Spanish squadron bound our way. As result, for the first time in our history, all Army operations were predicated upon and in support of the actions of the sister service, although in fact the spirit of coordination just didn't exist.

General Miles, stout Indian-fighter, was in command of an Army comprising ten regiments of cavalry, seven of artillery (the 6th and 7th had been authorized after the *Maine* was destroyed), and twenty-five of infantry—some two-thousand-odd officers and approximately twenty-eight thousand enlisted men, scattered throughout the United States. The militia—it was the National Guard now in most states, a title which had grown in popularity—was controlled by the same old home-defense laws of a century past.

The Congress took three hurried steps: (1) all able-bodied male citizens between eighteen and forty-five were held liable to military duty; (2) the volunteer system of 1861, with all its mistakes, including state-appointed officers, was reestablished; (3) the Army was more than doubled, by permitting larger company strengths and the addition of a third battalion in each regiment. The new legislation did contain two good elements. In contrast to the Civil War situation where the professionals were shoved aside in the new formations, it was now provided that these men could hold volunteer commissions. Provision was also made, in light of the probable tropical campaign, for enlistment of ten regiments of "Immunes," men who had already had yellow fever.

A frantic whirl of misdirected activity ensued, as the President called for one hundred and twenty-five thousand volunteers. They came rushing, many of the National Guard regiments volunteering in toto. Office-seekers and commission-hunters poured into the various state capitals and to Washington. A "Rip van Winkle" War Department, lacking a General Staff and completely unprepared, awakened, stirred and floundered. Supplies, uniforms, modern arms and ammunition were in but negligible quantity. The Regulars had the Krag-Jorgensen but the volunteers had to be equipped with the old-style, single-shot Springfield, burning black powder.

The newcomers were funneled into mobilization camps. Alger, at Falls Church, Va., and Thomas, at Chickamauga, Ga., were the first, but others shortly dotted over to the Pacific coast. National Guard outfits with some semblance of discipline mingled with the much larger group of willing but war-ignorant civilians trying to become soldiers.

The surge fell on the Army like a lightning bolt on a power line. Its fuses blew out, while harried detachments of Regulars tried to bring order out of chaos. It was Boston in 1775, Washington in 1861, all over again. Most of the new arrivals had not even the slightest idea of sanitation. It was a case of improvisation and snap decisions; there was no mobilization plan. And in the midst of this turmoil, a second call brought seventy-five thousand additional volunteers to the colors.

Meanwhile, as Regular units were being slowly gathered at Southern ports, the war fever burned. The nation, still in short pants in foreign relations, was prosperous as well as bumptious; its citizens convinced that an American could do anything better than any foreigner could. So, jingos all, we clamored "On to Havana!" just as in 1861 we had clamored "On to Richmond!"

The only trouble was that no one knew how this was to be accomplished. Certainly the War Department didn't. No plans had been drafted for an invasion of Cuba—or of any other place, for that matter. So General Miles and an improvised staff pondered the matter, sought information upon the most basic subjects—such as, for instance, the availability of transports, our own railroad capacity and the status of the enemy in Cuba. We had no communication either with the Cuban insurgents—whom we hoped would be our allies— and no inkling of their strength and location. That was why Lieutenant Andrew Summers Rowan was sent, single-handed, on that amazing journey immortalized in Elbert Hubbard's *A Message to Garcia*.

The tide of volunteers came from far and near, from all stations in life. In Nebraska, ex-Presidential candidate William Jennings Bryan, fluent apostle of "Free Silver," wangled himself an appointment as colonel of a volunteer regiment. "Fighting Joe" Wheeler and Fitzhugh Lee, ex-Confederates and ex-Regulars, too— men who once knew war—came gladly back in their old age as brigadiers general.

From the land-grant University of Nebraska, where a certain 1st Lieutenant John J. Pershing had been military instructor in 1892, came the 1st Nebraska Volunteers—the initial fruit of what one day was to become the R.O.T.C. And out of the mid-West, heading the

20th Kansas Volunteers, came a thirty-three-year-old soldier of fortune who, in the American tradition of the citizen-soldier turned
Regular, was later to leave his stamp on the Army: Frederick Funston.

But the most remarkable aggregation of them all was the 1st
Volunteer Cavalry—dudes, cowboys, hunters and what-have-you,
personally recruited by Theodore Roosevelt, who had resigned his job
as assistant secretary of the Navy to go to war. Taking the lieutenant
colonelcy himself, Roosevelt obtained for the command of his "Rough
Riders" a quiet, soft-speaking, steel-nerved and iron-willed assistant
surgeon of the Regular Army: Leonard Wood.

It was the beginning for both men of an adventure leading one
to the Presidency, the other to a post still to be created—Chief of
Staff. Between them they accomplished the rebirth of the United States
Army.

In the midst of the hurly-burly flashed the news of Dewey's victory
at Manila Bay, May 1, with the postscript that troops would have to
be rushed there to land, defeat the Spaniards on shore and occupy the
Philippines. Unexpected as this was, it at least presented an objective.
On the West coast a force was flung together—two volunteer regiments with a leaven of six companies of Regular infantry—and set
out for a goal the climate and other geographic features of which were
unknown.

While they were at sea—in more ways than one—Schley's "Flying
Squadron" on May 29 discovered Admiral Pascual Cervera's will-o'-
the-wisp Spanish ships (which for a few weeks had sent cold shivers
of apprehension along the East coast) in the harbor of Santiago,
Cuba. And for the second time the Navy forced the Army's hand.
Land forces had to invest the place where the Navy had bottled up
Cervera.

In agony of haste, an expeditionary force was scratched up from
the teeming camps. Miles, who had hoped that by October he could
put seventy thousand trained men in the field, could only assemble
sixteen thousand with any semblance of training for the Santiago
campaign. These were crammed into transports at Tampa, sweltering
in heavy wool uniforms, and at long last disgorged on June 20 at
Daiquiri and Siboney, little coastal villages some fifteen miles east of
Santiago.

It was another surge of mismanagement. Civilian transport skippers wouldn't go close to shore. The Navy took the troops in its small boats—a twenty-mile trip for some. Horses were unloaded by the simple expedient of dumping them overboard to swim ashore; many swam out to sea instead and perished. It took five days to land the entire force, and for weeks afterward the haphazard cargo-loading made supply a piece-meal day-by-day operation.

Commanding the expedition—the V Corps—was corpulent, elderly Major General William R. Shafter, afflicted with gout. Once a fine, gallant soldier who had won the Medal of Honor at Fair Oaks in the Civil War, Shafter was now so fat he had to be boosted onto his horse on the rare occasions he went abroad in Cuba. Most of the time he spent lying in a hammock in a state of semi-heat prostration. There is no satisfactory explanation for the choice of Shafter.

The Army could not be proud of the direction of the Santiago campaign. It could be proud of the bravery, initiative and individual resourcefulness which its junior officers displayed in what developed into two uncoordinated little battles on July 1, and of the disciplined Regular units whose steadiness compensated for the effervescent valor of ignorance of the volunteers.

Shafter's V Corps outnumbered the enemy actually opposing it, but was handicapped by climate, jungle, and the Spaniards' skillful use of barbed wire. The black powder of our artillery and of the volunteers' Springfields (the Rough Riders alone had Krags, received only the day before the battle) gave away our positions in the jungle by their dense white smoke puffs. Spanish sharp-shooters picked off men whose comrades could not see their enemies who were armed with smokeless powder weapons.

Bogged in the narrow trail, the 71st New York faltered. The cavalry dismounted and pressed on regardless. The yelling "Rough Riders" stormed the crest of Kettle Hill, "Teddy" Roosevelt in the lead, while the steady Negro troopers of the 10th Cavalry forged beside them. San Juan Hill to the left was swept by Regular infantry. Two miles away to the north, at the same time, another battle was being waged where volunteers and Regulars with equal valor and misdirected energy stormed and won El Caney.

Best example of the helter-skelter "up-and-at-'em" spirit of these Cuban battlefields is furnished by the story—probably apocryphal— of "Fighting Joe" Wheeler buzzing like an angry bee in front of San

Juan Hill and urging his men on against the Spaniards with the cry, "Get those damn Yankees, boys!"

It was all very gallant and very picturesque. It was also unnecessarily costly and stupid, for had this headless, staffless Army of ours been schooled and trained in the higher art of war, the Spanish forces in Cuba—cut off from all overseas help by the U. S. Navy—would have fallen like ripe plums for the picking. But this was the American way: the way demanded by a nation inflamed.

Worse was yet to come. While Shafter's troops began the investment of the city of Santiago itself, and Cervera and his squadron steamed out in gallant but futile gesture to their doom, July 3, tropical disease laid hand on the besiegers. The Spanish surrender of the city came, July 17, as half our troops already were down with dysentery, typhoid and Yellow Jack. "This army must be moved at once or it will perish," declared division and brigade commanders in an amazing "round robin" laid before Shafter, August 3, and next day he so cabled the War Department.

Homeward movement began and regiments of "Immunes" replaced the disease-racked troops who had been rotting in Cuba. It was about this time that the nation—and the Army—really began to realize what was happening. In the training camps and in the field, lack of sanitation and medical attention had been abetted by rotten meat foisted on the Army by unscrupulous contractors. Food poisoning was added to the other agents of destruction. The toll of death from disease and other causes in the war was to rise to 5,083, compared with only 379 battle casualties. That tells its own story.

Smartly handled in contrast to the Santiago campaign was the Puerto Rican expedition led by General Miles in person. This force occupied the island after minor enemy opposition.

The original expedition to the Philippines had landed, and with Emilio Aguinaldo's Filipinos invested Manila. The Spanish garrison had surrendered on August 13. The treaty of peace between the two nations, signed December 10, ceded to the United States Cuba, Puerto Rico, Guam and the Philippines, for which latter possession Uncle Sam, to boot, had thrown in twenty million dollars. So 1899 dawned with the United States in the "Big League"—for the first time in its existence a colonial nation—faced by two immediate tasks of military government and reconstruction: one at its Caribbean door-step, the other six thousand miles across the wide Pacific from its Western coast.

Both line soldier and medico had their jobs cut out for them. In Cuba Leonard Wood and Tasker Bliss were working administrative wonders, while William C. Gorgas and Walter Reed were battling Yellow Jack.

The story of the Medical Corps' conquest of yellow fever is one of tireless energy, tenacity and skill, and of the highest degree of pre-meditated courage. It is one of the great victories of the Army and of the Medical Corps in particular. It began in June, 1900, when four medical officers were assigned to go to Cuba and investigate the scourge which had defied mankind for centuries.

Majors Walter Reed and James Carroll and Contract Surgeons Aristides Agramonte and Jesse W. Lazear—all of them pathologists and already interested in combatting the disease—had been picked. The four physicians enthusiastically threw themselves into the job, recklessly exposing themselves to infection.

Becoming convinced that in no other way but by the bite of one particular species of mosquito could the plague be transmitted, it was up to them to prove their theory (already, incidentally, concurred in by Dr. Carlos J. Finlay, prominent Cuban physician of the day).

Volunteers were called for: some to sleep in the soiled bedding of previously smitten patients and to wear their clothing, some to be inoculated with blood serum drawn from these patients, and others to permit themselves to be bitten by mosquitoes who had already fed on yellow-fever victims.

The volunteers came: John H. Andrus was a private in the Hospital Corps; John R. Bullard a young civilian then in Cuba; Robert P. Cooke was an Army acting assistant surgeon; Albert W. Covington was a Coast Artillery sergeant; William H. Dean, a 7th Cavalry private; Thomas M. England, Levi E. Folk and Wallace W. Forbés were Hospital Corps men; Paul Hamann, a private in Battery N, 2nd Artillery; James L. Hanberry, James Hildebrand, Warren G. Jernegan, John H. Kissinger, John J. Moran, William Olsen, Charles G. Sonntag, Edward Weatherwalks and Clyde L. West were all Hospital Corpsmen.

That's the Roll of Honor; printed annually in detail by direction of Congress in the *Army Register*. They couldn't qualify for the Medal of Honor, these men; they were not fighting a human enemy. But to all of them, or to their families, went a special gold medal.

What happened to them?

Majors Carroll and Lazear, together with Andrus, Bullard, Covington, Folk, Forbes, Hamann, Hanberry, Jernegan, Kissinger, Moran, Olsen, Sonntag and West caught the disease. All of them had been either mosquito-bitten or inoculated. Lazear and Andrus died; the others recovered. Those men who had been exposed only to the bedding-clothing test were unharmed.

The theory had been proven, the enemy unmasked. Victory was in hand.

Major William C. Gorgas, General Wood's medical chief in occupied Cuba, at once adopted rigid sanitary clean-up and preventive measures ridding Havana of mosquitoes and Yellow Jack was licked.

It would be churlish not to add one more name, which appears on no honor roll and for which there was no gold medal. Clara Louise Maas, Army nurse, tending yellow-fever patients in the line of her duty at Las Animas Hospital in Havana in 1901, contracted the disease and died.

While these things were going on another problem had risen in the Philippines. Aguinaldo's people, feeling that the war had been, for them, simply a change of masters, revolted.

With open warfare on its hands, the Army in the Philippines was forced—as in Mexico fifty-two years earlier—to swap horses in midstream. Half our forces there were volunteers enlisted for "two years or the duration" of the Spanish-American War—which now was over. Back, of course, they had to come, while Federal volunteers—thirty-five thousand—were called for to be ·organized into twenty-seven regiments of infantry and two of cavalry. Another makeshift this— for these men were to be discharged in 1901—but as it turned out, an incubation bed, too. Their field officers came from the Regulars, the others in the main were men who had already served creditably in state volunteer organizations during the war against Spain. And when this "little war" was ended many of these men, professionals by this time, were recommissioned in an enlarged Regular Army.

This was indeed a "lieutenants' war," in which, after a few short pitched battles with the Filipinos—brave but totally inferior to the Americans in fighting know-how and equipment—it degenerated into a long series of skirmishes, of punitive expeditions, of hit-and-run action in which the art of troop-leading was learned the hard way. Long-forgotten now are most of these actions in which Americans suffered, fought and died in *cogon* grass and jungle, hampered by climate and—for some time—by the very uniforms they wore, unsuitable for the tropics.

But initiative was being developed, and, under the wise leadership of General Arthur MacArthur, something else, too. Tolerance and understanding were slowly to complete the work which bullet and bayonet had, unfortunately, to commence.

March 23, 1901, General Funston captured Aguinaldo by a daring ruse. Posing as prisoners, he with three of his officers were marched to the Filipino leader's headquarters by a detachment of Philippine scouts masquerading as *insurrectos,* and there arrested him. The back of the insurrection had been broken, but much remained to be accomplished.

In the midst of this the Army had found another job. In China the Boxer troubles flared. Their legations in Peking besieged, their nationals murdered in other places, Britain, Germany, Austria, Russia, France, Japan and the United States acted in concert to quell the menace. The 9th and 14th Infantry, part of the 6th Cavalry and a battery of the 5th Artillery came from the Philippines as the American share of the expeditionary force.

Tientsin was stormed, the 9th Infantry taking prominent part. In its mess today the Liscum Bowl—a punchbowl made of melted Chinese silver ingots—stands as memento to its colonel, Emerson H. Liscum, killed in taking Tientsin. The Allies pressed on against Peking. The Army could be proud of its people there, too: such men as young Bugler Calvin P. Titus, E Company, 14th Infantry, the first to scale the twenty-two-foot wall of the Chinese city; and Lieutenant Charles P. Summerall, walking calmly under fire to the gate of the Imperial City to chalk a mark for his guns of Light Battery F, 5th Artillery.

The Boxer episode ended, the Army continued its wrestling with the Philippine problem. But in the United States public opinion fluctuated, progressive imperialists rallying to the old cry of "manifest destiny" while isolationists protested, in what became a major political issue. And again the "do-gooder" clamored as garbled reports of American excesses and atrocities reached the homeland.

As far as the Army was concerned, here was the old back-seat driving of the Indian wars rampant once more. The American soldier was no angel; the court-martial records of the Philippine campaigns attest to that. But neither was the Filipino. The peaceful *peons* of the daylight hours became the snipers of the night. All the horrors of guerrilla warfare in a tropical land fell on the soldiers' shoulders; crafty pitfalls, treachery, ambushes and throat-slitting.

At Balangiga, on the island of Samar, for instance, Company C, 9th Infantry, was almost wiped out as a peaceful village treacherously flared while the men were at breakfast. Three officers and sixty-two men were butchered by slashing bolos; twelve wounded survivors managed to fight their way out.

The Army, chasing a will-o'-the-wisp enemy through hostile territory, lacked information of his whereabouts. It had to be obtained, frequently by devious methods and at times, unfortunately, through torture. Distorted tales of wholesale "water cure" and other alleged brutalities filtered back home, stirring public indignation, and became political ammunition which resulted in pillorying of the Army.

General MacArthur took drastic steps to stamp out the insurrection. At the same time, with infinite patience, he offered an olive branch. He managed to convey to a proud, sensitive race the fact that armed resistance was futile, but that generous mercy and a better life followed acquiescence. In the doing he became to the Filipino a symbol of justice and fair play—just as, one might point out, his son (also idolized by the Filipino) was to become to the Japanese people of a later day.

As a result, on July 4, 1902, President Theodore Roosevelt was able to proclaim peace, amnesty to all Filipinos taking the oath of allegiance, and the establishment of civil government throughout the Christian-inhabited portions of the Islands. And in so doing the President, in the name of the American people, thanked the Army for its accomplishments.

Fighting still continued against the fierce Moro Mohammedans of the southern islands—Jolo and Mindanao. Meanwhile a new element entered the Army's ranks: the Philippine Scouts, recruited from the little brown men who took to soldiering like ducks to water. These units were at first mainly officered by Americans. But a few Filipinos were commissioned, too, and a reservoir established for the future by legislation permitting Filipinos to attend the U. S. Military Academy. To assist the long arm of the Insular government, now a civilian chore, the Philippine Constabulary was formed. This was not part of the Army, but its initial commanders were Army officers and its training and equipment provided by the Army.

It was at this time, too, that in the Caribbean another distinctive regiment joined the Army list: the Puerto Rico Regiment of Infantry. First organized in 1899 as a volunteer unit, this regiment was in later years to become the 65th.

So the Army settled down, a goodly part of its Regulars once more engaged in a frontier established far from home in little garrisons dotting the Philippine archipelego. Back home, the remainder struggled in a pattern expanded and actually bulging a bit at the seams as Congress and the Military pulled different ways to make it fit an awakening of new ideas.

In 1900, Army women, taking relief matters in their own self-sufficient hands, organized the Army Relief Society, a voluntary organization furnishing advice and financial assistance to widows and orphans of Regular Army personnel. The officer corps itself, chafing under the then arbitrary rules of commercial insurance companies—which either refused them insurance or charged exorbitant rates for what was considered an extra-hazardous profession—had already taken steps in that line. In 1879, the Army Mutual Aid Association had been organized to provide life insurance to our professionals. Both institutions, run by volunteer personnel and employing no paid agents, still thrive today. So, too, does the Army Cooperative Fire Association, formed in 1887 to give more effective fire insurance to all Regular commissioned officers, including Navy, Marine Corps and Coast Guard.

New legislation in 1901 authorized a strength of 3,820 officers and 84,799 enlisted men, exclusive of Philippine Scouts. With five regiments added to each, the cavalry now had fifteen regiments, the infantry thirty. The artillery regiments were dissolved and their components rearranged in an Artillery Corps of thirty batteries of field and one hundred and twenty-six companies of coast artillery.

Actually the new Regular strength was never realized; in 1903, Congress took pruning knife in hand to cut the enlisted men to approximately sixty thousand (excluding the Scouts again). But the increase in regiments had given room for admittance of twelve hundred new officers. Some of them came from the ranks, but in great majority they were officers already proven in campaign in the volunteer forces who had found a new vocation. It is not too much to say that this was the finest block of erstwhile citizen-soldiers ever to enter the Army.

In 1902, the officer corps consisted of two thousand, nine hundred, of whom eighteen hundred and eighteen had been appointed since the opening of the war with Spain. Of all these newcomers only two hundred and seventy-six were West Pointers. In fact the corps was a composite of approximately half from West Point, half from other sources—a balanced ration, so to speak.

This fact is worthy of note, for it was about this time that Congress, always wary of "the man on horseback," began to express that truly American complex in an odd fashion by making it hard for Army sons to obtain appointments to the Military Academy. It was no crime for the son of a lawyer, a physician or an engineer to follow in his father's footsteps, nor for the son of a graduate of a great university to attend that same school. But, it appeared, there might be something nefarious in the desire of a soldier's son to don uniform, particularly if that father was a West Pointer and the young man, too, wanted to enter the nation's great school on the Hudson (a similar situation confronted Navy men and Annapolis).

Some of our legislators expressed their fear in so many words. Already some Army families had had three generations of West Point graduates; was this not evidence of the build-up of an "Army caste"? Parenthetically, was it not also a waste of patronage? Army folk couldn't influence votes. It was all very natural, very political, and— to the Regular—affronting. It was a situation which would last for a long time, alleviated to some extent by the institution of competitive Presidential appointments for sons of military personnel.

However, all in all, a new era was dawning, a new page in Army history turned over. The Congress, for the first time in more than a century, glanced at the militia and did something about it. The so-called "Dick Bill," passed January 21, 1903, divided our citizenry into two classes—the Organized Militia (the National Guard) and the

Reserve Militia which included all other male citizens between the ages of eighteen and forty-five.

National Guard organization, armament and discipline were to be the same as that of the Regular Army. Pay was granted for summer camps and other activities; target practice, drill and instruction periods were to take place twenty-four times each year. Regular officers were detailed as instructors. True, service was optional and response to a Presidential call was also optional with each state Governor. Archaic still was the limitation of nine-months' Federal service when called up. But it was a beginning, and a good one. The National Guardsman, no longer merely a play-soldier, perked up. The thinking Regular began to perceive that at long last he might have a junior partner.

Something bigger still had happened. In 1903, the Army got a Chief of Staff and a General Staff. That this occurred through the action of a civilian, inspired from within the Army itself, was once more in the American tradition. How it happened is worth the telling.

Russell A. Alger, Secretary of War when the Spanish-American War started, had been hurled out of office in 1899 as a result of the general incapacity of the War Department disclosed by a Congressional Committee investigating the abominations of 1898. President McKinley appointed to succeed him a brilliant, patriotic, far-seeing but at times most irascible lawyer named Elihu Root. McKinley's assassination brought Theodore Roosevelt to the Presidency. He looked on Root, liked what he saw, and backed him to the hilt in clearing the Augean stable.

Root's insatiable curiosity caused him to read a dusty manuscript in the War Department files—an analysis of the defects and needs of our military system written by a brilliant West Pointer perfectionist, Major General Emory Upton. Upton, star pupil of Dennis Hart Mahan, a student and a combat soldier both, had devoted the last years of his life after the Civil War to the work.

His reward had been the oblivion of a pigeon-hole, as predicted in pencilled handwriting scrawled across the work:

"I doubt if you will convince the powers that be, but the facts stated, the references from authority, and the military conclusions are most valuable and should be printed and made accessible. The time may not be now, but will come when these will be appreciated, and may bear some fruit even in our day.—W. T. Sherman."

Root was looking upon a blueprint for a real military establishment, including a system of military education. Its most vital ingredient was a live, flexible general staff, whose members would be rotated from the line and back again, and whose chief would bridge the gap between the paramount civilian command and the military.

With the hearty support of the President and of a Congress brought to an appreciation of military needs by the bungling of the Spanish-American War, a War College was established in 1900. The framework of what became the Command and General Staff School blossomed in 1901, and in 1903 the General Staff Act was passed.

In 1904, twenty years after its author's death, at Root's direction, Upton's *Military Policy of the United States,* the most valuable single contribution towards the shaping of the nation's military policy, was published at government expense, to become required Army reading.

Seven more years passed before the bureaucrats in the War Department were fully divorced from their overlordship; but uplift had hit the Army, its impact still very gentle indeed.

*   *   *   *   *

• • • •

● ● ● ●

11

SEMI-CLOISTERED ARMY

Ours was a tight little Army of some three thousand officers and fifty thousand enlisted men in 1904; shirt-sleeved and slouch-hatted in the field, but with dress uniforms, spike helmets, horse-hair plumes, parades and spit and polish in garrison. At home it lived a semi-cloistered life on some forty-odd military posts scattered through the United States in a pattern mostly based on the exigencies of lately-ended Indian-fighting days.

For the nation this was the era of "The Big Change," as the late Frederick Lewis Allen so well put it. There were changes in politics and government, in education, scientific research and invention, in industry, business and society. Americans were changing in the way they lived and the way they thought and dreamed.

Two "madmen" named Wright had actually lifted themselves off the ground in a flying machine. Another man named Ford felt that the automobile—that millionaire's playtoy—had come to stay. Female suffrage was a live issue. Gargantuan fortunes and stark poverty went hand in hand in a land where the horse, the bicycle, the cable- and trolley-car constituted the sole prime movers of local land transportation.

The Newport set, an odd mixture of pseudo-aristocracy and robber baron, was—one learned from the Sunday newspapers—bartering its daughters and its money for European antiques: human, architectural and artistic. The national melting pot was simmering in city slums and factory districts, with new ingredients added by the stream of immigration flowing through Ellis Island: the Pole, Italian and Hungarian along with the East European Jew were replacing the Irish, German and Scandinavian immigrants of a previous day.

The Grand Army of the Republic was fading as a factor in American politics in 1904, its surviving members a bit on the crotchety side. Their noses were put out of joint by a younger generation of veterans relating new, strange tales of war in odd places: of black-eyed senoritas, of El Caney and San Juan Hill, of battle and death in rustling *cogon* grass, of loot in Peking.

There were no radios, no television, no electric labor-saving devices. The telephone was a rarity in homes where, while the discreetly covered spittoon was bowing out, the antimacassar and the what-not were still standard front-parlor equipment.

Most Americans of that period would stare blankly at mention of the name of Karl Marx, though every once in a while out of Europe came black tales of anarchists and nihilists who went about blowing up Tsars and pistolling Empresses. We had our own Mafia scare, drowned in blood by an irate citizenry of New Orleans. Before that we had the Haymarket "massacre" in Chicago.

In the White House that irrepressible extrovert Theodore Roosevelt was doing much to bring about what Allen aptly termed "a revolt of American conscience." Capitalism, it appeared, was slowly but irrevocably becoming democratic, economics evolving as a science, and all to the betterment of the American people. The brash young giant among nations was coming out of swaddling clothes.

The Army with its thirty-one regiments of infantry, ten of cavalry, and its artillery corps was more an aggregation of arms and services vying with one another than one highly integrated battle team. The spate of service journals springing to life between 1888 and 1911, each of them touting, so to speak, the component whose name it bore, indicates the truth of this observation.

Branch associations, each devoted to its own particular part of the Army, had started to form. Each in turn brought out a periodical of its own. The *Cavalry Journal* was first published in 1888; the *Military Surgeon* (this, of course was highly professional and quite properly so in its own field) in 1890; the *Artillery* (later *Coast Artillery*) *Journal* in 1892.

When the *Infantry Journal* (now *Army*) was born in 1904 the *Journal of the Military Service Institution* editorially noted "this latest recruit to the small but increasing army of service periodicals" and gingerly added its hope that this did not "necessarily imply undue competition with or independence of other branches of the service."

Actually the United Service Institution read the handwriting on the wall. Its spokesman pointed out that "In the past, one of the weak

points in our 'officers' corps' has been a lack of cohesion in the promotion of army interest and a tendency to break up into cliques, each
working to improve his own condition, regardless of the welfare of
the others . . ."

The splintering continued. The fore-runner of the *Military Engineer* was launched in 1910; the *Field Artillery Journal* in 1911.
With the advent of World War I the Military Service Institution and
its periodical withered away, doomed as much by the more parochial
objectives of the arms and branches as by the fact that during wartime no officers were available for such editorial duties.

Additional service publications followed that war—such as the
Quartermaster Review, Army Ordnance and others—each adding its
bit to the rivalry. Not for many years did this active intramural bickering die, although in France the efficacy of the infantry-artillery team
as combat partners pointed the way towards unity.

The Army, as it stood in 1904, saw no financial betterment,
however; a parsimonious Congress had too many other things to
think about than any changes in the Pay Act of 1854, which still
governed the cash drawer. Not until 1905 was the thirteen-dollar-
a-month pay for the lowly private soldier increased a princely two
bucks.

In our new-gained area of trusteeship, the flames of the Philippine
Insurrection had been quenched. The volunteers—those citizen soldiers
who had gone to war singing "There'll be a Hot Time in the Old Town
Tonight," and "Ta-ra-ra Boom-de-ay"—had come home. The Regulars were establishing there a rule of life which, forty years later, paid
immense dividends. There was still stiff fighting in the Moro islands.

The leader of our first adventure in allied operations—the Boxer
Expedition—General Adna R. Chaffee, himself an active link with
the Civil War, was now Chief of Staff. In Korea young Lieutenant
Douglas MacArthur, one year out of West Point, was seeing war at
first hand as an observer with the victorious Japanese armies in the
Russo-Japanese War. Lieutenant George Catlett Marshall's commission was a scant two years old, while Lieutenant Lesley J. McNair
—who thirty-seven years later forged the mightiest war machine the
nation ever put in the field—had just doffed cadet gray.

The ruckus caused by mismanagement during the Spanish-American War with its "embalmed beef" scandal, its utterly incompetent

and outmoded system of supply and transportation, and its holocaust of disease in mobilization camps, had died down. Such soldiers as Leonard Wood, Hugh L. Scott, Tasker H. Bliss, John J. Pershing, Frank R. McCoy and many others were showing the nation—not that it gave a tinker's damn—by their wise administration in far places that the military mind was not so narrow, after all.

Ours was an Army without vote. True, a statute stood on Federal books to the effect that military service did not affect legal residence. But few if any states had an absentee ballot provision, and many still had laws stipulating specifically the denial of franchise to "idiots, paupers, Indians, soldiers and sailors." So our 1904 Army, though its personnel did sometimes engage in hot political argument, rarely went to the polls. Far different this from today when, with few exceptions, the states recognize the absentee ballot for all members of the armed forces.

Class-conscious was this army; the hierarchy of rank and command a living thing—from the Chief of Staff down to the most junior corporal who ever impressed his fist upon a slothful recruit, and from "Mrs. General" to the corporal's wife. It was a class-consciousness that embodied a healthy professional and communal pride.

We should look well upon this aspect of military life at the beginning of the century, for unless one can understand it, this attitude of RHIP—"rank has its privileges"—can be misunderstood by those outside the circle, and abused by some of those within. Here was a deep-rooted condition which would withstand the buffets, the ridicule and the hatred of the people who did not understand until a very few years ago.

To examine this, one must begin at the beginning. Socially, the status of the commissioned officer of the Army and the Navy by this time was unquestioned; the military ranked with the church, the law, and medicine as the cream of the professions. But that was all.

The average American civilian knew little about and cared less for the Army in 1904. Civil War memories had faded into mellow reminiscences. The Spanish-American War and the Philippine Insurrection—in sharp contrast with today when few indeed are the American families without some affiliation with the armed forces—had drawn but lightly upon the next generation. The continuous bickerings of the Indian wars, and the accomplishments of the Army on the plains were embraced, as far as the man in the street was concerned, in a nebulous atmosphere of Custer's last stand, and Buffalo Bill's Wild West.

Hero worship there was, of course. To the roll of great names of the Civil War had been added those of Dewey at Manila Bay, and Roosevelt and his Rough Riders at San Juan Hill (Kettle Hill it actually was). But the Army—and the Navy, too—as a living, breathing entity, part of the national structure, was *terra incognita*.

The most interested segment of that 1904 population was the generation of male teen-agers who, between dips into dime-novel exploits of the train-robbing James boys and Nick Carter, were revelling on the more succulent fare of G. A. Henty and our own Captain Charles King. More than one member of the West Point classes graduating during the next decade, as well as the young men coming in from civil life, had imagination titillated and career settled by King's vigorous, entertaining and veracious novels of Army life.

The general lack of civilian interest may be laid in part to the difficulties of transportation. To visit the average Army post in 1904 meant spending time and trouble. One had to have a definite reason to take the trip to these little islands of isolation. Those civilians who did participate in social events on nearby posts—with exception, of course, of relatives and close friends of Army people—saw in fact only what might be termed the tinsel of Army life. Conversely, the Army had but a partial and disorganized glimpse of civilian life. In consequence, a somewhat self-centered and certainly self-sufficient and self-contained Army and an uninterested civilian population had few common bonds.

Thus the enlisted man coming into the Army in 1904 found himself in an isolated community; a monastic society of sorts, whose father superior was a two-fisted first sergeant and the abbot his company commander. This recruit was a volunteer who had held up his right hand and solemnly sworn to devote his services to his country for a specified period—usually five years at that time. He slept, ate and worked by bugle call. Even his baths were regulated, and God help the uncleanly one—a pair of huskies armed with scrubbing brush and yellow laundry soap took quick action to wash away any body odors as well as dirt.

Even in those days, when eggs were selling at twenty-five cents a dozen, and bar whisky at ten cents a glass, when a good pair of shoes could be had for three dollars and an excellent civilian suit for twenty-five dollars, thirteen dollars a month and found was no princely emolument. To say it lacked attractiveness would be an understatement. So the man accepting this contract was the one to whom it offered more than the pay.

Was the attraction, then, security? Was it a chance for adventure? Was it—remembering that in those days the present system of criminal investigation and identification was in its infancy—evasion of the law's clutch? Yes, these and many other considerations all affected enlistment. When the nation was prosperous, enlistments fell; in times of panic and depression they rose, and with them rose the quality of the man enlisting.

To sum it up, the enlisted man with a few exceptions was not the cream of the crop of our citizenry. Ours was a combination of Rudyard Kipling's British Army and the French Foreign Legion. Not for nothing was it customary for first sergeants at monthly muster to warn recruits to "remember your Army name." The private soldier was the ne'er-do-well, the adventurer, and sometimes—but this one either mended his ways or was thrown out—he was a bum. But the American people, sad to say, felt that way about all enlisted men.

Certainly the fact is significant that by 1911 Congress had to place on the Federal statutes a law imposing a fine of five hundred dollars upon the proprietor, manager or employee of a public house or place discriminating against soldiers in uniform.

During the middle 1900s, Brigadier General Pershing, in mufti, about to enter a swank hotel, observed that the doorman was clad in the full dress uniform of a general officer of the Army. He called a policeman and insisted on the arrest of the man on the well-taken charge of impersonating an officer. His action, which made front-page news, had a very salutary effect.

Our recruit of that day lived in a red-brick barracks. He ate—usually well, although the food was not Delmonico's—from thick ironware crockery laid upon an immaculately scrubbed bare table top. He learned the feel of his rifle, he shot for record—there were two extra dollars a month for the man who made marksman and five dazzling bucks to him who qualified as expert rifleman. Were he in the artillery, there was extra pay to be gained, too, if he qualified as gunner, observer, gun pointer, and the like. Other branches also had extra pay to offer for qualified specialists.

He learned his way to the post exchange, where, at prices well below those on the outside, he could obtain his toilet articles, tobacco and other knick-knacks. More than that, he speedily found that if he kept his nose clean, he could obtain those things on credit to be later subtracted from his pay.

Receipt of this pay was contingent upon two things. First, he had to be present at the monthly muster—a ceremonial roll call dating back to the times when in Europe a regiment was the property of an individual who received its pay in bulk and might therefore have interest in padding his payrolls. Next, our soldier, to the merry notes of "Pay Call"—one of the first calls he learned—lined up in dress uniform, side arms and white gloves, the right one neatly folded in his belt. When his name was called, he stepped smartly up to a blanket-covered table, saluted and received his pay from the paymaster, over whose shoulder breathed the first sergeant and the company commander to identify him.

Then, carefully herded back to his company office in barracks, he underwent the painful process of subtraction, to pay his accrued debts to the post exchange and the company tailor and barber—all carefully listed by the company clerk on a large collection sheet. If he was a Regular, he gave up twelve and one-half cents each month for the Soldiers' Home in Washington.

There might be an additional subtraction, too, from his now rapidly melting thirteen dollars—illegal this, but widely prevalent. For there was always in a company some individual usurer, ready and eager to lend his impecunious comrades and requiring in return only what barracks slang termed "the soldier's one per cent"—a dollar a month for each ten dollars advanced!

And on payday night, in some carefully curtained back room of barracks or down in the stable area, might be found the musical click of the ivories rolling on a taut blanket, the muffled thumps of a black-jack game, or the tense concentration of poker, to bring clandestine pleasure and pain to the gamblers' senses. Strictly against regulations, this, but wise was the company commander who left this matter to the non-commissioned officers, after insuring, by drastic action if necessary, that non-coms and privates did not gamble among one another.

On the other hand, there were always some men who found it quite possible to save money—depositing a few dollars at a time with the Army—toward a tidy nest egg payable at expiration of enlistment.

For entertainment, this soldier of 1904 had comparatively few outlets as contrasted to today. But neither did his civilian contemporaries. In barracks there was the dayroom, fitted up with easy chairs and pool tables, where a man might sit and read—the company subscribed to a variety of periodicals, with *The Police Gazette* the mainstay—or play pool or just chew the fat. There was a post library, too, usually; but movies had not come into vogue, so that post movie theaters did not appear for a decade.

Athletics, in the shape of unit baseball and football teams, were popular, as was boxing. But not until after World War I would they become an organized cult and soldier athletes gain special privileges. Not infrequently officers played on such teams. We learn of one good soldier baseball team with the skipper and the topkick as its battery, a very appropriate combination!

Men whose conduct was good could always obtain passes to seek in the nearest town what slight entertainment was offered to those with slim purses. Payday, of course, brought a rash of requests for passes. Above all, the old soldiers—the men who for a month, two days excepted, were models of deportment and discipline—sought passes for that essential periodical roaring drunk in some civilian dive.

Well knowing this, the company commander would issue these passes with a sigh, perhaps, but then "single men in barracks don't grow into plaster saints," and he could only hope that he would not later get a message to come to town and bail his erring lambs out of the local calaboose.

This brings up the post commander's problem with relation to the adjacent civilian population. The town nearest to an Army post in 1904—is it any different today?—made money out of the Army. Its shops were patronized, as were its public utilities. And, on the seamy side, its red-light district and its gin mills depended upon Army pay. In some towns municipal officials found there was money to be made by jailing soldiers "on the loose." And the very pillar of the local church who complained of the licentiousness of the garrison might be drawing fat rents from purveyors of illicit pleasures.

As a result, relationships depended upon the tact and efficiency of the post commander. The local chief of police and municipal judge frequently found that better conditions and cordial relations prevailed if, although erring soldiers might be locked up, they could be called for next day by the provost guard and attended to at home by military courts. But if the post commander was tactless, or if the venalities of the municipal organization waxed fat upon the bonds and fines extracted from frothing company commanders, relations could be and were sometimes very strained.

All in all, it was a tough, two-fisted aggregation into which our recruit of 1904 was dropped. The company commander was king; he was to remain so for many more years. Army opinion in 1904—and in fact until World War II—was unanimous in agreeing that by far the finest, most exacting and most exhilarating command in the service was that of company, troop or battery commander.

Except in line of duty, the enlisted man spoke to the company commander only after he had sought and obtained the first sergeant's permission. He spoke, too, in the third person. Since the first sergeant was appointed by the company commander and held office only at his pleasure, it might be expected that the sergeant could make appropriate decision as to when and why the skipper should be disturbed. However, the company commander usually made it plain to his top that permission should never be refused unless the request be absolutely unessential.

Somewhat similar was the first sergeant's authority for confining men, in emergency, to the guardhouse; a delegated authority, recognized in the slim blue bible—Army Regulations. One might add that in our 1904 Army this measure was infrequently used; no self-respecting first sergeant would normally hide behind regulations when he had a strong right arm to use.

The officer-enlisted man relationship, then, was both autocratic and paternal. It was a very real relationship, for the platoon and company commanders knew their men. Units might change station, but individual rotation of officers was comparatively uncommon. As a result, warm friendships grew up between faithful men and appreciative officers—friendships lasting for lifetime, much to mutual pride.

The line between commissioned and enlisted personnel was plainly marked. It was, however, a line and not a barrier as many fine, self-respecting young soldiers had already proved.

Did not the official record of the Chief of Staff himself, General Chaffee, lead off with this terse listing: "Pvt Sergt and 1 serg K 6 cav 22 July 1861 to 12 May 1863"? And James Guthrie Harbord, one-time private, corporal, sergeant and quartermaster sergeant in the 4th Infantry, was now a captain in the 11th Cavalry. German-born Walter Krueger, who after a Spanish-American War hitch with the 2nd U. S. Volunteers had enlisted in the 12th Infantry, had since 1901 been sporting the then blank shoulder straps of a 2nd lieutenant, 30th Infantry.

And in the 10th Cavalry, a Negro officer who was to be personally respected by two generations of American Regular officers, had stepped across that line, too. He was Benjamin O. Davis, first commissioned a lieutenant in the 8th U. S. Volunteers, and honorably mustered· out at the end of the Spanish-American War, who promptly enlisted in the 9th Cavalry. Rising from private to squadron sergeant major in two short years, he had won his commission in 1901. He bridged a half-century to see his soldier son, a graduate of West Point in 1936, wearing general's stars in the Air Force.

No, that line between enlisted man and commissioned officer in our Army of 1904 was no caste barrier; rather was it a challenge to the ability of the man who would raise his sights beyond it.

It was a bachelor Army, in the main, as far as enlisted men were concerned. Old non-commissioned officers, true, were frequently family men, and quarters were provided for them on post as far as possible. Or they could live off post and draw separate rations. But mainly because of the quarters and fiancial situation, the marriage of private soldiers was looked upon with disfavor. There was no law or regulation against it, but an enlisted man who married without the permission of his company commander could be refused the right to separate rations, and he was not entitled to quarters on the post. More than that, he could be denied re-enlistment, and that meant a great deal in a professional army.

What of the officer, the leader of this aggregation of professional soldiers, whose trade—as Kipling has it—was parade? In 1904 the officer corps—a cross-section of our citizenry— was a formalized group, governed by a rigid etiquette and century-old customs of the service. Its segments were West Pointers, men from the ranks, men from civil life, and men who had come in from the Volunteers and the militia after the Spanish-American War and the Philippine Insurrection. The pattern was fixed; immutable, some would say. There had been a ripple of unrest and some bitter feeling when the increase in Army strength in 1901 had brought those twelve hundred new officers into the corps, for some of them had been commissioned in high grades, disrupting the flow of seniority. "The crime of 1901" was what the discontented had called it, among themselves. But not until 1905 did the Presidential appointment—perfectly legal at the time— of Captain John J. Pershing to brigadier general, over the heads of many heavy-breathing oldsters, cause another ripple of dissatisfaction.

One thing all these officers had in common: they were in uniform because they wanted to be in the Army; it was their chosen profession.

Certainly it was not chosen for financial gain. A new 2nd lieutenant got $116.67 a month. He might expect, before he reached the age of statutory retirement, to rise perhaps to the grade of colonel for a brief space (generals were another matter, politically appointed, and therefore a gamble) and the princely salary of four thousand dollars a year. (In fairness, that sum was worth a great deal more in 1904 than it is today.)

Out of his salary the officer provided his own uniforms, his food, the required arms and equipment—from saber and revolver and field glasses to mess kit and bedding roll—as well as the civilian clothing he needed. Were he in the mounted service or on staff duty he provided his own horse—field officers without any compensation, the lower grades drawing an additional one hundred dollars annually with, later, fifty dollars additional for any second mount. And, of course, the mounted officer furnished all his horse equipment.

Out of what was left then of his salary the officer of 1904, were he so minded, could also support a wife and children. Or could he? Well, he did. And, unless the fortunes of war intervened and he went to the Mexican border to live in an adobe hut, or to the Philippines under *nipa* thatch, the officer of 1904 did have spacious quarters in which his family could live with a graciousness certainly far above most of those existing in the Army today. A light-and-heat allowance governed by a complicated seasonal and isothermic chart was of bare sufficiency; loud cries of anguish frequently followed the post quartermaster's presented bill for excess use!

These factors, plus medical care for himself and family, and the right—privilege, if you will—like the enlisted man, to purchase at commissary and post exchange at lower prices than on the outside, were ameliorations to the small pay. Above all, there was that anchor to windward, the guaranteed retirement pay.

But these things, these so-called "fringe benefits," do not tell the whole story of why a man should choose the Army as a career. They do not explain the relinquishment of that basic right of every American to battle with other Americans in the field of individual enterprise in which—it was certainly apparent by 1904—the good man could rise to financial and social success by survival of the fittest in business or the professions, other than military.

They do not explain why a man, foregoing these opportunities, should willingly embrace a life governed by rigid concepts of discipline and all that goes with the *noblesse oblige* principle of leading men to war, and possibly death on a battlefield.

The answer to the why is both simple and complex. "Arms and the man I sing," wrote Virgil. There is no space here for psychological research, so let us leave it at this: the Army officer of 1904 was a man with a vocation for a profession of honor and prestige that demanded a complete self-abnegation to duty and country. The "fringe benefits" constituted a pat on the back.

Rectitude was one common characteristic possessed by this corps of officers. The corps was governed by a code—partly written, partly unwritten—some of the principles of which reached back through the ages since the profession began and which may be expressed very simply. An officer was expected to be a straight shooter. Conduct unbecoming an officer and a gentleman was punished by dismissal from the service. So read the Draconian Articles of War. There was no quibbling, no sliding scale of punishment. Read it:

"*Art. 95.*—Any officer or cadet who is convicted of conduct unbecoming an officer and a gentleman shall be dismissed from the service."

This concept of honor by no means meant wearing a halo. Nor did it mean that every individual who took that solemn oath "to uphold and defend the Constitution of the United States against all enemies both foreign and domestic" was by that act endowed with this precious characteristic. Individuals from time to time fell short of the standard; the group itself did not.

Some of these officers—graduates of the U. S. Military Academy —had had this quality instilled in them by virtue of their four-year stern novitiate, governed by the precept of Sylvanus Thayer: "A cadet does not lie, cheat or steal." Others had attained it first through background and upbringing, retained it later by virtue of the unseen pressure of the West Point leaven on the Army.

Newton D. Baker, our World War I Secretary of War, expressed this essential quality in language explicit and crystal clear: ". . . Men may be inexact and even untruthful in ordinary matters and suffer as a consequence only the disesteem of their associates or the inconvenience of unfavorable litigation, but the inexact or untruthful soldier trifles with the lives of his fellow men and with the honor of his government."

The very fact that this corps of officers lived in a close 24-hour-day contact—socially and professionally—made this code a living thing, not just a posture assumed during an eight-hour job and to be cast aside in leisure moments. Its expression cropped out in a thousand different ways, of which perhaps one example suffices: the officer's word was his bond. He did not—except for the initial act of accepting his commission and during the process of military justice (an inheritance from the common law)—take oath or make affidavit. He *certified* that such and such was the case when necessary. That was sufficient. Wasn't it inscribed on his commission—as it still is, by the way—that the President of the United States reposed "special trust and confidence" in him?

The officer's basic responsibility—as any shavetail soon found out —was to the enlisted man, whose health and physical well-being were paramount, be it in garrison or in the field. Only when the soldier had been bedded down, so to speak, could the officer take his leisure. That, be it said, was the foundation, too, of the system of soldier-servants—strikers, dog-robbers—voluntarily serving for a few extra dollars out of the officer's pocket, who would relieve the officer of the little drudgeries of life while that officer was attending to the duty of looking out for his men.

The majority of these officers had had combat experience either in the Spanish-American War or in the Philippines. Except for a very few, these operations had been small ones. Few indeed were those officers who had as yet attended the Staff College or the War College.

And the restricted life of a small garrison was no breeding ground for grand strategy.

Garrison life was an ordered existence, with practically all work —except court-martial and boards—completed by noon for officer and enlisted man alike. Each officer in turn did his routine chore as officer of the day and officer of the guard. Let us not minimize these routines, either. No one does who has turned out at midnight into pelting snow at twenty degrees below zero at Fort Ethan Allen, or crawled on hands and knees against a typhoon's clawings in the Philippines, or fought Texas floods to inspect a sentinel on post.

Schools were carried on at each post—garrison schools in which officers studied regulations and manuals, military law, and the techniques and tactics of their respective arms, all expounded by older officers whose experience was more technical than tactical. Methodical precision was the rule: close-order drill, the alignment of a row of tent pegs, the parrot-like memorizing of the Manual for Interior Guard Duty, the exact respective dimensions and use of garrison, post and storm flag (what officer can tell you that today?), the layout and drainage of a camp site, the customs of the service. Such things were paramount.

Perhaps they went in one ear and out the other. But certainly the men who in 1904 were reciting, and insisting that their enlisted men recite, letter-perfect, the general orders for a sentinel on post, never dreamed that a day would come when both the commanding general of an immense fortified island outpost, and the admiral commanding the fleet supporting that outpost, would forget them!

The immaculate uniform, the varnished wheel spokes, the glistening metal work, the shining pots and pans, that shocking speck of dust on a locker shelf—all these were things occupying the mind of our 1904 officer. Minutiae, idolizing of technique and eyewash? Yes. But also stimulation of a sense of responsibility and self-discipline, therefore good up to a certain point.

Tactics were something else. Volley-firing, advance by rushes, even —shades of Balaclava!—the forming of square to repel cavalry, rather than the use of cover or the fine points of holding force and maneuvering mass. Parades and ceremonies were carried out with minute precision and rubric, beginning, as one remembers who was at "tin" (private military) school in those days, with a sonorous "Pass in review! Companies break from the right to march to the left! Right company, right forward, fours right!"

But mark this well: it was a hard-shooting Army. The Springfield rifle, Model 1903—still, so argue a number of small-arms experts, the finest military rifle ever produced—had just been issued to our infantry. Individual marksmanship was becoming a fetish: a doctrine definitely opposed to that of most, if not all, foreign armies whose conscript soldiers were given but rudimentary training in small-arms firing. Over there—even for Britain's professional army—the rule was the cone of fire; that is, the spraying of an area by men incapable of better aiming.

So American infantrymen—by a gamut of incessant training, from sighting and aiming exercises to the gruelling competition of the firing range (and for the gun bugs, the rarer altitudes of Camp Perry's perfection—in the National Rifle Matches) were building a reputation. It was one which would pay off handsomely at Belleau Wood and on the Marne a decade later, when amazed Germans were dropped at a thousand-yard distance by cool, competent marksmen firing at will. These were men who could judge distance, adjust for windage, and find their individual targets at ranges which led the enemy to believe they were being machine-gunned. And all American soldiers, Regular and National Guard, prized the little silver markmanship badges they wore.

As for the strategy in this "old" Army, it was true that Moss's *Officers' Manual,* bible of the shavetail in the mid-1900s, listed suggested readings of the Great Captains and of past campaigns, and Wagner's *Service of Security and Information* was on many an officer's shelves. Upton's *Military Policy of the United States,* just rescued from the oblivion of dusty War Department files, was there, of course. The cavalryman probably had Carter's *Horses, Saddles and Bridles.* And the West Pointer, although memory of Dennis Hart Mahan was fading, had been indoctrinated by Gustav G. Fiebeger. But in general this was not a studious officer corps; the club was so comfortable, and the evenings were so frequently taken up with post entertainment and visiting.

Actually, the minimum requirements for an officer's professional reading in those days consisted of four volumes. These were: the slim, blue-bound *Army Regulations,* with its incessant changes neatly pasted into its pages; the *Manual for Courts-Martial; Manual for Interior Guard Duty;* and the short, fat, pocket-sized *Drill Regulations* of his arm or service, which contained "all the answers."

Garrison life was pleasant on the whole. Once in a while there were field maneuvers—and always, of course, there was small-arms firing. But the mess, the bar, the club, and occasional trips to town, took up the bachelor's time. The married officer had his own home life. Both met on the frequent social occasions: garrison dances and card parties —ingrown affairs, one might call them.

The officers' mess was a formal association with its own quite rigid rules of decorum. The seating of the senior officer present governed the opening of the evening meal; officers arriving late made stiff, formal apology to him before taking their chairs. Blues—or, in summer—whites—were worn; the officers of the day and guard alone might be excused for appearing in service olive drab. One appeared in civilian clothing only if he were hurrying off post on leave, or returning therefrom. The mess was a man's world, too, for although all officers of the post were members, ladies were accommodated only in a side room—and this but in emergency.

If the garrison were large enough to include a regimental band, it was in frequent demand on social occasions: its concerts in fine weather, its orchestra for the post dances.

There was open house, of course, at the Commanding Officer's quarters on New Year's Day, when the garrison officers and families went calling *en masse.*

A few times each year both officers and men intermingled quite formally. Attendance by most of the officer population, male and female, was expected at enlisted men's dances. The co had to go— custom of the service. He and the sergeant major's wife led off the opening grand march, followed by the sergeant major and the ranking lady of the post, and other officers and ladies present. Then the commissioned personnel quietly and gracefully withdrew. On Thanksgiving and Christmas, attendance of officers and their families in the unit messes was expected and relished.

Evening parade was the highlight of daily garrison life. As the troops formed, the edges of the parade ground sprouted little groups of femininity along with the children, in chattering clumps, upon which, as the line stiffened and the sunset gun boomed, silence fell. Down came the colors slowly to the strains of the National Anthem while all faces turned to the tall flagstaff, the tots emulating their elders, with hand salute. To that cynical sentimentalist, the soldier, this simple poignant ceremony, always heart-catching, was and still is something never to be forgotten.

All this post life was bound up in a rigid code of etiquette, a composite of customs of the service that could not be learned at once, and violations of which would stamp the violator as being outside the circle. For instance, in that Army of 1904, so military in many other things, officers in uniform doffed their hats to ladies instead of saluting. Just why, even Captain James A. Moss, the Army's "Emily Post," could not explain. One called at once on newcomers, they—who by custom on arrival also called immediately on post commander and immediate superior—rendered return calls upon the garrison, cards being exchanged in all cases.

All, however, was not always beer and skittles. If the post commander were a martinet, his officers' official life could become uncomfortable, indeed. But, individuals of this type were usually ramroddy characters motivated less by spite than by zealous interpretation of regulations, and their lashes fell impartially. One unwritten law there was: official and social relations were two different things. Thus the frosty commander who had verbally crawled up and down an unfortunate subordinate's frame during the day's work could and did dine and drink and joke with that same subordinate at the club or in quarters that evening.

Among the officers of the garrison there was, of course, the normal cordiality to be expected in any group of gentlemen. There were also, for all these men were human, the other cross-currents and frictions of human relationships. And no matter how cordial their relationship, even if the senior did socially call the junior by his first name, rarely indeed would the junior call any officer of captain's grade or higher by his. In the first place, there was a wide disparity of age between captains and lieutenants; in the second, it wasn't done. And while the senior might call his subordinate "Jack" or "Bill" off duty, on official occasions it was "Mr. Soandso" for the lieutenants and the rank for the others.

The young officer arriving on station, whether in all the pride of a just-graduated cadet or fresh from civil life, found himself plunged into this sea of convention. Unaided, he might well sink despite the rigid provisions of *Army Regulations* with its pages of small-type injunctions. For even this official book had its blind spots.

For instance, take its finger-pointing admonition: "The interchange of compliments and visits between officers of the service is of great importance. Failure to pay the civilities customary in official and polite society is to the prejudice of the best interests of the service. The well-established customs of the Army in this regard will be carried out."

But there was a life-saver. It was the *Officers' Manual,* an almost five-hundred-page volume compiled with loving care by Capt. Moss, 24th Infantry, and dedicated "to the Subalterns of the Army who some day will be our Colonels and Generals."

"This Manual," so reads the preface, "is a compilation of 'Customs of the Service' and other matters of a practical, worth-knowing nature —*things of value and assistance to the inexperienced*—most of which cannot be found in print, but must be learned by experience—often by doing that which we should not do or by failing to do that which we should do."

It was all there, from the correct wording of an official message ("the commanding officer presents his compliments") to a recipe for champagne punch—a good one, too; from the duties of staff and company officers to advice to ladies going to the tropics (who should include in their baggage an American washboard and a galvanized tub as "great protection against the rapid wearing of the clothes with paddles, the native method").

Extravagance and debt were to be shunned, warned Moss. The young officer should watch his cash, but he must always be well-dressed. The minutiae of visiting-card procedure, the necessity for paying attention to one's hostess, gifts of candy, books and flowers in return for hospitality, all were included in its etiquette.

And the entire philosophy of the dedicated life of the professional officer was summed up in the following:

"Officers just starting their career should be most careful to make arrangements for messing which will enable them to live with the quiet dignity becoming their station. An officer's pay is given him for this purpose; it is sufficient to cover his expenses, and he owes it to the service to dress and live, though simply, yet always 'like a gentleman.' "

Thus far we have surveyed the scene on the larger posts where garrisons were of at least battalion strength. In the smaller posts, one- or two-company affairs—and there were not a few of them—life could be grim, as it always is where men and women are isolated for long periods in small groups. There is told, for instance, of an island one-company artillery post where there were only two commissioned officers, whose wives were not on speaking terms!

That brings us to the ladies of this Army—God bless 'em!—who were, and still should be, part and parcel of its life and customs. The wives of officers and soldiers were as far apart as were officers and soldiers—and also just as near. The soldier's wife might be the officer's cook or laundress, if she so chose. These women knew one another. Their children played together, went to school together, visited one another's homes, and made lifelong friendships. But aside from the formal occasions mentioned previously, there was no social intercourse between the adults on Officers' Row and "Soapsuds Row."

Soapsuds Row no longer exists. The name dates back to the days when, as we have seen, women, as laundresses, were actual components of the Army and wedded to soldiers and non-coms. Hence, in Army slang, the non-coms' row of quarters had become, without any intentional slur, Soapsuds Row.

There was other contact, however, between the wives of officers and enlisted men, outgrowth again of this close association. No soldier's wife ever hesitated to come to the company commander's wife for advice and counsel in times of trouble. And, by custom of the service, she was kindly and warmly received.

At the top, the commanding officer's wife—the cow to the initiate —could make or break the serenity of post life. And we must remember this, too: the bosomy dowager in shimmering evening gown who ruled the garrison's social side, whose dinners were impeccable from napery to dessert, had once been an Army bride. A shirtwaisted young woman, she probably rode in a Dougherty wagon on a hundred-mile hike from railhead to join her lieutenant in a stockaded post in the Bad Lands. Like any other Army woman of her vintage, she had come to know the chilling sound of the Indian war whoop. She had probably known the sharp pang of a hurried "Call to Arms" in the night, and the tense waiting until the column came riding back, gaunt, unshaven and hungry, bearing behind them on pack mules or escort wagons grim, 'paulin-covered bundles. In that case, too, she had heard the shaking sobs of Army sisters from both officers' and enlisted Rows, to whom the sight of those bundles meant the end of happiness.

She had sent her husband off to Cuba and to the Islands. She had later made that nightmare trip across the Pacific on a trooper to join him in a *nipa* shack somewhere in the *bontocs*. She had, not infrequently, cooked and slaved for her family under primitive conditions. And her children, as the "old" Army had it, cut their teeth on a bugle.

You could, if like Owen Wister's cowboy you smiled when you said it, call her a camp follower; for that was how Army Regulations and the Articles of War rated women. But had you termed her a "dependent," she would probably have risen in all her wrath. No dependent she, indeed.

Small wonder, then, that *Mme. la Colonelle* should consider most of her civilian sisters with some indifference—those women who didn't know and never would know. Small wonder that she bossed the younger Army wives, clucking and fluttering among them like a mother hen with chicks. They had joined *her* Army; they must learn its pains and its pleasures, and they must obey its customs. One of these, by the way, was that while flirting and philandering might be part of human relationships, the Army wolf was supposed to confine his more serious depredations to the area "ten miles beyond the post flagpole," as the old service unwritten law put it.

Most of these women contributed to the Army's welfare, but there were vixens, too—female martinets scaring the wits out of younger women, meddling at times through weaker husbands with the careers of such officers as they disliked.

The arrival of such a one on a post was something to think about. Should she not be satisfied with the set of quarters provided for the co, and prefer those already occupied by Major x—who at his own expense had just redecorated the interior, perhaps—out went the xs, to oust in turn the ys, who then nudged the zs. There was one case where seventeen officers moved because the cow "ranked out" someone else! Thankfully such characters were the exception rather than the rule.

The Army wife of 1904 led a more leisurely life in garrison than her sisters of today. She had a servant, of course; nearly all American middleclass families had servants in those days. And the government houses were built that way; with big kitchens, butler's pantries, and third-floor servants' quarters. She didn't have to spend hours in line to shop, although at times she might visit the commissary to choose groceries and meats. But it was much simpler to write the order out in the book she left on the back porch to be picked up by the Quartermaster messenger who passed daily. And before noon the groceries were delivered.

She had to count her pennies, of course. Pay checks could be stretched just so far, and the demands for entertainment and other social intercourse were exacting. But she made do, and she kept up a front. There was no necessity for keeping up with the Joneses, however, for officers' pay was no secret; everyone knew just how much each one was drawing, knew that Mrs. General had more money than Mrs. Lieutenant. Outside income was something else, and rare; to boast of it was, as Moss put it, "offensively vulgar."

Purchases from commissary and post exchange were on credit; all bills rendered promptly on the first of the month. A delay in payment beyond the tenth day following not only would result in tart official demand for explanation "by endorsement hereon," but it also just was not done.

And the Army wife, by contrast to her Navy sister, usually accompanied her husband when the unit changed stations. Exceptions were, of course, when exercises or campaigns took the troops out. Up until World War I, when the influx of replacements flooded each post as the troops moved out, the families remained in their government quarters while the men were in the field.

That unit change of station! Who, having made one, could ever forget it? Usually it was by train, although infrequently Army units went hiking across country from camp site to camp site, like a group of disciplined gypsies, while families followed as best they could by commercial transportation and—be this remembered—at the expense of the individual officer and man concerned. This was true also when the unit moved by rail; wives and families did not move at government expense until 1920.

The long ride on a troop train was tiresome. An old Regular recalls a move from Fort Hancock, New Jersey, to Fort Scott, California—eight days of cross-continental jolting—the men, three to a section, in tourist sleepers; the few officers (and one wife, one small boy and one bulldog) in the last car; and a caboose trundling behind. The view of the Feather River Canyon and the Royal Gorge from the cupola of a caboose is unforgettable.

A boxcar carried the kitchen—the Buzzacott field ranges embedded in sand—with the smoke pipes poking jauntily out the door. There were at least two scheduled long halts a day at some dreary way station, to let the men get out, march and double-time to take the kinks from their muscles. But half the time was spent, it seemed, waiting on sidings while passenger trains and legitimate freights slid by; troop trains until long after World War I rated behind freights in priority.

In 1906, the Army was shocked by a most unfortunate incident in Brownsville, Tex., sparked by race prejudice. A group of soldiers of the 25th Infantry, Negro, goaded by what they considered to be unjust discrimination, "shot up" the town. Because the culprits' identity could not at first be discovered, President Roosevelt summarily discharged the entire personnel of the three companies involved. Three years later, after a Congressional investigation, those guilty were punished and the innocent restored to duty.

On September 17, 1908, a group of Army people gathered on Fort Myer's parade ground, across the Potomac from Washington, inquisitive but all unwitting that they were about to witness both the first human sacrifice to heavier-than-air aviation and the birth of the United States Air Force.

Wilbur and Orville Wright fussed about the box-kite on wheels standing there. Then Orville climbed in and 1st Lieutenant Thomas E. Selfridge, California-born field artilleryman, swung up beside him. The little motor roared. The clumsy biplane wobbled along its launching track, rose, then lurched down to crash in splintered debris. Orville Wright was badly injured, but Selfridge was dead.

This had been the first official Army field experiment since the organization, in 1907, of an Aeronautical Division in the Signal Corps, with Major George O. Squier in charge. Squier, investigating the Wright invention, took a flight with Wilbur, liked it, and reached out for bold young officers. To him came cavalryman 1st Lieutenant Frank P. Lahm, who in 1906 had joined the newly-formed Aero Club of America and had piloted to victory the American entry in the first James Gordon Bennett international free-balloon race in France. To him also came Selfridge, spurred by Lahm's example.

Now, despite Selfridge's death, other souls of vision and daring came in to carry on the work. Lahm and engineer Lieutenant Frederic E. Humphreys, instructed by Wilbur Wright, became the first two Army pilots.

Mars had taken wings. He still had a very long way to go to attain recognition.

In such fashion our Army in the continental United States went through life for another decade.

There were interservice frictions, true. And there was one intra-service break which, for a number of years, led to some hard feeling. In 1907, the Artillery Corps had been rudely split into Coast and Field Artillery, six regiments of these latter being formed. So the "redlegs" became, respectively, "cosmoliners" and "wagon soldiers." The former were highly scientific; the latter played by ear, so to speak. The field artilleryman, become a virtuoso of improvisation, sneered at fire control which included plotting boards, wind-component indicators and mathematical computations of conditions of the moment. The coast artilleryman, waving his slide rule, hooted at the idea of popping little white shrapnel bursts into the air to bracket a moving target. Ten years later, on the stricken fields of France, it was proved that both were right, that each had something to learn from the other. And out of that came the magnificent American system of artillery fire control and direction that so amazed our allies and confounded our enemies in World War II.

Root's efforts to revamp the high command were still being hindered during the period by reactionaries in the War Department. Finally, long after he had left the Secretary of War's office, the old State, War and Navy Building in Washington rocked as two strong-willed men—Leonard Wood and Fred C. Ainsworth—clashed in what was the Waterloo of bureaucracy. That both men had started their Army careers as Army surgeons added some piquancy to their battle to head the Army. It was 1911, and Henry L. Stimson, protegé of Root, and like him imbued with constructive ideas, had just become Secretary of War.

Major General Fred C. Ainsworth, Adjutant General of the Army, meticulous master of paper-work who knew little of and cared less for the real functions of the military—he had sat in Washington from 1892 until 1907 as chief of the Records and Pension Office—detested the idea of a General Staff which would clip his wings. His wide acquaintanceship on "the Hill," and general knowledge of official Washington gained during his Pension Office tenure, enabled him to retain power in his own hands despite the new staff framework until Wood's advent as Chief of Staff in 1910.

The men, so the story goes, locked horns at once. Wood, dropping in on Ainsworth in friendly fashion when he first took office, received a brush-off:

"When I have anything to discuss with you, General, I will be glad to send for you."

In quick riposte Wood accepted this gage of battle.

"And I, General, whenever I have orders to give you, will as gladly send for you!"

The friction grew. The explosion followed when Wood appointed a board of officers, with Ainsworth as president, to study War Department administrative procedures. Under the Adjutant General's influence the board submitted a majority report retaining archaic features. Wood approved the progressive minority report instead. So, too, did Stimson.

Ainsworth, in fury, protested in an insubordinate memorandum criticizing "incompetent amateurs."

Stimson, stirred by his sense of rectitude and discipline, at once relieved Ainsworth and ordered formulation of charges and selection of a court martial. The Army sat and watched, preparing for a battle between giants, for Ainsworth had the reputation of a fighter. But the fight never came. Through Wyoming Senator Francis E. Warren's mediation, Ainsworth's request for immediate retirement was approved by President Taft. The tail no longer wagged the dog.

So, here at home, while big business spread, skyscrapers rose, and dynamos hummed, the Army drowsed in its isolation. Dot-and-dash telegraph was spanning land and sea. A national road system was evolving, to knit together an aggregation of American villages, towns and cities into an articulated whole. Automobile-building was becoming a national industry; but hitching posts still dotted the streets of Army posts and garrison business moved on foot or behind clopping hooves.

From time to time the soldier did emerge, but it was momentary and quickly forgotten. The San Francisco earthquake, Mississippi floods, great forest fires, strikes; each in turn brought the Army out to save, salvage and bring order. And, of course, the Army Engineers and Medical Corps were building the Panama Canal. General George W. Goethals and Colonel William C. Gorgas—and Walter Reed— were household names.

The service schools, too, were growing, although as yet but a fraction of the officer corps had felt their influence. Some few combined field maneuvers from time to time brought the professional and part-time soldier together for a short while.

Army pay had been boosted a bit. The buck private was getting fifteen dollars a month now, the topkick a minimum of forty-five dollars, the shavetail $141.66. And the country was still on the gold standard. There was the Cuban Pacification of 1906-09—the peaceful occupation by five regiments of infantry, two of cavalry and several batteries of field artillery—tactfully carried out without ripple or friction.

And, although there was much grumbling from chair-bound staffers and foot-conscious doughboys, the officer corps each year went through Teddy Roosevelt's famous hundred-mile-ride physical endurance test, now long forgotten.

Overseas the picture was different.

*   *   *   *   *

• • • •

12

DAYS OF THE EMPIRE

In the Philippines, Hawaii and Panama, the national expansion was doing something to the Army. It had exchanged the old frontier of the West for another frontier: exotic, romantic, and of the utmost importance to the national welfare. All these new areas had certain common climatic and ethnic elements. Not only were they all tropical, but their peoples were strange to most Americans and their languages foreign. In the Philippines, too, the established legal code—the Code Napoleon—was foreign except to Louisianians.

What had happened was that the United States by now had assumed what our British cousins, already bearing it, chose to call "the white man's burden." Consequently, the Army was becoming increasingly engaged in an overseas service having a number of points in common with that of the British Army in India. Particularly was this true in the Philippines. And as this service, bridging World War I, continued until 1941, materially affecting not only Army life and thought but also—through that Army—our national destinies, it will be well to linger on it for a moment.

From the beginning the Army took a tremendous part in the role of the United States in the Philippines: the role first as a conqueror, then as administrator, educator and advisor, while at the same time developing the fields of commerce and industry. One can definitely say that without the Army nothing advantageous either to our own nation or to the Filipinos could have been brought about. Without pursuing the subject further, one simply points to the fact that when the Japanese in 1941 launched the Greater East Asia Co-Prosperity Plan in its sea of blood, the Philippine Commonwealth maintained full allegiance, alliance and support to our flag and nation.

During those long years from 1904 to 1941, two generations of Army officers fought and lived in the Philippines. It would be hard to find an Army family some member of which had not at some time

been stationed there. More than that, the higher commanders of
World War I served their apprenticeship of combat in the humid wildernesses of Luzon, Samar and Mindanao. And when, in our own
United States, the high cost of living began to curtail the little leisures
of life, tropical service became all the more popular.

Garrison life in the islands was intriguing, from the first installa-
tion of Army homes in *nipa* shacks, to the later developments of fine
concrete barracks and quarters. All the concurrent trials and pleasures
of life in the Orient were experienced, from flying cockroaches to deft
and nimble servants. It began, of course, with the month-long voyage
out, in one of those ancient, creaking wayfarers of the sea we had
purchased in 1898. They had been cattle boats on the North Atlantic
run—the *Sheridan,* the *Sherman* and the *Thomas* and their smaller,
even more ancient sisters.

One remembers such things as the crowded troop quarters, the
diapers on the lines rigged athwart the officers' promenade deck, the
steady sway and thrust of the ship's movement, the band tuning up for
the afternoon concert, the bridge and poker parties in the smoking
room, the early-morning setting-up exercises on the troop decks, the
"Abandon Ship" drills, the boxing matches on the forward deck, and
the baby food packages stowed about the staterooms (you bought and
brought your own in those days).

Soldiers of all ranks found a social system strikingly different from
home. In the first place, Filipino "boys" were available for kitchen and
barracks police, taking away much of the normal drudgery of soldier
housekeeping. For the Army wife and her husband, too, as well as for
the bachelor, servants were plentiful and cheap. Houseboys took care
of the officers from changing buttons to ironing the stiffly starched
uniform always laid out: khaki for the morning, whites for evening
wear. The *lavandera* was constantly on the job, washing and ironing.
The *amah* rode herd on the children. The cook could do amazing
things with canned milk—there was no fresh, of course—and such
other staples available from a commissary where Stateside delicacies
arrived in small quantities and were exhausted promptly after each
transport's arrival. Were he a Chinese cook, he was really a prestidigi-
tator.

Such things were some compensation for the friendly little green
lizard which might plop from the dining-room ceiling into the soup,

or the army of ants suddenly appearing from nowhere to march in column of battalions across the living-room floor.

Of course, the bed- and table-legs were kept in cans filled with kerosene to discourage creeping things like tarantulas, scorpions and centipedes, and only a fool would disobey orders and sleep without a mosquito bar. The drinking water was boiled, and fresh vegetables were scalded—for obvious reasons.

Incidentally, the common practice of keeping the drinking water in the icebox in gin bottles—after the original contents had been removed —necessitated some care in selecting the ingredients for the evening cocktail.

Dinners and dances were frequent. Probably one of the most intriguing things about those affairs was the amazing facility with which the houseboys and cooks rallied to help one another at parties. Somehow the grapevine always brought the news, with details of the guests expected. So one might find one's own houseboy serving at someone-else's table, and one's own cutlery, napery and china eking out the hostess' store. The only unpleasant elements were the continuous feuds between Chinese and Filipino house servants, which sometimes turned into battles royal, ending only when a file of the guard came charging down to disperse the howling combatants. A berserk Chinese cook spitting like a cat, with cleaver or carving knife swinging free, chasing a screeching Tagalog houseboy down the back row of officers' line, was something to see!

Manila was, of course, the locus of official and social life, not only for the posts in and near the city but also for transients on leave from provincial stations, the most important of which was Zamboanga, south on Mindanao.

Fascinating was the former Spanish stronghold, old Fort Santiago, where department headquarters was situated, and also the 31st Infantry—the one American regiment that had never been stationed in the United States. Army life pulsated inside its frowning escarpments and battlemented curtain walls four hundred years old.

Pinpin Street in Manila was a favorite rendezvous for soldiers on pass, while shopping took the ladies along the Escolta or into the little musty Chinese shops of Binondo and the Japanese Osaka Bazaar.

Golf was indulged in by Army and the European civilian colony along the greensward in the old moat of Fort Santiago and the Intramuros, the walled city. Tennis, too, was popular, while the equestrian-minded rallied around the Polo Club. Socially, Filipino and European mingled little, with two exceptions: the official functions at Malacanan Palace and the swank Spanish Club—almost exclusively Filipino—where annually the King of Spain's birthday was celebrated lavishly.

Up in the mountains, Baguio was a mecca for Army folk on leave. Occasional visits to China were also popular, to obtain china, rugs and furs, to visit friends in the 15th Infantry in garrison at Tientsin, and to get a real glimpse of the mysterious Orient.

The jungle was always close by, with its hazards such as pythons. They told a story up at Stotsenberg of a python found wrapped about a limber wheel, which, in its dying convulsions when shot, snapped the stout spokes like so many matches. James Ravine on Corregidor's slopes was named after an unfortunate lieutenant who never came back from a ride there—having met a python which left only the officer's hat behind as evidence. And it was the sight of a battery pounding along a Luzon jungle trail that inspired Lieutenant Edmund L. (Schnitz) Gruber to compose in 1908 the Field Artillery's "Caisson Song."

The horses today are long gone; so, too, are the caissons, except for the ceremonial rig at Arlington National Cemetery where old soldiers "take their last ride, on the top of a rolling caisson." But as long as there is a "red-leg" left in the Army, Gruber's words will ring out:

> Over hill, over dale, as we hit the dusty trail,
> And the caissons go rolling along.
> In and out, hear them shout,
>   Counter march and right about,
> As the caissons go rolling along.

Chorus

> Then its hi! hi! hee! in the field artilleree,
> Shout out your numbers loud and strong.
> Where e'er you go, you will always know,
> That the caissons go rolling along (Keep 'em rolling!)
> The caissons go rolling along.

Professionally, there was fighting—and hard fighting—in the Moro

islands of Mindanao and Jolo for many years after 1904, as small
punitive columns beat their way through tropical jungles to the
fastnesses where fanatic Mohammedan warriors of a robber-baron
type held out. And throughout the period, as the defense of the archi-
pelago grew in importance, particularly after World War I and Japan's
bid for Manchuria developed, the Army was intensely interested in
strengthening our positions.

While defense plans coalesced, with the path of conquest down
from Lingayen Gulf plainly marked, the Army again and again in
paper war and maneuvers operated through central Luzon, with Corregidor—Gibraltar of the East—as the keystone of the arch of
defense. We must not forget that the withdrawal to Bataan Peninsula
in 1941 had been long planned and practiced—since 1921, in fact.
As for the means available for defense, it was always a case of make-
do, particularly in the years following the Washington Disarmament
Conference which halted, in transit, additional armament for the
islands. In 1922, the single anti-aircraft gun mounted on Corregidor's
Malinta Hill—a 75-mm. piece—was mute evidence of national som-
nolence. The breechblock for this gun still lay in a Honolulu ware-
house, a victim of that conference.

Of such stuff was the thought that lay in every Army mind in the
Islands during the early 1920s. The U.S. Army in the Philippines was
earmarked—its destiny plain—a pawn to be sacrificed to Congressional indifference. But black clouds faded in tropic nights with the
haunting scent of the hibiscus and a jazz band playing in the Army
and Navy Club—where beaming Ah Moon presided over the dining
room—or over across the square in the Manila Hotel.

It might have been later than one thought, but why consider the
inevitability of Japanese invasion when caressing a frosted julep on
the Polo Club veranda, with the moonlight rippling across Manila
Bay? Why think at all when swaying to "Three O'Clock in the Morning" with plenty of Watson No. 10 and Tansan water waiting on the
table? Eat, drink, and be merry, for tomorrow we die!

So it was Kismet, the Brussels ball before Waterloo, or life on the
slopes of Vesuvius . . . with a run later to Santa Ana's rattan-divided
dance floor and a glimpse of the piquant little Filipinas with their
quaint shoulder-of-mutton-sleeved dresses, and a final tour to Tom's
Dixie Kitchen for ham and eggs before going home to bed. Tom him-

self, black as the ace of spades, and his brother-in-arms, Casey of the famous "Hospital for Shoes" where every American woman in the Islands had her footgear made, were notable, for these two were ex-9th Cavalry soldiers who had married Filipinas and settled down to a new life after a tour of duty in the Islands.

And all the while, a stout military organization—the Philippine Scouts, warriors loyal to their salt—was slowly growing to become the nucleus in a later day of the Philippine Army. Some of its officers were Americans, others Filipinos. Some, old-time Army non-coms, dated back to the early days as did a few of the native officers.

There were some Filipinos, like one elderly major, whose living-room in a pleasant set of quarters was festooned in true Filipino fashion with drying fish! And there were others, graduates of West Point, like stout Vicente Lim—"Cannibal" was his Academy nick-name—and gallant Pastor Martelino, who one day would make the supreme sacrifice for their Stars and Stripes.

Recreation for this overseas Army fell into several categories. Baseball, which became a national game for Filipinos, was most popular in both American and Scout units, as well as in civilian circles. The competition in the Island leagues was fierce.

Soldier diversion off-post followed what might be called normal channels with Oriental trimmings. The soldier drank his beer in Pinpin Street barrooms, he walked and talked and haunted the dance halls with attractive Filipina girls. One of his most popular and harmless stunts was to pile with several comrades into a *calesa* and go singing and shouting down the street. *Calesas,* two-wheeled pony-drawn gigs with the native driver perched almost over the animal's rump, were long the sole means of public transportation, except *carabao* carts. They vied with the later automobile practically to the end. Everyone took *calesas.*

In Panama, while the tropical garrison life resembled closely that in the Philippines, the setting was somewhat different. In the first place, the Canal Zone was within easier reach of the United States and so there was less sense of isolation. And while military maneuvers were incessant and rigorous, and alerts continuous, there never was any of the jungle warfare of the earliest days in the Philippines. Thanks to the vigorous sanitary precautions, life was as pleasant as tropical life can be. And for the ladies, the free-port facilities of the Zone and of the Republic of Panama brought wide variety of bargains in fine English chinaware and linens at this busy crossroads of empire.

The early days in Panama, while the Canal was abuilding under the imperious but just rule of Colonel Goethals—"the man who stood up in Panama and the mountains stood aside"—had been hectic, of course. They were seven years of toil, in an atmosphere of dogged determination and fiery enthusiasm, while Goethals conquered incessant obstacles. The task was monumental. Take, for instance, the great slide at Cucaracha in 1913, when slimy mud engulfed in a moment months of heart-breaking work.

"What are we going to do?" wailed one of Goethals' lieutenants in a frenzy of despair, when the leader arrived on the scene on the run.

"Hell!" barked Goethals. "Dig it out again!"

The job had been turned over to the Corps of Engineers in 1907, four years after work had been started on it by the best civilian engineers in the United States. The task had been bogged down by red-tape, dissention and the ravages of disease. Except for some work on the Culebra Cut the great engineering project was still a drafting-board dream. Locks, dams, dredged channels, breakwaters, power plants, piers and docks—and, of course, the fortifications—were still to be constructed. Misfortune, which had dogged the steps of all Panama Canal builders since the days of the ill-fated Frenchman Ferdinand de Lesseps, could not be conquered, it seemed.

But the United States needed that canal, and President Theodore Roosevelt turned to the Army. Goethals was put in charge and given free rein.

Goethals had had much practical experience in Tennessee River engineering projects. No one could fool him, as the thirty-five thousand civilian employees—five thousand were American—soon found out. They were hostile in the beginning, those turbulent hard-rock men, muckers, drillers and gandy-dancers. They worked hard and they played hard, and they didn't want military discipline. But they got it, willy-nilly, from a leader who was a square-shooter. He could drive them ragged and make them like it.

Goethals' word was law in the Canal Zone. There was no appeal from his decision. At the jerk of his thumb the grafter, the waster, and the incompetent went back home on the next boat. He was all over the place, from six in the morning until ten at night.

But all of Goethals' engineering knowledge and leadership would have been in vain had not the Medical Corps cleaned up that pest-hole. It was a by-word in Panama in the old days that every tie laid on the Panama Railroad had cost a human life. And from 1881 to 1889, more than twenty thousand laborers working on the old French canal project had died of yellow fever, bubonic plague, malaria and small-pox.

Yellow Jack was flaring when the United States took over the Canal Zone in 1903. Major William Gorgas, Medical Corps, who had cleaned up Havana as soon as Walter Reed's discoveries had shown the cause of the disease, was sent down. Under his preventive measures disease was coming under control by the time Goethals took over. Under his iron rule, which brooked no departure from Gorgas' sanitary regulations, the Zone blossomed into a garden spot where people from temperate zones could live, work and maintain health.

The Atlantic and Pacific Oceans met; the first ship went through the Canal August 15, 1914. Between them the Corps of Engineers and the Medical Corps had produced another wonder of the world. Well may the "old" Army be proud of that accomplishment.

The great job done, the Army settled down to the development and maintenance of an impregnable fortress area guarding the country's vital military trans-hemispheric bypass.

Hawaii, like Panama, had developed into a protective bastion. Both expressed, in theory at least, the interdependence of Army and Navy in joint cooperation. There they differed from the Philippines, where the Army garrisons dangled before the maw of potential Japanese invasion. Thus in both Hawaii and the Canal Zone areas the garrisons became larger, the military aspect more vigorous.

Hawaii, differing from both Panama and the Philippines in that its climate was even and salubrious, was a pleasant place in which to live—with much the atmosphere of a summer resort. While the Coast Artillery on Oahu manned its forts ringing the great Navy base of Pearl Harbor, the mobile forces up at the growing cantonments of Schofield Barracks spent a great part of their time in incessant maneu-vers and field operations. They worked hard in Hawaii, and they played hard, too, for it was there that the Army really developed its system of athletics. Some feel that the semiprofessionalism of Army athletics has been overdeveloped. In any event, it was on Oahu that the old hit-or-miss Army sports programs began, in 1919, to change—for better or for worse—into a regimented scheme, and Army athletes to receive preferential treatment.

In Alaska, another side of this new frontier was developing, as tiny garrisons wrestled with totally different problems of life in that wilderness. Cut off from communications during the winter, fur-clad Army folk, frequently on snowshoes, went about their work. Living costs were high in so far as supplies from Stateside went, but there were compensations in this sportsman's paradise, provided one was either hunter, fisherman or both.

And over across the world, in Tientsin, China, was another sort of outpost again. There the 15th Infantry—part of the Allied occupation force imposed on China as a result of the Boxer Rebellion—rubbed elbows with the mysterious East. Spectators rather than participants, the doughboys and their families watched the warlords come and go, saw the encroachments of the Japanese, and attended battalion maneuvers in the hills. Trips to Peking, short summer leaves at Peitaho, occasional journeys to the brooding Great Wall, and some hob-nobbing with their colleagues of the European garrisons were all part of the 15th Infantry's life.

*　*　*　*　*

13

THE FIRST CRUSADE

In 1910, Mexico seethed into revolution. Porfirio Díaz, iron dictator, was ousted by Francisco I. Madero's liberals. General Victoriano Huerta's reactionary revolution, followed by the assassination of Madero, ignited a jumble of conflagrations that stepped on American business toes. European string-pullings and the rise of Venustiano Carranza followed fast. President Taft and his successor President Wilson, by opposite courses of action, attempted in turn to allay our neighbor's troubles but only succeeded in arousing resentment south of the border. It was "dollar diplomacy" suddenly put in reverse. The chain reaction startled the nation to some realization of its paucity of armed strength.

Up to that time combined maneuvers and large-unit training in the Army had been practically nil. Occasionally, it is true, Congress had been induced to spend a little money on such folderol, but it was only a drop in the bucket. There had been an attempt at concentration at American Lake, Washington, and one remembers two combined field maneuvers in the East: one at Pine Camp, New York (now Camp Drum) in 1909, with both Regular and National Guard units attending, and the other the next year in Connecticut. Of this latter one recalls two events: The daylight charge of the 1st New York Cavalry in column of fours, up a long hill road closely defended by the "enemy"; and the presence of two old biplane crates, one belonging to the Regular Signal Corps, the other to the New York National Guard.

To concentrate one so-called "maneuver division" during 1911-13 along the Rio Grande absorbed practically all available Regular and National Guard troops, including the Army's fifteen "military aviators." When the border flared in 1914, resulting in the Vera Cruz Expedition under General Frederick Funston, and, two years later—following Pancho Villa's raid upon Columbus, New Mexico—General

Pershing's punitive expedition into Mexico, the military power of the nation was shown to be so pitably small that Congress did take some reasonable steps. Leonard Wood's "Plattsburg idea," stimulating military interest among professional and business men in 1915, contributed to a national preparedness.

The National Defense Act of 1916 was the greatest piece of constructive military legislation this country had yet seen. By its provisions the Army of the United States became a tripartite entity: the Regular Army and its civilian components—Organized Reserves (commissioned and enlisted), and the National Guard, at long last recognized officially by that name. The Organized Reserves embraced an Officers' Reserve Corps and a Reserve Officers' Training Corps to feed it—the military units of colleges and of other institutions, including in particular such long-established all-military schools as Norwich (founded in 1819), Virginia Military Institute (1839), the Citadel (1842), and others whose instruction conformed to War Department requirements. The Morrill Act of 1862, expanded in 1881 to include schools other than land-grant colleges, had come of age.

Insofar as the National Guard was concerned, however, the Act still limited its participation; only "while in the service of the United States" was it to be a part of the Army. Nevertheless, our citizen-soldier, the militiaman of the past, had come a long way—a way which would bear good fruit, despite the hamperings of State politics that interfered more or less with the efficiency of his high command in peacetime.

The new blue print called for a peacetime Regular Army of one hundred and seventy-five thousand fighting men, organized into divisions and brigades upon tactical basis. The rub was that peacetime was running out, and except for paper wars at the schools, the Regular officer was without professional experience with large units.

Let us look at it as that soldier-historian, Colonel William A. Ganoe, in his *History of the United States Army,* saw the picture:

"When April 6, 1917, tossed the American spectators onto the European gridiron, they had not even a high school squad to meet the professionals. The 1916 Defense Act had been merely the promise of a team for which only a few freshmen had reported. The army had no large tactical units in a modern sense, few weapons, a dearth of officers, no experience with trench warfare, little training and less strength. It had 9,750 officers of all grades and experience, while 180,000 of the utmost efficiency were immediately necessary.

"On the other hand it had received a signal blessing in disguise. Few have ever regarded Pancho Villa as a benefactor. But his crossing our border the previous year had given our President the excuse for training a large portion of the Regular Army and about 150,000 National Guardsmen on the Mexican border. The hardening, discipline and schooling in the field were the finest to date for the army and made possible later the ability of the American forces . . . to turn the tide in March, 1918, in France. There has been much speculation since as to what might have happened had not Mr. Villa done us this temporary or ultimate ill-turn or favor."

The war that set Europe aflame in 1914 had sharply divided sentiment in the American people and in their Army, too. Our Germanic element of population quite naturally sympathized with their forebears. Those of Irish strain, the hatred of England running in their blood, chimed in as did the vocative few still raising the somewhat childish warwhoops of "perfidious Albion" and "the Redcoats are coming." Against them were pitted at least equal numbers of Anglo-Saxon Americans convinced that blood was thicker than water. With these stood people still reminiscent of France's help in our Revolutionary days, as well as our population segments hailing from Poland and from the captive races of the Austro-Hungarian Empire.

But most of this was sympathy alone. The hungry maw of war reaching out for munitions set American industry humming to provide them, and poured millions of dollars into American pockets. Prosperity waxing on war could continue only if America remained neutral. It took a long time to convince the United States that this war against the Germanic powers was hers, too. It took such things as a German offer of alliance with Mexico, German sabotage—the Black Tom explosion being the worst example—and, finally, unrestricted submarine warfare, to arouse the United States.

On April 2, 1917, President Woodrow Wilson, just elected on the slogan "He kept us out of war," sparked the Congress with his war message, announcing "the world must be saved for democracy." Four days later war was declared. The plunge made, the United States whirled into action—the keynote of uninamity its acceptance six weeks later of a Selective Service Act drafting the country's manpower to the national disposition.

The Selective Service Act of 1917, the nation's second experience in conscription, deserves consideration both for its effect on the Army itself as well as on the American people. Carefully drawn to avoid the stupidities and injustices of our Civil War experience, it allayed the fears that another nightmare of violence would result. Its product, our National Army soldier, was an average young American who in general assumed his civic obligation with good will. Sixty per cent of our armed forces were drafted men, as contrasted with the two per cent obtained by draft in Civil War days.

Gone were the "hand-cuffed volunteers," the bounty-jumpers, the substitutes. Gone was the power legally open to the craven to buy his way to exemption. There were draft-dodgers, of course, human nature being what it is. But most of these were caught and punished, while public opinion branded them all. The most notable case was that of Grover Cleveland Bergdoll, wealthy young German-American, whose mother connived to spirit him out of the country (Bergdoll, long years afterwards, returned to serve time in a Federal penitentiary).

The man who, by reason of his religious belief, would not fight, became a problem new to an Army accustomed through the years to voluntary enlistment. This "conscientious objector" had a rough road ahead of him when he donned uniform. He might be transferred to a non-combattant branch of the service; he might, and some did, become convinced of his duty to the team, in which case his problem ended. But in general he was looked upon with suspicion, and for a very common-sense reason which had nothing to do with religious grounds.

The fact was that no officer or enlisted man wanted to go into battle beside a man who wouldn't fight either for his own life or for the lives of his comrades. He was more than a fifth wheel; he was a menace to his squad and to his Army. The individual who carried his objections to the extent of refusing to put on uniform, or to do duty of any sort, was simply considered to be a malingerer, was tried by court martial, and was punished.

Some conscientious objectors, of course, simply broke the conscription law by refusing to register or to obey the call-up. Such men fell

into the category of draft-dodgers and the Justice Department took
care of them.

It was all rough and, certainly as far as the other enlisted men were
concerned, no holds were barred. In general public opinion concurred,
while at the same time subscribing, of course, to the Constitutional
right of freedom of religion and recognizing the magnificent welfare
effort of the Society of Friends in particular, and other such non-
warlike sects as the Mennonites.

But Mr. and Mrs. Smith, of Main Street, Anytown, U.S.A., could
not see why, if the government forced their son to face enemy bullets,
someone-else's son should be spared just because he said he did not
want to fight. And if, as the war went on, a gold star appeared in
the window of the Smith home, the resentment was acute.

The generally cheerful public acceptance of the law lay in the
bright brain of Newton D. Baker, our great Secretary of War of that
period. One gloomy Senator had at first predicted its passage would
cause the streets of St. Louis "to run red with blood." An equally
gloomy Representative announced that in his locality "a convict and
a conscript were synonymous terms."

But Baker, in drafting the bill, had introduced the proviso that
final selection of each draftee would lie in the hands of his neighbors.
The initial registration was voluntary, the call-up by lottery. The
inductee came before a board of residents of his local community,
who could be expected to know him and his necessities. Classification
and exemption lay in their hands. The enforcement of the law was a
duty of the Justice Department. It was all fair, honest and democratic.
There was no saber-rattling, no vestige of impressment. It was the
American way. And it worked.

The one really sour note resulted from the blanket deferment of
all ship-building labor. This was caused by the stark necessity of
producing shipping to replace the losses caused by the German U-boat
campaign. But some hundred thousand able bodied men in the ship-
building trade who would otherwise have gone into uniform were
deferred, as it turned out, and much local indignation resulted from
men and their families in other trades not exempted.

This new legislation also abolished the old volunteer system and
—because all officers above the grade of colonel were to be appointed
by the President by and with the consent of the Senate—there would

be no state-made political generals leading men to death in the valor of ignorance. It put all officers and enlisted men of the new army on the same footing as Regulars for pay and allowances. Having done this much, Congress pushed up its specs on its startled forehead—as it realized there would be voters in this new army—and raised enlisted pay all around: the buck private beginning at a dollar a day.

Cantonments and training schools blossomed all over the country, some around existing Army posts, others in isolated areas. The Regular and the newcomer found themselves thrown into a hectic life totally different from the past. Gypsying wives, following their menfolk, found lodgings where best they could. Some newcomers, brought into immediate contact with existing garrison life, floundered, bewildered by a code and customs of which they had known nothing. Welcomed warmly by some, they were snubbed by others of the "old" Army. Both newcomer and oldtimer suffered equally from scrounging landlords and shop keepers when they attempted to settle in the vicinity of outlying camps. It was an era of frustration and anxiety.

This was a mass-production Army, built upon the existing Regular units, the entire National Guard and the totally new draft colossus called the National Army, all neatly packaged into divisions. The four-million-man aggregation quite naturally lost—or rather never quite gained—the individual regimental team-spirit of the "old" Army. No longer to the common query of marching men who pass in the night—"What outfit, soldier?"—would the answer be an identification of the regiment. Rather, it was, "The such-and-such Division!" for his division was the only common bond this new soldier knew.

The war-time President, Woodrow Wilson, and his Secretary of War, Newton D. Baker—whose stature waxes as history matures—laid their trust on two remarkable West Pointers, Peyton C. March, Chief of Staff, and John J. Pershing, commanding the American Expeditionary Force.

Granite-faced and inflexible were these twain. The Army looked to them in vain for the flamboyance of a Scott, the homely simplicity of a Grant, the hat-waving of a Sheridan. But it found a hidden spark of leadership expressed in their dedication and their knowledge of their profession. They brooked no opposition; they feuded as only two strong-willed men can feud (the enmity lasted until death); they accepted no excuse (many hearts were broken in that process); but the one forged the new Army, and the other led it to victory as an entity.

It was March who, turning deaf ears to politicos seeking commissions by favoritism, also turned down Theodore Roosevelt's patriotic but ill-advised attempt to organize a division of elite volunteers based on the concept of his "Rough Riders" of the Spanish-American War. March rightly felt that such skimming of military cream would only weaken the morale of the rest of the Army.

This was, in the high command—from the General Staff down through division and to regiment—a Regular Army's war in the main. Its leaders were mostly the captains and the lieutenants of Philippine Insurrection days, and of our Army of 1904, tempered and groomed by further schooling—Elihu Root's donation to the nation. They were, as General James Harbord said, men "who speak the same language."

Utilizing the know-how and the resources of a nation at last convinced that if war does come it is the problem of civilian and soldier both, prodigies of extemporization were accomplished. It couldn't all be done at home, of course; the nation wasn't geared for it. Artillery, tanks, machine-guns and other special weapons had to be provided by France for American soldiers to man.

So, too, with three-quarters of the planes of an Army Air Force emerging full-blown from the tiny Aviation Section of the Signal Corps (we had in the beginning but fifty-five airplanes, none fit for combat). British and other foreign ships, including German vessels held here, helped take our men to France. Overseas, ports and railroads and telephone lines were built and operated by American soldiers.

For the first time in American history our soldiers learned to go to war in shrouded secrecy, lest the dreaded U-boat meet them on the way. However, for one regiment of Coast Artillery the mingled thrill and heart-wrench of the old days were granted. It marched on board the old excursion boat *Grand Republic* at Fort Hancock, N. J., with the rest of the garrison drawn up and the bands playing, while families watched. The big paddle-wheels plunked away to New York and the waiting transport to the tune of "The Girl I Left Behind Me." It was a pretty good way to go to war.

But the AEF as a self-existing entity would never have known victory had it not been for Pershing. Body and soul it would have been squandered, had the Allies had their way, as replacements—mere cannon fodder—in their own depleted ranks. However, Pershing had his directive; a ringing one:

"In military operations against the Imperial German Government you are directed to cooperate with the forces of the other countries employed against the enemy; but in so doing the underlying idea must be kept in view that the forces of the United States are a separate and distinct component of the combined forces, the identity of which must be preserved. This fundamental rule is subject to such minor exceptions in particular circumstances as your judgment may approve. The decision as to when your command or any of its parts is ready for action is confided to you, and you will exercise full discretion in determining the manner of cooperation."

Pershing kept the soldier's faith against the blandishments of Lloyd George, the fulminations of Georges Clemenceau, the explosive reactions of General Ferdinand Foch. He kept it, once making the council table shake under their very noses as his fist crashed down before he stalked from the room in flat refusal.

In battle at last, Pershing's AEF in two hundred days of battle— thirteen major operations (eleven were joint enterprises with the Allies)—broke the back of the Kaiser's Germany. Europe, dubious at first of American fighting ability, saw such things as Belleau Woods, where the 2nd Division—half Marine, half Army—held the enemy's best; the 3rd Division at Chateau Thierry and its 38th Infantry Regiment, "Rock of the Marne," with the 10th Field Artillery, "The Rock's Support," fighting and throwing back a battle-wise enemy attacking it on three sides. It saw Cantigny, where the 28th Infantry Regiment achieved success in the first American offensive move. Finally, it saw the 1st and 2nd Divisions at Soissons spearhead to victory General C. M. E. Mangin's Aisne-Marne offensive.

The St. Mihiel operation, American-planned and directed, bit further into the German strength. That was followed fast by the Meuse-Argonne; forty-seven days of incessant combat, the largest and longest battle the Army had ever engaged in until World War II. There occurred such incidents as the 35th Division's gallant but unwary thrust that ended in collapse; the 77th Division's "Lost Battalion," surrounded and cut off, but undefeated, in the gloomy Argonne Forest for five dreadful days. There was the 1st Division's epic but unortho-

dox drive that carried it straight to the walls of Sedan—and incidentally across the path of both French and U. S. armies to their mutual
exasperation. In the end came victory.

It was a victory emphasizing the character of the American soldier.
For of the many in France who received the cherished Medal of Honor
for gallantry in action "above and beyond the call of duty," two
individuals stand out—Samuel Woodfill and Alvin York—differing
perhaps in every characteristic except personal valor and devotion to
duty.

Woodfill was a professional soldier commissioned as a lieutenant
in the 60th Infantry. York, a conscientious objector until he learned
why the Selective Service Act had put him in uniform, was a corporal
in Company G, 328th Infantry; a Tennessean and a fit descendant of
mountain men. Both soldiers attained glory in the Meuse-Argonne,
within a forty-eight-hour span, and less than eight miles from one
another.

Woodfill, leading his company, single-handedly attacked in turn
three machine-gun nests. Using his rifle, pistol and finally a pick, he
killed or captured all the occupants in hand-to-hand combat. General
Pershing later proclaimed him the outstanding hero of the AEF.

York, his superior officers killed, assumed command of a patrol
of seven men in an assault on a German battalion occupying a string
of machine-gun nests. In a one-man offensive he engaged the enemy
with rifle and pistol, killing fifteen and bringing back one hundred
and thirty-two prisoners, including five officers.

In France, too, American artillery had brought new techniques to
the battlefield; the most revolutionary since the days of Napoleon's
grande batterie. The flexibility of modern artillery fire was utilized in
extent previously unrealized—to pour mass concentrations on target
after target as needed. This shifting and grouping, not of guns but of
their shells, was the brain-child of General Charles P. Summerall,
master artilleryman.

Over there, also, the Army learned the use of the new agents of
war; the airplane, the tank, and chemical warfare.

There were American sideshows to the main struggle. The Army
was in Italy in small fashion; one regiment of infantry. It was in North
Russia; a regiment of infantry and a battalion of engineers fighting
Bolshevists in that ill-fated and badly-conceived Franco-British effort.

It was in Siberia; William Graves' 27th and 31st Infantry regiments were scattered along the trans-Siberian railway from Lake Baikal to Vladivostok with every man's hand, it seemed, against them, Allies and Russians alike.

By November 11, 1918, when the firing died away on the Western front, we had an Army tried in battle, an instrument of national power commensurable with the stature of the United States in a new world from which so much of the old foundation had gone. Forty-two divisions with additional masses of corps and army troops made up the American First and Second Armies overseas—some two million men. Twelve more divisions were in training in the United States and four additional were being organized.

But the build-up had been painful. This national Army, when it came into being in 1917 as a cross-section of our citizenry, squeaked and chafed at the joints.

The Regulars first sniffed at the National Guard, and then both took a good hefty sniff at the "ninety-day wonders" of the Officers' Training Camps—predecessor of ocs.

Sergeant Alexander Woollcott of *Stars and Stripes* told of how the drafted men of a National Army division made a counter thrust against a passing National Guard regiment: "Draft dodgers!" they taunted.

It was, of course, just what happens to new boys at school; just as childish and at the same time serious. All did join together as an irresistible team after the shakedown, but the duration of the war was too short for the civilian soldier's amateurish inferiority complex to have been erased.

The Regular found out that the civilian made a good soldier, and took the lesson to heart. But the civilian, remembering only the iron discipline that had trod on his personal toes, took back to civil life a dislike for those taskmasters whom—frequently inaccurately—he lumped as "West Pointers."

It was a smart Army that Pershing led in France. Gone were the slouch hats and shirt sleeves of 1898; collars were tight-hooked, blouses buttoned, saluting fast and furious. But it was light-hearted. One heard slogging doughboys sing on the march and in bivouac, "Pack Up Your Troubles in Your Old Kit Bag" and "Tipperary" which we had borrowed from the British, but George M. Cohan's "Over There" and "Mademoiselle from Armentieres"—praise her bawdiness!—became our very American own.

Some old-time officers, it is true, soon found that their years of restricted service had so lowered their sights that they were unable to see the divisional woods for the company and platoon trees. Such men went to "Blooie," as the reclassification center at Blois was popularly called.

Others, around the hard core of the few graduates of the Command and Staff School, went on to high places. And that handful of Leavenworth graduates did the job—the men who had studied war despite the childish tantrum of a President shocked in 1915 by a newspaper article asserting that the General Staff was preparing a plan "in case of war with Germany." An interesting angle to this Fort Leavenworth study was the fact that in its early days the school, hard put for maps, had been forced to place its problems on German-made maps of the Franco-German border of 1870-71. So in 1917-18 our leaders in the AEF found themselves working out the real problems of a real war over terrain already familiar to many of them!

The Regular learned in this conflict the dependency in war of the armed forces upon the civil economy, of which, as Douglas MacArthur once said, they are "but the keen, cutting edge." So industrial preparedness went into the books and into the schools, and the Regular, particularly in the technical branches, moved out into the world of production.

Because this had been a people's war, the home-folk had rallied generously to help their men in uniform. For the first time since the Civil War and its Sanitary Commission, the nation united to bring comfort and entertainment to soldiers in camp here and overseas. The American Red Cross led; its representatives were scattered everywhere. Close behind came the Y.M.C.A., the Salvation Army and the Knights of Columbus. Tobacco manufacturers donated cigarettes by the ton. The entertainment world volunteered, with prominent stars leading, to bring their talents before cheering crowds of men.

The very abundance of the effort by the various relief and welfare agencies cluttered the supply lines; their offerings competed with the essentials of war for space on transports going overseas. Abroad, the soldier gave his whole-hearted preference to the Salvation Army lads and lassies whose doughnuts and coffee were served amid the very mud and debris in which he fought.

Early in this war we had learned from the French the utility of decorations: those little tangible evidences of a national pat on the back. So the old American aversion to military decorations was over-ridden. The Distinguished Service Cross, for valor, and Distinguished Service Medal, for exceptionally meritorious service, came into being. Up to that time, except for the rare Medal of Honor, all an American soldier could expect for outstanding bravery had been a parchment Certificate of Merit. A third award for bravery was the Silver Star, attached to the Victory Medal ribbon (in 1932, the Silver Star became a separate medal).

This Victory Medal is notable, too, as a departure from the by-now-accepted simple service medals issued since 1907 after each of our wars. Everyone in the armed forces received the Victory Medal, but its added battle-clasps (bronze stars on the ribbon) denoted actual battle participation in various campaigns. To the soldier it was evidence that he "had been there," and he liked it.

More remarkable was the Congressional legislation permitting, for the first time in our history, the automatic acceptance and wearing of decorations bestowed by the various allied governments with whom we had been associated. The wheel had indeed turned.

Out of this war came, too, something new to the Army: *Stars and Stripes*, its very own whimsical weekly, published in the AEF by General Pershing's directive. The Paris edition of *The New York Herald*, which had wide circulation among the troops, furnished daily news. But Pershing felt that the soldier needed something more, a sort of home-town newspaper devoted to his own doings which would, thereby, raise his morale.

They were not long on discipline, the youngsters who staffed the sheet. But they were newspapermen, writers and would-be writers, and they got out a paper. And when they got out of uniform, which they did in a hurry when the war ended, many of them went places. There was Alexander Woollcott, for instance, and Harold W. Ross, whose whimsy, developed on the *Stars and Stripes,* led him to establish in 1925 the one and only *New Yorker.*

The Armistice concluded, the nation at once began to take its

Army apart, as it has always done. The National Guard and the drafted men went home in a stupendous flood. The Regular and his family looked forward to returning to the familiar life of the garrison. Some fortunates saw service in occupied Germany (that lasted until the troops came home in early 1923), or in the Philippines, Hawaii and Panama. But in the continental United States, while some reoccupied good quarters on permanent posts, many found themselves living in makeshift huts in squalid cantonments.

One officer, for instance, from 1919 to 1921 occupied, at Camp Lewis, Washington, a former dental clinic. The first floor consisted of two rooms at opposite ends of a large central area—probably a waiting room—which served as an admirable race track for the boy of the family to exercise his toy auto. There was no kitchen equipment; all cooking was done on two small portable electric grills on which the lady of the house performed culinary miracles. Upstairs was what had been the dental operating room, with battery of wash basins still installed. The propensity of this formidable apparatus to freeze in winter and, upon thawing, to flood the living quarters, furnished interesting seasonal thrills. Incidentally, the reason for staking out this claim was the fact that this was one of the few buildings in the brigade area having indoor plumbing!

Picking up the pieces from 1918 to 1920 was a nightmare, as was the two-year period following. The great mass of former emergency officers now commissioned in the Regulars had to be assimilated, with all the vexing problems of indoctrination of both them and their wives. Some of these people did not fit; the majority did and were welcomed into the corps to be welded into another generation of Regulars.

The famous "promotion hump" with its actuarial tables proving to the youngster bent on a military career that if all went well he might retire as a major, affected morale to some degree. (That some of these same puzzled youngsters are today sporting two or more stars is due not to the Congress, but to Tojo, Hitler, Mussolini and Stalin, with an assist from Neville Chamberlain.)

Came the fine National Defense Act of 1920, with a much-needed pay increase of twenty per cent all along the board, and with its dream of a National Army organization complete with regular and civilian components. But hot on its heels came, too, the reduction of 1922, with all promotions stopped, more than six hundred line officers thrown out and with them a hundred thousand enlisted men.

We could stand the loss of the enlisted men. For in 1920 the increase had been recruited by a drum-pounding ballyhoo promising an education and a trade for a one-year hitch. Want to play the flute? Learn wood-carving? Be anything, except a fighting man? The answer was prompt, as a puzzled Regular corps soon found out.

They came, these one-year men, from all over the country—a number of them one jump ahead of the sheriff. They went to school while the older Regular soldier did the chores. And the depredations of the riff-raff among them shocked nearby civilian communities.

An incident arising from this mess is worthy of mention. At Camp Lewis was the 31st Artillery Brigade—three veteran regiments containing a hard core of old-time grizzled Regulars. Here arrived the 4th Infantry Division, its ranks swelled by a horde of the one-year recruits who rocked nearby Tacoma by their lawbreaking—including robbery, murder and rape. An ill-advised editorial in a local newspaper comparing the exemplary conduct of the artillery brigade to the depredations of the division resulted in the mugging of a brigade soldier by a gang of division men.

That evening, after supper, the enlisted men of the 31st Brigade, led by their non-commissioned officers, came swinging down toward the 4th Division cantonment in a cadenced silent column of fours. They were clad in dungarees, they were armed with clubs and stones— and they meant business.

A quick-witted brigade staff officer dining at the club, saw the column and realized what was happening. Dashing out to the head of the troops he halted them, faced them about and marched them back to their own barracks. One man, a leader invoking discipline and training, had averted what might well have been a tragic outbreak.

Yes, we could well spare the scum who had so aroused the wrath of self-respecting Regular soldiers. But we couldn't spare the officers who were spread thin. The Army's obligations to the civilian components—a growing National Guard now definitely become a Federal element, an ORC seventy thousand strong, an ROTC of two hundred and twenty-three units, and the increased attendance at service schools —bled troop units white of leaders. The necessary shuffling of individuals rotated for such detached service knocked out a major prop—

that intimate mutual acquaintance of officer and man so essential for teamwork. What was left of the Army was still further burdened by summer camps—and particularly by that new element, the Citizens' Military Training Camps, which for more than a decade was to attract annually thousands of fine youngsters. Good things, all these, in themselves; they would pay off in the future. But the Regular scratched his head as he tried to make a twenty-four hour day contain a forty-eight hour schedule.

Such was the Army world of 1922; the "old" Army was gone, said the pessimists. So it was; gone with the America of the "Gay Nineties" and "Life with Father." The age of Andrew J. Volstead's Noble Experiment was upon us, complete with hip flasks and rowdiness. The Newport Set surrendered to Cafe Society, the rest of the nation to flappers, Rudolph Valentino and cheesecake art. The gangster became a force of national evil. A cynical younger generation was tired of war and the mistakes of its elders. A few years later undergraduates were to form "The Veterans of Future Wars" as a collegiate prank, if not social protest, that was based on common misinformation.

An America transformed by the machine age was money-crazy. The click of the stock ticker kept pace with the rumble of earth movers widening our network of concrete roads. Air expansion, wanderlust, and religious scepticism, marched side by side with the flouting of the Prohibition laws. It was not for nothing that a wag at the Field Artillery School in 1924 nicknamed the post "Fort Still."

In 1924 the Congress, acting upon the Army's recommendation, took a step which would pay immense dividends in the national future. It established the Army Industrial College—an institution unprecedented in any of the world's existing military establishments.

The function of the College was to plan the nation's economic mobilization. It was an agency under the civilian Assistant Secretary of War, who organized a small staff corresponding, on the industrial side, to the General Staff. The immense value of such study to all the services at once becoming apparent, naval personnel were shortly added to both the faculty and student body of the new school. The next step was the coordination of economic mobilizational planning of the two services, through the Army-Navy Munitions Board.

The professional soldier thus found himself being groomed to assess and to harness the national potential in emergency. His horizons were further widened through the increasing participation of political and social scientists from various colleges and universities, and their welcome analyses of the patterns of civil-military affairs.

It was only a beginning, of course, of the complex national machinery which twenty years later would gear the nation to the awesome scope of effort which would bring victory. But it was a beginning, and through the lean years our professionals struggled with it.

One lingers on this development for two reasons. In the first place it was a demonstration of the wiser side of the Congressional prerogative to "raise and maintain armies," and in the second it would enable the maintenance of civilian control of the armed forces of the United States when the world was later plunged into total war. It was the American way. And it worked.

But the Congress in 1926 did find time to add two more decorations to the Army's list. The Soldier's Medal was authorized for award to members of the armed forces who, while serving in any capacity with the Army, should distinguish themselves by heroism not involving actual conflict with an enemy, and not in aerial flight. At the same time the Distinguished Flying Cross was authorized as reward for heroism or extraordinary achievement while participating in an aerial flight. Since its provisions dated back to April 6, 1917, the date of our declaration of war against Germany, it was a much-needed and appreciated compliment to the now fast-growing Army Air Force.

It was during this period that a long-smoldering schism in Army circles flared with the court-martial and conviction of General William (Billy) Mitchell. When the Army had first taken to the air, in 1908, the new power had been in the hands of a few devoted souls in the Signal Corps. Not until 1914 was there established a nucleus for air power—the Aviation Section of the Signal Corps, to become, when aerial combat became a fact in World War I, the Air Service, and later, the Air Corps.

After the war was over the devotees of the air arm quite naturally waxed vociferous in urging its development as a major element of our military forces. Loudest of all was General Mitchell. What developed was the clash of a militantly proselytizing group with the reactionary elements of the old faith. But when the crusading Mitchell overstepped the bounds of propriety by publicly accusing our high military and naval command of "incompetency, criminal negligence, and almost treasonable administration of national defense" he was tried, not for advocating air power, but for his violation of the 95th Article of War: conduct prejudicial to good order and military discipline. Regretfully, during the winter of 1925-1926, a court composed of high-ranking officers who were to a man close personal friends or acquaintances of Mitchell had to find him guilty.

As the late General H. H. Arnold later remarked: ". . . the thing for which Mitchell was really being tried he was guilty of, and except for Billy, everybody knew it, and knew what it meant."

But public opinion made Mitchell a martyr to the new cause. The ill feeling thus engendered continued through the years, ameliorated to some extent as both airmen and ground soldiers began to realize both the growing powers and the limitations of the new arm.

By 1935, the service schools had evolved a doctrine of air-ground operations, which as time went on was elaborated. The magnificent performance of the Army Air Forces during World War II needs no further accolade. Many ground soldiers continued to feel that the airmen carried always a chip on their shoulder. The intense argument in the AEF air components that air units should "cooperate" tactically with ground troops, rather than "support" them, was an indication of this feeling. It was indeed best for all concerned that the Army Air Forces with its tremendous and ever-growing responsibility in the strategic field, should attain complete independence as a member of the trinity of military power.

By that time the ground forces had developed their own observation and command aviation—the little liaison planes first initiated in World War II by the field artillery and then adopted throughout the combat forces. The Navy had long since gone its own way successfully in the air. Korea saw the flowering of the helicopter as an adjunct to ground operations. And the end is not yet in sight.

But we have gone far ahead of our story.

Dress blues were back by 1927—voluntarily. They did not become obligatory until 1937. Those prewar officers who had all these years kept their expensive uniforms carefully tucked away were in for a costly disappointment: the cut and specifications had been changed. Everyone was in the same boat, new officers and old, and military tailors chuckled fiendishly as they prepared for a killing. Slacks, too, had been decreed; an innovation at first deplored, then welcomed. The

Sam Browne belt, one of Pershing's few mistakes in the AEF, and one of General March's abhorrences, became regulation for all. And a fetish was growing up for harmony in leather—not a bad thing in itself as far as looks went. Unfortunately, different commanders held differing views upon the hue; as a result, a change of station might mean a costly re-investment in belt, boots and shoes, if one's leather did not match that fashionable on the new post.

Among enlisted men (and officers) there was first the debate over whether the roll-collar blouse was militarily superior to the traditional choke collar. Choke-collar wool blouses—remnants of World War I overstocks—were still being issued as late as 1927, complete with black-painted buttons and collar insignia. An enlisted man paid ten dollars to the post tailor to convert the blouse to the required roll-collar for off-post wear. As for converting the buttons and insignia to standard brass, that was solved by several nights' application of paint remover and elbow grease. To go with the snappy roll-collar blouse, he must wear a white, collar-attached shirt—not an article of issue, either. You couldn't leave the post in a combination of roll-collar and khaki shirt.

There was that "peg" in the breeches. From no peg at all, in some years and some places, the peg became almost a skirt flapping at every step. But always there was the detestation of "wrap leggings"— spiral puttees. Even those soldiers who had the secret knack of being able to encase their ankles and calves in taut and neat yards of woolen o.d. had little use for them. And old soldiers whose legs were blue with varicose veins invariably blamed them on the wrap leggings. Men who abhorred horseflesh and the odors of the stable were jealous of the mounted soldier's canvas leggings with facing leather on the inner sides. Wrap leggings were to stay for many years and through several changes in uniform cloth. In the early 1930s, the Quartermaster Corps came out with a new cotton uniform for summer wear in a shade still known as "sun tan." It was a neat uniform, and handsome. But in Panama, by command decision, the sun tans were dyed a sickly green and soldiers returning from the Canal Zone to Stateside outfits to finish out the last year of their three-year enlistments, found themselves buying new uniforms out of clothing allowance savings that represented cash in hand at the end of the enlistment for the soldier who thriftily had cared for his clothing.

And the fatigue uniform! Was a more demeaning, respect-destroy-ing, unsoldierly garment ever devised? Its cloth was cheap, its tailoring abominable. The hat was beyond belief. The first time a soldier wore fatigues he felt more like a candidate for the chain gang than an honest American soldier-workman. Only the fact that all of one's fellows also wore it, saved the situation.

The Army had other things to think about, professionally. The officer was reading more, studying more. The urge to go to Benning (Infantry School), to Sill (Field Artillery School), to Leavenworth (Command and General Staff School), and to the War College was rampant—and that was good. Not all the men best fitted did go to the last two, unfortunately; favoritism expressed in efficiency reports some-times broke hearts. But the important thing was that the Regular officer was becoming a professional theoretician of the art of war.

The Army's roof blew off, like most American roofs, in the chill tornado of the Great Depression following 1929. Aside from personal losses for those individuals with outside income, and those who had been dabbling in stock gambling, an administration reaching for straws forced upon the Army a payless furlough annually, which meant a net pay loss of eight and one-third per cent. The dawning New Deal in 1933 went farther; a straight fifteen-per-cent cut in federal salary and the freeze of all longevity pay increases, left bitter tastes. But small though Army pay was, many an unemployed civilian father or brother received financial help from his soldier relative.

Not since the days of 1784, and the dissolution of the Continental Army, had Congress placed its Regulars in such jeopardy. Pacifistic reformers urged abridgements and cuts; advocates of chimerical doc-trines of war sniped—the loudest being Rep. Ross Collins of Missis-sippi. Douglas MacArthur, then Chief of Staff, boldly and eloquently faced the Congress with the fact that after having produced the brave blue-print of 1920, the reductions in appropriations had brought the Army "below the point of safety."

Meanwhile, in the midst of all the hubbub, MacArthur was en-gaged in continuous efforts at modernization within the Army itself. The clank of tank-treads was slowly replacing the rataplan of hooves. Most important of all, in 1932 the framework of a national mass army had been set up. Nine corps areas comprised the territorial compart-ments, in an over-all concept of four field armies. Regular, National

Guard and Organized Reserve had alloted part in each. The skeleton was complete in command and staff. For the first time the United States Army had a mobilization plan for national emergency.

And on the blouses of those still comparatively few officers who had completed at least two years of duty on the War Department General Staff began to appear a new decoration—a green and gold badge, worn on the right breast pocket. To this day few people outside the Army recognize this General Staff badge, known to the initiate as the "liver pad."

It was at this time that another new problem came into Army life: the Civilian Conservation Corps. The Regular officer assigned to this duty had an interesting problem while smarting over his own pay cut, to explain to the Regular private soldier also detailed just why that private's pay had been cut to seventeen dollars and eighty-five cents a month while the pampered pet of the CCC for whom he was caring got thirty dollars plus complete immunity from military discipline!

But this hurriedly conceived CCC hurled into the Army's lap—there was no other element of the government capable of the task—had, as it turned out, beneficial effect upon practically all officers involved. It was a job to be done, and a tremendous challenge to personal leadership to be met. These CCC men were not the malleable youth of the CMTC. They were youth in the raw, with more than a dash of Dead End Kids and of irresponsible veterans added; both tough. In handling this conglomeration successfully, the Regular and the Reserve officer learned a lot that would stand them in good stead in 1940 and 1941 when our great draft armies stirred in unrest.

The CCC was not the only emergency chore entrusted to the Army. In February, 1934, the task of carrying the U.S. mail fell into the lap of the little Army Air Corps, all civilian domestic air-mail contracts having been suddenly cancelled. For three months, mostly under gruelling winter conditions and in open-cockpit combat planes entirely unsuited to such work, more than seven hundred and seventy-seven thousand pounds of mail were carried safely over a distance of one and one-half million miles.

By the mid-thirties the Regular officer's mind was, to put it mildly, confused. He was closer to the civilian than he ever had been in past years; and the civilian should know more about him, too. But, with some few outstanding exceptions, there was no more meeting of minds than there ever had been. Something had happened to the American civilian and his viewpoint. Overseas the handwriting was already plain on the wall, but indecipherable to our public.

Over here the Pied Pipers of Fascism, Nazism, Communism and Pacifism were tootling their cacaphony into the ears of a generation embittered by the Depression and cynical of the motives behind our War to End Wars of 1917-18. The "Bonus March" of 1932—disgruntled jobless veterans stirred by Communist infiltration—shocked the nation. The Ku Klux Klan and shirts of black, brown and silver strutted. The Oxford Oath, the accusations hurled at "international bankers" and Merchants of Death, and not infrequently the direct objurgation of "butcher" and "warmaker" applied to the military, met all arguments for preparedness. Patriotism was a laugh; "What's in it for me?" a slogan.

It is doubtful if the officer corps as a whole realized what was happening, although a few devoted souls in Military Intelligence here and abroad kept fingers on the feverishly throbbing world pulse, and followed—by watching—the hate campaigns of sedition in the United States. Modern Cassandras, they laid their findings before the higher-ups, to no avail. But what all Regulars did know was that things were in bad shape and that there was no money forthcoming to mend our military fences.

Another thing that all Regulars knew by this time was their profession. Sill, Benning, Leavenworth and the War Colleges had well accomplished their job, as had the other service schools. So when the dam burst, there was ready a corps of professional officers, talking a common language, thinking along common lines. It was a corps ready and able to divide and subdivide itself again and again to provide commanders and staffs for combat army groups, armies, corps and divisions; to train a huge new crop of emergency officers; and to gear the national resources to the national common effort the world over.

*　　*　　*　　*　　*

• • • •

14

WAR FOR SURVIVAL . . .

The storm clouds rolling up broke September 1, 1939, when the Nazi invasion of Poland began to put out the lights in Europe. The American people, confused, then apprehensive, watched a tragedy of terror unfold, its trade-mark a new word—*blitzkrieg*.

Curiously, enough, though but little noted at the time, this pattern of fire and movement, of lightning strokes and nerve-shattering swoops from air and ground both—that overwhelmed Poland and later ripped westward through France and the Low Countries—was not new.

Here, expanded to heights of inhuman brutality undreamed of by their author, was essence of the century-old doctrines of Dennis Hart Mahan, "No great success can be hoped for in war," he had written, "in which rapid movements do not enter as an element . . . in the presence of an enemy who having lost his communications is entirely disorganized and demoralized . . . we have only to throw our forces into the midst of these broken-up fractions to determine them to fly. We may here attempt any blow; no movements can fail to turn out well except those which are too slow and methodical . . ."

Mahan's pupils had proved the truth of his theories on Civil War battlefields. Their campaigns, studied and restudied overseas, had given basic impulse to a *Wehrmacht* governed by a satanic despot. The results were being shown a shivering world, emphasized in propaganda of written word and documentary film.

France's fall, the evacuation of Dunkerque, the U-boat depredations off our coast, stirred the Congress on September 16, 1940, to enact the nation's first peace-time compulsory military service Act, that brought—for one year only—one million, two hundred thousand men into the Army.

This was something for the Regular to set his teeth into. It was a big bite for a permanent force of some fourteen thousand officers and two hundred and forty-three thousand enlisted men to digest at one gulp. But the framework, as we have seen, now existed, and General Lesley J. McNair, commanding GHQ, set about the task.

The wheel had made a complete turn. Instead of what Col. Ganoe characterized as "not even a high school squad to meet the professionals" in 1917, a competent professional officer corps was now leading an amateur Army. This corps was able to spark the latent intelligence of the draftee—who had a higher IQ rating than his 1917 forebear—and finally was able to penetrate the facade of indifference to, and ignorance of, world events which in 1940-41 characterized the heroes of "OHIO" ("Over the Hill in October") and "Yoo-hoo!"*

The problem of the conscientious objector, too, was squarely faced in the Conscription Act of 1940 by a simple proviso dividing such persons into two classes. In the first class were those who, unwilling as they might be to enter combat, had no objection to fulfilling their civic obligation by serving in non-combattant branches of the service. By Executive order such individuals were so placed, mainly in the Medical Department. There they did their duty faithfully, under the same conditions as other general service soldiers, and received the same pay and privileges. Some twenty-five thousand draftees came into the Army under this classification.

On the other hand, a draftee who refused any military participation at all, read the law, "shall . . . in lieu of such induction, be assigned to work of national importance under civilian direction." This, of course, took them out of the Army and out of our field of interest here. However, the soldier was glad to note that these men—there were some twelve thousand of them—who engaged in labor of various kinds throughout the United States, in sixty-seven camps, received no pay, family allowances or other remuneration than a pittance for their incidental personal needs. The American Legion spearheaded public opinion to action in this matter.

It must be noted, too, that some of these "conchies," as the Army called them in derision and contempt, did serve their country. The President's Advisory Commission on Universal Training, in 1947 had this to say:

---

* In 1940 a battalion of drafted men cat-called "yoo hoo" at two young women on a golf course as they were passing in trucks. General Ben Lear, the Army commander, happened to be on the golf course. He ordered the battalion to make a forced march as punishment. The incident made front-page news at the time.

"Perhaps one of the outstanding contributions of the conscientious objectors [of this type] was their participation in research, or so-called "guinea pig" projects, in which they served as volunteers in experiments to develop certain correct rations and clothing and to check the efficacy of certain drugs. These programs were under the Office of Scientific Research and Development and under the Surgeons General of the Army and the Navy. Forty-one units were operated for this purpose."

Of different caliber were the thirteen thousand draft-dodgers who went to prison, and the additional three thousand who were fined or placed on probation, as result of actual violations of the Selective Service Act. According to the Advisory Commission's report, some four thousand, five hundred of these belonged to the sect of Jehovah's Witnesses, who had all claimed deferment as full-time ministers of the Gospel, and about fifteen hundred others claimed some type of conscientious objection.

As in 1917, the mobilization brought complete upheaval to the Regular's social life—as it did to the citizen soldier, too. Once again we had the spectacle of Army wives and families—there were more enlisted families this time than in 1917-18—traipsing about the country to huddle in makeshift housing as their soldiers shifted from camp to camp. Once more gouging landlords and shopkeepers had their innings, at the expense of Army folk—Regular, National Guard, Reserve and draftee. This time the gypsying was of longer duration.

Meanwhile the United States stirred in a fog induced by political and ideological propagandists. Even substantial citizens were affected. As example, Charles A. Lindbergh, returning from a Goering-conducted inspection of Nazi technological might, announced that democratic inefficiency could not compete with it. The late Senator Robert A. Taft declared we should wait until the German threat reached our shores before we took "the steps that may be necessary to meet the particular kind of German 'blitzkrieg,' if there is such a blitzkrieg, at the time we find out what it is."

The stroke that ripped through France was at first unbelievable to Army people convinced that the French Army was the best in Europe. Then the pendulum turned. There were inklings of a certain fogginess of thought and a statistical pedantry spotting our high command, which overlooked the will of a people to win. When Britain stood alone and Churchill's lion-roar blared defiance world-wide over the radio, some General Staff people discounted it; they expressed the opinion that Britain would throw in the sponge at once. At a General Staff Conference shortly after Hitler invaded Russia in 1941, a colonel who had apparently never studied Napoleon's Russian adventure emphatically predicted the German army would be on the Volga River line in thirty days.

That the nation in general was in any way prepared by 1941 was due to the fact that President Franklin D. Roosevelt was convinced that war would come, that the United States must enter it on the side of the free world, and that when it came it must be fought as far as possible from our shores. So for more than two years he had taken all steps that Congressional appropriations and national sentiment would permit.

Some of these steps were devious, some obvious. They added up to the humming of factories, a stiffening of the Navy, the extension of our Atlantic frontier all the way to Greenland and Iceland, and to all aid "short of war". to Britain and Russia. In the Pacific, despite the growing intransigence of Japan, the Congress had not followed him. The ocean was wide, our Navy held it. So proposed fortification of Guam was turned down and little attempt made to strengthen our garrisons in the Philippines. There, since 1935, General MacArthur, retired and made a field marshal by the Filipino people, was engaged in developing the Commonwealth Army—a ten-year program.

In July 26, 1941, as Japanese-American relations worsened, Mac-Arthur was recalled to active service and placed in command of all troops in the Philippines—the American forces, some fifteen thousand strong, and the now nationalized but still only partly trained Philippine Commonwealth Army.

At home, our mass army was still a flabby affair in mid-summer, when the one-year service of National Guard and draftees was almost up. The majority of these enlisted men, reflecting the national uncertainty, had no definite objective. Most of them had no idea of why they had been dragged into uniform, and the leaven of discipline and tradition was still thin. The Congress deliberated on an extension of the draft. A bill extending the service for eighteen months went through the Senate but only after sharp debate and by a margin of one vote did it pass the House on August 12.

Four months later, on December 7—"that day of infamy"—the

Japanese surprise attack upon Pearl Harbor galvanized the United States into action. War against Japan was declared next day. By December 11 we were at war world-wide against the Axis, while the nation, agonized, watched its Army in the Philippines fighting a hopeless fight against Japanese invasion.

That invasion swept across the Lingayen beaches of Luzon to be met by American and Filipino Regulars, and by the part-trained Philippine National Army. The defense was forced back in a series of delaying actions until MacArthur's skill diverted it from the Japanese pincers into the Bataan peninsula. The Army's mission was to deny the enemy the use of Manila Bay and its installations as long as possible.

For MacArthur's men on Luzon there was neither help nor hope. Our Pacific Fleet lay shattered in Pearl Harbor; Japan now held the seas. These men knew it while they fought and starved. They put it, as only American soldiers can, into cynical soldier doggerel:—

> "We're the battered bastards of Bataan,
> "No pappy, no mammy, no Uncle Sam."

On Bataan they clung for more than three months of jungle-fighting until, starved and disease-ridden, the defense collapsed April 9, 1942.

Some thirty-five thousand soldiers—American and Filipino—herded by bayonet, boot, rifle-butt and club, went stumbling in captivity, in hunger, thirst and misery, for two hundred miles of tropical agony from Bataan to Camp O'Donnell in Central Luzon. Some nine hundred Americans perished on that Bataan Death March, butchered by their guards as they fell in final exhaustion.

General Wainright, with what was left, held the fortress of Corregidor until May 6, when the American flag came down. At home, angry tears gushed as the stuttering key of a lone radio signalman on the Rock, giving a blow-by-blow description of the final agony, went dead.

The survivors, after a march as penible as that of their Bataan comrades, but, thankfully, shorter, were locked up in Bilibid Prison in Manila. Behind them, on the beaches and in the city streets, were strewn the bodies of those sick and feeble who couldn't keep up and had been bayoneted or shot.

The Army in the Philippines was gone. But its soul remained.

From out of the debris a few stout-hearted men—American and Filipino—who refused surrender, had drifted into the hills to organize a
guerrilla movement which later, linked to MacArthur in Australia by
short-wave radio, hamstrung the enemy.

Thanks to the sacrifice of Bataan and Corregidor, time was given
to our nation to get its second wind for its greatest effort. The United
States, its Navy crippled, its Army struck a body-blow, rose in rage
from the depths of humiliation and chagrin to face a war world-wide
in scope and as yet unplumbed in lethal potentialities. It flung wide
its treasure chest of manpower, technology and scientific resources for
its armed services to dip into and to use.

The Regular, planning for war on what Frederick Lewis Allen
terms "a truly majestic scale," found that his plans could be activated.
The American economy, once the brakes were off, produced in
amazing quantity and quality the new engines of war of the machine
age, and thanks to our sea and air power, could supply and subsist its
soldiers the world over. In the doing, our Regular found his own
horizons broadening as he plunged into the world of industrial technology and science.

Gone in the shuffle was the tinsel; gone the buttoned-up, shiny
side. The Army, which in 1937 had ridiculed General Johnson
Hagood's recommendation that soldiers get into dungarees to do their
work in the field found itself in 1942 climbing into overalls and
baseball caps to do its job. Dennis Hart Mahan's precept that the
musket and spade went hand in hand in war was still valid; but this
time it was the bulldozer that went side by side with the self-propelled
gun and the two and one-half-ton truck.

Down through the hierarchy of command, this Army was professional. The teachings of the great array of service schools were im-
printed in the minds of the leaders. It was an Army preparing to carry
out a war of fire and movement, in the spirit of the offense long ago
emanating from Dennis Hart Mahan. On the battlefield the successors
of Grant, Lee, Jackson, Sherman, Sheridan and Pershing led our
citizen-soldiers in a *blitzkrieg,* blasting the inventors of the word.

General George Catlett Marshall, Chief of Staff, soon found that
the immensity of the global war necessitated not only a revamping of
the General Staff, but also a recasting of the Army's combat machine.
The broad resultant picture was a tripartite affair—the Ground Forces,
the Service Forces, and the Air Forces.

A balance-wheel was needed: a nerve-center through which the Chief of Staff's directives should flow, while at the same time it should transmit back to him, through observers, the successes and failures on the battlefield of existing procedures and training methods. So from the old War Plans Division of the General Staff grew a new, super-duper General Staff which Marshall called his "command post"—the Operations Division.

The three new empires of Ground, Service and Air alike absorbed manpower. They absorbed it in such great gobs that the Ground Forces, the essential fighting arm, suffered at the expense of its own technological branches and the service of supply. Bright plans for a one-hundred-division field strength, with appropriate corps and army troops, had to be cut down to eighty-nine divisions. Actually, in this great new Army, which before war's end had grown to more than eight million men, only thirty per cent were combat soldiers. Two million of these were in the Ground Forces, some three hundred and eighty thousand in the Air Forces.

The tempo of training rose. McNair's objective was simple—to ensure that no American went into combat either unprepared to fight or ignorant of use of his weapons. The keynote was teamwork. He put it briefly in his own words:

"The mission of the Army Ground Forces is to create units and train them so that they are fit to fight. . . . Our soldiers must have the fighting spirit. If you call this hating our enemies, then we must hate with every fibre of our being." And then he rang the bell:

"It's plain murder to send boys into battle under incompetent officers."

McNair was referring, of course, to combat officers. He had no control over the commissioning of civilians to military rank for the performance of specialist jobs. His hands were upheld by Henry L. Stimson, the indomitable Secretary of War. Stimson was firm in the conviction that the uniform's dignity should be reserved for the combat soldier. Even he, however, had to bow to the fact that some commanders, who needed high-class civilians as specialists, and needed them very badly and in a hurry, found, as Stimson sadly wrote, it was "much easier to get them by pandering to the itch to wear the Army uniform . . ."

McNair was never able to carry his training objective to full fruition, though he did his best. The stark necessities of time and the demands of a two-front war sucked the manpower overseas too fast. But in the over-all picture, no American citizen-soldiers had ever before gone into combat so well trained as our Army of World War II. "Made by McNair, USA," was a good product. The nation has real reason to thank him.

Amphibious war, airborne war, tropical war, all produced new problems. Our artillery tactics and techniques were proved to be sound, and were amplified and refined to amazing degree, all to the benefit of the infantry-artillery team.

But lack of time and the multiplicity of hand weapons hindered development of what to this period had been the basic element of the American soldier—individual marksmanship. That was unfortunate. With few exceptions, no longer was the individual infantryman a calm, cool marksman who called his shots and "squeezed off." Instead, he fired from the hip in an unaimed so-called "marching fire." This gave confidence of sorts to troops advancing in attack, but was wasteful of ammunition and scanty in lethal effect.

None of our combat strength could be used unless it was equipped, transported and supplied world-wide, when and where it was needed. That would be the job of Brehon B. Somervell, commanding the Army Service forces, linking the agricultural, industrial and technological resources of the United States to its Army.

It was a problem of astronomical proportions: depots and railway management from the Rocky Mountains to Iran, a highway through Alaska, a Pentagon, pipe-lines under the English Channel, clothing for arctic and tropical weather. It was measured in millions of tons and thousands of miles. The build-up for the Normandy invasion pumped seven hundred and fifty-three thousand tons of supply and matériel a month to Britain through 1943, rose to one million, nine hundred thousand tons by the time of jump-off.

Electronic equipment; tanks, guns and rockets; ammunition in billions of rounds; bridging material for the Rhine, the Danube and the Irrawaddy; harbor improvements and rebuilding from the Persian Gulf to the English Channel and the Mediterranean; all these would be included.

Not only were our own Army air and ground needs to be ministered. To Britain and her Commonwealth forces went vast store of munitions and equipment as well as aircraft to equip four air forces.

To Soviet Russia went four thousand tanks, twenty-eight thousand jeeps, two hundred and eighteen thousand trucks and two hundred and fifty pieces of heavy artillery besides clothing, locomotives, rails and rolling stock. France received equipment for twelve divisions of fighting men. Before 1945 was over, China had received five million dollars worth of war matériel.

Production, allocation, distribution and transportation of all this was the Service of Supply's chore. It built the Army's camps, roads and hospitals; it operated the largest radio network in the world. For every American soldier sent overseas went from five to ten tons of equipment, followed by another ton in food, clothing and ammunition for each month every month.

Henry H. Arnold was archpriest of air power. It was his concept which brought his Army Air Forces to become the mightiest striking arm of aerial warfare ever seen, founded on his simple simile of "a three-legged stool—pilots, planes and airfields." His slogan was "Keep 'em Flying"; the long-range Strategic Air Force was his ultimate in arms. The Army Air Force wrote its signature in fire from Ploesti to Tokyo and from the Mediterranean to the Baltic. And that, as the doughboy of 1917 used to sing, was "about all one feller can do."

This organization, too, was more than a combat arm, for it had its own Air Transport Command, its Troop Carrier Command to lift the airborne ground soldier, and its own construction and maintenance forces to build flying fields—from elaborate bases to fighter strips— that came into being almost before the assault troops had cleared the ground.

But before all these immensities had come to full operation the Army's come-back had already started on the battlefield.

It was accompanied by developments aimed to assist the American people and the Army to understand both one another and themselves. Army public relations activities grew into an immense organization. Laboriously picking their way through this somewhat sticky publicity-minded cocoon first woven in the early 1920s, a few bold souls who thought this was the people's Army and the people should know all about it, managed to build a machine to guide and assist war correspondents who, as someone said, "put the war into the nation's lap."

In the Public Relations Division of the War Department was born, too, a so-called Orientation Course. This was nothing more nor less than an attempt to carry out von Steuben's discovery of Revolutionary War days—that the American soldier had to be told why before you could expect him to fight.

Long before our great offensives started, camp newspapers—most of them rolling off mimeograph machines—had started to flourish for soldier consumption throughout the country. They were more or less trammeled by military overlordship, but from them grew something bigger and more audacious as we went overseas—the fantastic, happy-go-lucky *Stars and Stripes*.

This soldiers' daily, staffed and edited by soldiers for soldiers, combined the pugnacity of a California gold-rush camp newspaper and the more titillating features of the *Police Gazette*. A tabloid designed to end all tabloids, the *Stars and Stripes* probably ruined more general officers' breakfasts overseas than did all the enemy efforts put together.

Except for its mast-head the World War II *Stars and Stripes*, which by the end of the war was publishing independently-edited editions in five major theaters, bore little relation to its more sedate predecessor of Pershing's AEF, which had been a weekly. In 1917-1918 our troops in France needed no daily of their own; they had the Paris edition of the old *New York Herald*.

But this time it was different. Except in Britain, there was no press. So the *Stars and Stripes* rushed into the vacuum, in an attempt to establish a free press where none existed. To top it off, this was within the military establishment. It attracted newspapermen in uniform as a magnet attracts steel filings. Its self-appointed editorial policy—and what newspaper worthy of its salt doesn't have one?—was to defend G. I. Joe (that horrible nickname was a World War II product also) against the brass, while at the same time printing all the news that could be pushed within the confines of paper and type. It was as American as Main Street, and, at times, more libelous than the loosest "keyhole commentator."

But General Dwight D. Eisenhower approved of it; at least he did in principle, or it couldn't have published more than one issue. It did a lot of good. It also did some harm, for its "B-Bag" agony column would run the zaniest complaint that any guard-house lawyer could concoct. And—one likes to think unwittingly—its clamor added to the vast soldier unrest overseas in the demobilization days of 1945-1946.

Another Army publication was *Yank,* an illustrated weekly, featuring Army wartime activities in a lively way. *Yank,* it seemed, had wider circulation among the home-folk of soldiers than in the Army itself. But both these publications were legitimate, and their war correspondents rightly rated places in the Army's press box, beside *The New York Times,* the *New Yorker,* and all other representatives of the Fourth Estate.

It is interesting to note that staffers of World War II *Stars and Stripes,* like their predecessors in World War I, have risen high in their profession since they doffed uniform; with Bill Mauldin perhaps the best known.

Now let's go overseas.

*   *   *   *   *

● ● ● ●

15

ON LAND, SEA AND AIR

Manifestly it is impossible to compress into this book a blow-by-blow narrative of the war our Army fought around the periphery of the globe. One can only give an impression of the leadership and the devotion which characterized its operations world-wide.

Our first impression is the catholicity of the combat—the amalgamation of ground, air and naval power which was applied. From the time we entered the war the leadership on all fronts became predominantly American; MacArthur (and Navy's Admiral Chester W. Nimitz) in the Pacific, General Joseph W. Stilwell (later General Albert C. Wedemeyer) in China-Burma, Eisenhower in Africa and Europe.

Sometimes Army commanded Navy; sometimes Navy commanded Army. For a great proportion of his campaigns MacArthur controlled Admiral William F. Halsey's fleet which itself included Army components. Nimitz's Pacific Ocean operations included command of great masses of Army troops (at Okinawa the entire Tenth Army was under his over-all direction). And the Navy took the Army overseas on all fronts.

American commanders led troops of our Allies. But part of our Army at times was under Allied commanders of other nationality—Britain's Montgomery at the opening of the Normandy invasion, on one side of the Bulge and in crossing the Rhine; her Wilson and Alexander in Italy; her Mountbatten, Slim and Festing in India and Burma.

It was a crazy-quilt of war, woven into a pattern for victory. Not the least part of the pattern was that of air power, in which our own Army Air Force (in fact, if not in legality, an entity) so greatly shared.

So, in examining the highlights of our Army's part in World War II, it must be remembered that we are glancing at but one panel of a tryptich of ground, sea and air power. There was glory enough, and hard knocks, too, for all. But we are looking here at our Army only.

The come-back started across the Pacific, which in one way may seem odd, for the high command—personified in Roosevelt and Churchill—had decided that the primary objective was destruction of the German enemy, with all else subordinated to that. But the Japanese tide, seemingly all-powerful, had lapped over the southwest Pacific area, and was already lapping at Australia's door in New Guinea.

MacArthur, quitting his beleaguered troops on Luzon only after peremptory Presidential command, took up the Pacific leadership in Australia—a forlorn hope at the moment—March 17, 1942, with the terse statement:

"I came through and I shall return."

It was only May 20 when another American soldier spoke up. At Imphal, in India, where he had led to safety the handful of men salvaged from the Japanese flood in Burma, Stilwell—"Vinegar Joe" to his Army colleagues—commented flatly:

"I claim we got a hell of a beating. We got run out of Burma and it is humiliating as hell. I think we ought to find out what caused it, go back and retake it."

Both men kept their word.

MacArthur's campaigns, which carried him back to Manila, constitute one of the most amazing sagas in the entire history of warfare. Beginning on a shoe-string, (with one American and one Australian division) in September, 1942, he took the offensive over the Owen Stanley mountains of New Guinea to close on the slimy jungle fringes of Buna-Gona. The daring thrust developed into a two-pronged fighting stroke as his forces grew.

It was a "hit-'em where they ain't" progression, in which surprise and initiative, combined under a masterly direction, carried out Dennis Hart Mahan's concept of leadership—to do the greatest damage to the enemy with the least exposure to ourselves.

While Halsey's amphibious force knitted its way up through the Solomon Islands, General Walter Krueger's Sixth Army troops leapfrogged along the New Guinea coast. MacArthur's men learned such names as New Georgia, Vella Lavella and Bougainville; Triobrand, Salamaua and Finschhafen; Arawe, Cape Gloucester and the bitterly-contested cliffs and caves of Biak. General Robert L. Eichelberger, who took that last-named place, termed it "unimaginable purgatory."

And when in September, 1944, MacArthur's shifting, side-stepping series of knight's moves on war's chess-board brought him poised for another, greater step, in concert with Nimitz, he had left behind him literally thousands of Japanese troops festering in useless garrisons, dying buds on the withering tree of the Greater East Asia Co-Prosperity Plan.

Far away in Burma, the forgotten theater of the war, Stilwell had indeed come back, had revamped and trained his Chinese troops, was beginning an offensive. Army Air Force planes were flying "the Hump," and new names—Merrill's Marauders, and the Mars Force—were fighting in the jungles in concert with Chinese and British troops.

Across the Atlantic the Army's might had begun to pour while the star of Eisenhower rose above it. The North African landings of November, 1942, culminated in the long, Tunisian campaign—frustrating in the beginning when our team in its opening game came up against General Erwin Rommel's veterans.

At Kasserine Pass, American troops in over-extended and uncoordinated line had been overrun, but resiliency and leadership contributed to the comeback. By May 13, 1943, the offensive rolled over the *Afrika Korps* to reach Bizerte, end of the North African line.

From Africa to Sicily the offensive had jumped to bring General George S. Patton's Seventh Army into sharp focus as he sliced the length of the island and reached Messina.

Up to and across Salerno's bloody beaches Eisenhower's men had gone—amphibiously once more—to gain foothold in Italy coincident with the announcement of Italian surrender. But the Germans were still there, to contest every foot of the way north in the chill of an Italian winter.

General Mark W. Clark's Fifth Army beat its head for a time against the mountains around Cassino, and the epic of Anzio had come and gone—the VI Corps' amphibious landing planned to envelop the Germans barring the way down by the Rapido. That had turned out instead to be a last-ditch struggle on a beach-head, despite the 36th (Texas National Guard) Division's gallant sacrifice across the Rapido to divert enemy attention.

For two years meticulous preparation on colossal scale had been going on in Britain. Soldiers quipped that it threatened to sink the British Isles under the weight of American men and matériel. Grosvenor Square won the nickname of "Eisenhower Platz."

All this culminated June 6, 1944, (Rome had fallen to Clark the day before), when Operation Overlord, the world's greatest armada and the world's greatest invasion, had been unleashed. More than two million, eight hundred and seventy-six thousand men, one million, two hundred thousand of them Americans—the mightiest force ever commanded by one man as an integrated unit—started pouring into Normandy under command of an American soldier—Dwight D. Eisenhower.

Our Army knew the crimsoned shelf of Omaha Beach, the stubborn fighting of the Normandy hedgerows, Cherbourg and St. Lo. It had swept down through Brittany to the Loire and across to the Seine. Paris had been liberated.

The nation watched its Army roll over the Germans in the Battle of France and, joined by the veterans of Anzio coming up from the south of France, poke towards the Westwall. The attempt to crumple the stiffening German northern flank at Arnhem—where airborne Britons died in vain because their troops could not reach them beyond the gateway opened by our 82nd and 101st Airborne Divisions—was just a momentary blurring of the pattern of victory.

Four American armies were now in Eisenhower's line-up: the First (Courtney H. Hodges), Ninth (William H. Simpson) and Third (Patton) forming Omar Bradley's 12th Army Group, with Montgomery's Britons and Canadians to their north and Jacob L. Devers' 6th Army Group below them; Alexander M. Patch's Seventh and the First French Armies.

Out of the Pacific flashed the dramatic word of MacArthur's next astounding leap—from Indonesia to Leyte in the Philippines. His "I have returned!" rose above the battle smoke where Krueger's men were locked in conflict with the best of Japan's ground troops, and above the Navy's great sea victory off-shore.

In far-off Burma Stilwell's offensive was on, the Myitkyina campaign concluded. Japan's designs on Asia had received a body blow.

A whiff of smugness rose at home; it would all be over soon. This smugness even infiltrated to some extent the thinking of our staff in Western Europe as the AEF prepared for the offensive which would carry it across the raging Roer to the Rhine. In the front lines this opinion was not shared. It wasn't shared by the men of the "Big Red One," the 1st Infantry Division fighting its way through Aachen and battling in the Huertgen Forest; nor by the 28th, who wore Pennsylvania's Keystone on their shoulder patch and called it the Bucket of Blood after their mauling at Schmidt near the Roer dams.

But the smugness was there. It was reflected in a SHAEF intelligence report decrying any further German offensive power. Men who had just read it gasped as Hitler's Sunday punch rammed into the Ardennes December 16, 1944, shattered the VIII Corps' thin cordon and reached for the Meuse.

The facts were simple. While our strength was being massed for an assault which would sweep over the Cologne Plain to the Rhine, the enemy hit our most loosely protected sector. We had taken a calculated risk. We were in the situation of the veterinarian, once depicted by Churchill. The "vet" made careful preparation to blow a dose of medicine down an elephant's throat; but the elephant blew first.

The blow fell on the 106th Infantry Division—just-arrived and green—ripping it apart and bagging two of its regiments. It fell on the 28th Division to the south, shaking it into bits. There was panic and confusion. But amid it all, too, was the stubborn, raw gallantry of men in those fragments who would not admit defeat; and of other men of other units who held the shoulders of the break-through.

In the midst were Robert W. Hasbrouck's 7th Armored Division at St. Vith, and Anthony C. McAuliffe's 101st Airborne at Bastogne. The one snubbed the Nazi push; the other, German-ringed, with its commander's famous "Nuts!" of defiance, held until Patton's amazing shift of his Third Army came driving in to link with it.

Doomed from the first, the German threat was ended as 1945 came in. With it had gone our nation's smugness, too. There had been panic over here in those first few days, when the German radio was blaring victory while SHAEF kept silence. Leadership and the resiliency of the American soldier himself restored the situation. But the reverberations of the Bulge and the command decisions involved will last as long as soldiers can still argue.

The chill and hatred that still makes American soldiers snarl at mention of the Malmedy Massacre—the cold-blooded mass murder of one hundred and forty-six men of an American field artillery battalion ambushed by a Nazi force and shot down after they had surrendered—will last long. It is today directed more against the Nazi ideology than against the stupid brutes who carried it out.

With the receding German tide from the Bulge went the sorry procession of American prisoners captured there during the initial surprise. They went to join the other Americans captured long before at Kasserine Pass in Tunisia, and those shot from the skies during our aerial offensives over Europe. Prison camps are not nice places at best, and our soldiers had a hard time of it. There were numerous instances of unnecessary cruelty, and some of starvation.

However, piecing together all the POW evidence, one comes to the conclusion that most of the privations undergone by our men in German hands were due to the shortage of food in Germany. The German authorities did accept Red Cross packages shipped via Switzerland, and most of them were delivered.

And against instances of brutality, one can balance the adventure of three American air force officers who escaped from a marching prisoner column in the spring of 1945. For nearly a month the trio, wandering through Bavaria undisguised and unmolested, were fed and sheltered by German farmers. Captured once, their guards, elderly reservists, let them loose and finally "recaptured" them officially only when stormtrooper patrols approached. This time they were locked up in Moosburg prison camp, to be released a few days later when the American armies overswept the place.

America could look both east and west as final victory drew near in 1945. MacArthur swept onto Luzon in the last and most imposing of his great amphibious leaps, and Eisenhower plunged over onto the Cologne Plain. The fall of Manila was followed close by the miracle of Remagen: an outstanding example of American initiative and leadership which brought the First Army across the Rhine.

The rest in Europe was history in a hurry. Patton in the Palatinate, Patton darting over the Rhine to strike east; Montgomery over too, with our Ninth Army's armor reaching to Paderborn to meet the First Army curving north—between them three hundred thousand Germans were caught in the greatest double envelopment ever known. Our Armed Forces radio was crooning "Don't Fence Me In" as that occurred.

From the Baltic to the Brenner Pass, where the Seventh Army linked with the Fifth coming up through Italy, Eisenhower's legions were sweeping to meet the Russians on the Elbe. Nazi emissaries sped for Rheims and surrender May 7, 1945, while the radio played "Heading for the Last Round-Up."

It was v-e Day in Europe; the planners were already preparing for the homecoming rush, for the battle for "points," and for redeployment towards Asia. Over there Burma had been cleared and convoys were rolling over the Burma Road—rechristened Stilwell Road—into China. Stilwell himself had been relieved, but Wedemeyer had carried out "Vinegar Joe's" plan.

MacArthur in the Philippines, his mission accomplished, prepared for an invasion of Japan, while our Strategic Air Force rained incessant bombs on Tokyo. That invasion would never be needed. On August 6, a lone Army Air Force plane circled lazily over Hiroshima and the atomic age was ushered in.

On September 2, 1945, Japanese envoys bowed low in formal submission before Douglas MacArthur on the deck of U.S.S. *Missouri* in Tokyo Bay. For the world the war was ended. For the United States Army honor had been retrieved—behind MacArthur stood the gaunt figure of Jonathan Wainwright of Corregidor.

Wainright's presence evidenced the end of a four-year martyrdom. Our prisoners in Japanese hands had come back—those of them still alive. They had starved on pittances of wormy corn, rice, soy beans, and such roots as they could pick up and gnaw. They had been beaten and tortured. Some had died of malnutrition, disease and brutality. Others had died penned up in the holds of prison ships sunk by our own bombing planes while on the way to Formosa and Japan.

Through it all the Japanese had behaved in most incongruous manner. Nipponese soldiers, who had just beaten to death an American trying to escape, could later stand before his body, bowing and shedding real tears in admiration for his bravery. A Japanese officer, pointing to the emaciated form of sixty-two-year-old Colonel Paul Bunker who was dying on his feet of starvation and blood poison, could respectfully remark: "Very old, but looks very brave." There was, it appeared, a remarkable similarity between the Japanese and the North American Indian insofar as their treatment of prisoners was concerned.

All these sufferings are symbolized today in West Point's museum by a ragged piece of red and white-striped bunting—one of the Army's most treasured trophies. It is all that is left of the flag that flew over Corregidor, which had been burned by order after being hauled down lest it fall into enemy hands.

This same Colonel Bunker, encharged with the destruction of the colors, had first cut off a piece which he sewed under a patch of his cotton shirt. Before he died in his prison camp, he turned it over to Colonel Delbert Ausmus, fellow prisoner, with the prayer that it be carried to the Secretary of War.

Ausmus in turn sewed the relic under his shirt pocket. Surviving, true to his trust, he presented it on his return to the United States to Robert P. Patterson, Secretary of War.

It is just a piece of bunting, but it symbolizes the soul of the Army.

*   *   *   *   *

• • • •

16

LESSONS LEARNED AND UNLEARNED

From Bataan to the Elbe the Army in four years of war had fulfilled the nation's trust. Its great leaders, from MacArthur and Eisenhower down, had waged a war of fire and movement on three continents. Their exploits speak for them. They had once again proven correct the American concept which had been first fully tested in the Civil War.

This business of leadership, as we have seen, expresses itself in various ways. The principle is always the same: the impulsion of one man's initiative, be he squad leader or Supreme Commander, at the right time and in the right place. Let us linger now for a moment on two men as example. One of them was an army commander who has become a legend; the other just one of many lieutenant colonels.

George S. Patton was to World War II what Stonewall Jackson was to the Civil War. His fame, first rising when he revamped a disorganized army corps in Tunisia, grew brighter in Sicily. It dimmed for a moment, then. His explosion of emotional rage—the cuffing of a man he believed to be a skulker—brought quick revulsion. No one at the time gave thought to any comparison with Thomas J. Jackson who in icy rage time after time shot deserters out of hand.

The fortunes of war brought Patton back into the picture. Eisenhower insisted that the man he considered (according to Harry Butcher, Ike's aide) "the best ground-gainer in the United Nations' armies," be given an army command in France. Omar Bradley correctly employed his talents.

Unleashed in the breakout from Normandy, Patton overran France north of the Loire from the Bay of Biscay to the Seine. It was a twelve-day-long tornado whirling over an area two hundred miles wide and one hundred miles deep. Later, in the Battle of the Bulge, the speed and power of his attack, after making a ninety-degree shift in full stride, was a magnificent demonstration both of tactics and logistics, for one doesn't change the course of an army in battle by a simple "Squads left!"

In the Palatinate, Patton shattered the German armies remaining west of the Rhine. His armored columns chopped all resistance into mincemeat so fast the bewildered enemy didn't know what had happened until it was all over. In ten days he raked four thousand square miles of territory and captured sixty-three thousand dazed Germans.

His Rhine crossing—unexpected to everybody outside his own army—was an operation long planned and prepared for. And when the guns ceased fire his spearheads were at Pilsen in Czechoslovakia and down in the Danube Valley below Linz—four hundred miles east of the Rhine.

These things were not just the hell-for-leather raids of some hard-riding cavalryman. They resulted from a forty-year span of war study by a soldier who once remarked "It's not the date of a battle that counts—it's what happened there."

Patton was embodiment of Jackson in the Valley, at Second Bull Run, at Chancellorsville; of Sheridan at Five Forks and Sayler's Creek; of General James H. Wilson driving to Selma. He was indeed personification of Mahan's "celerity is the secret of success." Within his sphere as an army commander he must rank as one of the great captains of history.

The Moslem scribe who composed the citation to the Grand Cross of Ouissan Alaouite which the Sultan of Morocco awarded Patton after the invasion of North Africa in 1942 must have been a bit of a prophet. It read:

"The lions in their dens tremble on hearing his approach."

Our second man changed the entire course of the war in Western Europe. When Lieutenant Colonel Leonard Engeman (he was a product of ROTC) led his task force of the 9th Armored Division—a battalion each of tanks and armored infantry—over the hill-crest looking down to the Rhine at Remagen March 7, 1945, Bradley's armies had just started to lap over to the river bank.

The unfordable Rhine was Hitler's last barrier, its broken bridges —destroyed by fleeing Germans—mocking the invader. Eisenhower's plan was for Montgomery's 21st Army Group to make an amphibious crossing above the Ruhr and plunge into the heart of Germany.

Bradley's 12th Army Group to the south was slated for a supporting part only.

But further south Engeman saw the unbelievable—a bridge, still standing. Through its cantilever skeleton little dots moved; Germans were still using it.

Here was a royal road into Germany, provided one could seize it before it blew. Engeman, rushing a message back, sent his infantrymen scampering on, covered by the fire of his tanks. Resistance was slight, but time was flying. One demolition charge cratered the roadway, another smashed a truss. But the doughboys got across, clipping blasting-wires as they ran, and they held the eastern end of a structure still intact.

To division, to corps, to army, in turn Engeman's message had flashed; to army group and up to Ike himself, igniting a chain reaction that shifted the center of balance of the AEF as each successive commander raced reinforcements. Bradley was over the Rhine. The main effort, the coup de grace, became his mission.

And that's the story of the Hindenburg Bridge at Remagen. One singles it out not as sole example of initiative—there were thousands of others, in both Pacific and Atlantic areas—but because of its effect on the fortunes of war.

In retrospect, Winston Churchill best pictured the Army's effort in World War II. Speaking in 1946 before the Army's brass at the Pentagon he said, in part:

"I greatly admired the manner in which the American Army was formed. I think it was a prodigy of organization, of improvisation . . . the rate at which the small American Army of only a few hundred thousand men, not long before the war, created the mighty force of millions of soldiers, is a wonder of military history. . . . This is an achievement which the soldiers of every other country will always study with admiration and envy.

"But that is not the whole story, nor even the greatest part of the story. To create great armies is one thing; to lead them and to handle them is another. It remains to me a mystery as yet unexplained how the very small staffs which the United States kept during the years of peace were able not only to build up the Armies and the Air Force units, but also to find the leaders and vast staffs capable of handling enormous masses and of moving them faster and further than masses have ever been moved before . . . .

"That you should have been able to preserve the art not only of creating mighty armies almost at the stroke of a wand—but of leading and guiding those armies upon a scale incomparably greater than anything that was prepared for or even dreamed of—constitutes a gift made by the officer corps of the United States to their Nation in time of trouble, which I earnestly hope will never be forgotten here, and it certainly never will be forgotten in the Island from which I come . . . ."

The Regular could take this tribute to his heart, for it acknowledged the debt the nation owes to Washington and von Steuben, to Sylvanus Thayer and Dennis Hart Mahan, to Emory Upton who clarified our national military policy and to Elihu Root who understood. It was tribute to the devotion and professional training of the Regular whom we have watched evolve through one hundred and seventy-odd years of tradition.

Churchill's tribute could go also to the inventive genius of the citizen-soldier, which flowered unhampered under this system. In particular it could go to Sergeant Curtis G. Culin of the 102nd Cavalry Group, a New Jersey National Guardsman who showed the Army how to lick the hedgerow defenses of German-held Normandy.

These age-old bunkers of earth and tree-roots held up the advance of our troops. Tanks were useless, because although they could climb them they exposed their unarmored bellies to deadly close-range enemy fire in the act. The AEF's advance, it seemed, might be turned into a foot-by-foot struggle for every field and pasture.

General Omar Bradley appealed to every man in the First Army for suggestions. And Sergeant Culin, experimenting in the portable machine-shop of his outfit, found the answer. It was a steel horn, to be bolted on the bow of a tank, enabling it to plough and rip through the obstacles. Bradley, down on the run to witness a demonstration, found it good. So "rhino-horns," made out of the steel of the enemy's own beach-obstacles and mounted on every tank in First Army, did the job.

Self-sacrifice was another part of the gift of which Churchill spoke; such self-sacrifice as that epitomized in the heroic death of four Army chaplains in the icy waters off Greenland's Cape Farewell, February

3, 1943. The transport *Dorchester,* hit by a German U-boat torpedo, reeled suddenly to destruction. Men scrambled for life-belts as they spilled into the sea from her canting decks. "Discipline and seamanship were lacking in her merchant crew," remarked the Navy historian Rear Admiral Samuel E. Morison.

The four chaplains—a Roman Catholic priest, two Protestant ministers and a Jewish rabbi—stripped themselves of their own life-belts to help others more unfortunate. When last seen by survivors, they were standing, arm in arm, alongside her rail, their voices raised in prayer, when the stricken ship made her final plunge.

Let us mark them well, these men: First Lieutenants John P. Washington (Catholic), Alexander D. Goode (Hebrew), and Clark V. Poling and George L. Fox (Protestant).

"Greater love hath no man . . ."

Looking at the war scene from another point of view, it was well, indeed, that our officer corps had the Army tradition of leadership and self-sacrifice to support them during that period between 1941 and 1945, for the going had been tough. The run-of-the-mill Regular, in particular, had had some very unpleasant experiences.

He would learn that sometimes the lust for power can do strange things to individuals who should know better; leading them to climb over other men's necks to attain it. He would see expediency, quibbling and political juggling enter into the rat-race of burgeoning staff empires. He would see civilians commissioned over his head.

The older Regular, too, was slapped in the face by an arbitrary combat-age limit; unnecessary, in fact, because endurance could be measured accurately by physical examinations plus demonstrated efficiency. He would see the wastage of money and much-needed professional experience caused by such practice.

Worse, all officers unblessed by stars would learn, too, the hard way, the humiliation of such things as "Yankee Doodle Rooms" and other conveniences reserved "For General Officers Only." Up to this time the American officer, like his British colleague, had been accustomed to an age-old code which, while acknowledging the right of any commander to rule his own headquarters mess, defined other common social meeting places—such as clubs and general messes—as gatherings of gentlemen, where rank *per se* was momentarily laid aside.

If he traveled as a casual (as an individual, not with a troop formation), he was in for another humiliation. Generals, of course, moved in state, with their personal orderlies to handle their baggage. But the sight of a group of other officers, including colonels of thirty-years' service, bent low under the burden of their own bedding rolls and baggage, bobbing like a line of weary stevedores past crowds of staring much-amused enlisted men, was helpful neither to the self-esteem of the one nor the discipline of the other.*

Socially, it appeared, American officers in the AEF were, like all Gaul, divided into three parts: generals, who were the landed gentry; colonels, the poor relations; and lieutenant colonels and under, *hoi polloi*.

Of such spiritual saddle galls was the material first fashioned to impair morale.

On the enlisted men's side the stresses of war and the sudden heady blooming of temporary rank produced sufficient injustices and unnecessary hardships to rankle. The majority of these men impressed into the Army didn't understand it, therefore they didn't like either its restrictions or its discipline. Some of them found themselves to be better educated than the leaders assigned to them by the fortunes of war.

Magnificent, of course, was the record of the individual American soldier in this war—in the slimy morasses of Asiatic jungles, the crumbly *djebels* of North Africa, Italy's grim hill masses, the hedgerows of Normandy. From Okinawa to the Elbe, whatever his origin, he proved himself a warrior.

One of the most remarkable aspects of the conflict came out of this national melting-pot. We Americans were fighting imperial Japan. Yet some of us were of that same blood and breed. It was natural, perhaps, that others of us should look with suspicion upon them. Had we not already seen Americans turn Nazi? Were we not, with some reason, suspicious of other Americans who toyed with Marxism?

The Nisei—American-born citizens of Japanese parentage—ignoring these suspicions of their neighbors, clambered into uniform to prove their patriotism in a big way. The 442nd Infantry Regiment (and the 100th Battalion, which later became a part of the 442nd)

---

* Lest this last observation be misconstrued, be it noted that the author, while observing such things frequently, never was subjected to this himself.

bears five proud battle streamers on its colors, as well as a silver band. It carries five Distinguished Unit citations.

Immortalized as the "Go for Broke" boys—it's the regimental motto—these Nisei came from Hawaii and from the West Coast to fight their way through Italy with the Fifth Army, and in the Rhineland with the Seventh. Individual Nisei soldiers at the same time were engaging in intelligence and counter-intelligence work in the Pacific.

To generalize, this American soldier of 1941-1945 seemed to have a different mentality from his father of 1917. In some ways he was more pampered, with such things as USO shows and post exchanges in profusion. On the other hand, the combat man didn't always get entertainment—fault of the war and not of the willingness of our stage folk. And sometimes he didn't even get such simple things as cigarettes—as example the 1st Division in the Huertgen Forest was rationed to one cigarette a man daily for several weeks, at a time when every night spot in Paris was selling purloined American post exchange cigarettes by the packet. He didn't like such things, and he was sometimes vocative about it.

Such irritations were caused by the fortune of war and by human frailty. Certainly they were neither the fault of the American people nor of the Army's desire to carry out the national will. From the very beginning of the struggle—in fact prior to Pearl Harbor, when the mass armies first began to form—the nation took up the problem of the soldier's well-being in fashion and scope heretofore unknown. Before the war ended the effort was consolidated into today's Special Services Division of the War Department, assisted wholeheartedly by civilian agencies throughout the country.

Ubiquitous, the American National Red Cross made the soldier's life easier by its activities at home and abroad. Its home service link, between the soldier and his home, eased family worries. Its canteens, clubs, recreation centers, snack bars and rest homes furnished him recreation. Through the International Red Cross it furnished food and delicacies to our men made prisoner by our enemies. Our wounded and sick in hospital received its ministrations, not the least of which was its life-saving blood-donor program.

This relationship between the Army and the Red Cross is unique, through the very nature of its incorporation in 1905 by Congressional charter. Its mission, in part, is ". . . to serve, in accord with military and naval authorities, as a medium of communication between the people of the United States and their armed forces." The President of the United States appoints its principal officer. It is "the only volunteer society authorized by the Government to render aid to the Medical Department of the Army."

All other civilian welfare organizations rallied generously to the war effort. It was realized from the beginning that something even bigger and better than the admirable but sometimes chaotic effort of World War I was needed. So the war relief activities of the Salvation Army, Y.M.C.A., Knights of Columbus, National Jewish Welfare Board and other units similar in character were channeled and focussed at the Army end through a newly formed Morale Division of the Adjutant General's Office. Through this pipe-line pulsated all the Army's recreation activities, reinforced by the civilian aid. High among such efforts was the USO Camp Shows, in which stage and screen stars participated, moving to all parts of the world where our soldiers were, in a definitely connected and controlled military operation.

Libraries, service clubs, a motion picture service (which had started in 1920), recreation centers (these came at the end of the war), organized sports, were among the many non-combat activities devised by the War Department to make soldiering easier; to gloss the fact that in war there are but two kinds of fighting men—the quick and the dead.

But they did relieve the long monotony; they did compensate, by their very existence, for the gougings and short-changings of the harpies and ghouls who flap heavy wings on the fringes of war. Best of all they were evidence that the people of the United States believed in, and wanted to care for their fighting men.

The soldier took such things in stride, thankful perhaps in heart, but always ready and willing to gripe. Griping is always a soldier's privilege.

Unlike our soldiers of past wars, this American soldier of World War II was not a singing soldier. Several efforts of Tin Pan Alley to produce synthetic melodies fell flat. "Praise the Lord and Pass the Ammunition" cheered civilian spirits in the early days, and Irving

Berlin's "This is Your Army, Mr. Jones" was good. But the average soldier left both these to the people at home. And "Dirty Gerty from Bizerte" enjoyed but a very brief life in Africa; she was too obscene. Only one real soldier song did emerge: "Dog-face Soldier," the particular property of the 3rd Infantry Division, who took pride in chanting the lilting words beginning—

> "I wouldn't give a bean to be a fancy-pants Marine—
> "I'd rather be a dog-face soldier like I am."

This soldier read more than his predecessors, too. In particular he devoured *Stars and Stripes,* his own newspaper, and chortled—as did all officers with a sense of humor—over Bill Mauldin's immortal cartoons of Willy and Joe. And when the folks back home sent clippings of Ernie Pyle's reports, our soldier read them with more than passing interest, for here was a reporter who somehow managed to get into words all the simple, elemental comedy, drama and tragedy making up the life and death of American fighting men.

But once the fighting was done, his resentments, real or fancied, came to the surface, and all too frequently he began to cry havoc upon the men who had led him and his country to victory. A vocative minority it was, with, ironically enough, its principal resentment voiced against what it termed "regimentation," although it is hard to see how one can make a regiment without regimentation.

In the end when peace and the "I wanna go home" frenzy set in, these things popped out. The stage was set; "Momism" and the usual American urge to get back when the business was over combined to bring about a partial chaos of insubordination. We had had taste of this in the past. In Philippine insurrection days the soldiers were singing, "Return us to our own beloved homes." They thundered it in 1918. But the bedlam in 1945-46 was appalling. The nation literally wrecked its Army in the mass demobilization. Like an angry child in a tantrum it wrenched the spokes from its little red wagon and strewed them for the world—and a watchful Kremlin—to see. General Eisenhower's term for it was "near-hysteria," an understatement if ever there was one. The flames were fed by a skillful communist manipulation.

Probably the region least affected by all the uproar was the Pacific

Ocean Area, commanded by the late General Robert C. Richardson, whose prompt action and efficient leadership snuffed out the first smouldering flame of insubordination.

The Regular became, as always, the whipping boy; target for a barrage searching to break down completely the authority of the officer corps of which our Regular was the hard but tiny core. The tomtoms beat in rhythmic tune—an old tune, now played in frenzy. "West Pointer arrogance," "caste privilege," "double standard," were some of the more polite allegations. In a democracy, whispered the party line, officers and men should be equal in all things; above all, that horrid custom, the hand salute, must be abolished. The stooges lapped it up and roared.

In September, 1939, there had been in the Army some fifteen thousand officers, commissioned, warrant and flight. By July, 1945, the officer strength had reached a peak of 897,777. Two per cent of this grand total were Regulars—half of them graduates of West Point; approximately three per cent more came from the National Guard, and fifteen per cent were from the Officers' Reserve Corps. Thirteen per cent came directly from civil life—doctors, dentists, chaplains and other specialists. Of the remaining sixty-seven per cent, half of them came from ocs, and the rest from aviation cadets, battlefield commissions, and direct commissioning from the ranks and from warrant and flight officer grade.

To expect from this mass, flung into command over an army of 8,291,366—mainly draftees—an absolute adherence to standards of judgment and probity evolved during years of peacetime training was impossible. Even the two per cent leaven of Regulars was not immune to the stress of war. So there were inequalities, there were delusions of grandeur, there was some stupidity and some ineffective leadership. The War Department tried from the beginning to weed out the unfit. A total of six thousand, seven hundred officers passed before reclassification boards; 327 were demoted, 4,123 separated from the service, and 2,250 were reassigned. In addition, 1,887 others were reassigned without board proceedings. The total number of square pegs in round holes—8,587—was, one notes, approximately one per cent of the peak commissioned strength.

So serious became the hue and cry that the Secretary of War in March, 1946, appointed the now famous Doolittle Board to look into officer-enlisted man relationships. There is neither time nor space here for critical analysis of the findings and recommendations of the board; anyone interested may easily obtain a copy. But it is the opinion of many professional officers that the board, finding that the standards of the "old" Army were so high that the "new" Army had not come up to them, instead of recommending such indoctrination as would bring the "new" to the higher standard, recommended *lowering* the standard to meet the situation. Without in any way questioning the motives of this board, it does seem that it looked at the situation through reversed glasses.

Net results of the following wave of experimentation included a complete revision of the Articles of War, now become, by the Act of May 5, 1950, the Uniform Code of Military Justice. And old AW 95, concerning conduct unbecoming an officer and a gentleman, deteriorated to Article 134:

"Any officer, cadet or midshipman who is convicted of conduct unbecoming an officer and a gentleman shall be punished as a court-martial may direct."

The fine edge of the officer's honor was blunted. Not dismissal—cashiering—as inevitable result of conviction of dishonor, but a loophole. There were, in this new code, degrees of dishonor. One might, so to speak, be a little bit pregnant without causing invidious comment.

This, of course, is a matter of personal opinion. But the situation exists, and must be taken into account in any consideration of the changes in the Army.

It was during this war period that the Army went on the pay-as-you-go, cash-and-carry system in its commissaries and post exchanges —with which no one can cavil. And about this time, too, the saber—symbol of authority—went by the boards. The Sam Browne belt, unwept monstrosity, had disappeared several years previous.

The war brought more flecks of color on Army blouses. The Legion of Merit, the Bronze Star, the Air Medal, the Good Conduct Medal and later the Commendation Medal blossomed. So, too, did the Army of Occupation of Germany Medal (belated, this, for it commemorated 1918-1923). The American Defense and the American, European-African-Middle East and Asiatic-Pacific campaign medals, all with appropriate arrow-heads and stars to indicate combat landings and battles, were issued. The Woman's Army Corps had its own medal. The World War II Victory Medal, a general catch-all for each participant, followed. And in the aftermath, came the Army of Occupation Medal for our troops in occupied countries around the world.

Combat and Expert Infantryman badges and Medical, Parachutist, Glider and Diver badges began to appear on uniform blouses also, in bright array. Foreign decorations flowered, too, for Congress once again had authorized automatic acceptance and wearing of such expressions of Allied esteem.

Little wonder that the soldier, with his usual Army irreverence disguising pride, promptly dubbed the variegated color scheme "fruit salad."

During those war years the Nation saw uniformed women in the service, expanding from the nurse's role to that of the Woman's Army Corps' general administration. The Regular, initially shuddering at the thought, accepted the fact, albeit as reluctantly as his grandfather had accepted Clara Barton. He accepted, too, almost complete elimination of the old Army's post social life. The Army had grown entirely beyond the capacities of existing garrison posts, and a nation by now become habituated to the wanderlust of the trailer, to the uprooting of its own home life by industrial processes which sent families by the thousands gypsying from place to place for work as well as for pleasure, saw no valid reason for perpetuating the past cloistered existence of the Army. Consequently Congress was in no mood to expand Army housing.

As a result in the post-war period the average professional, like his civilian colleague, became a commuter; his wife—were he married —a commuter's wife, uninterested in hubby's job, unacquainted with his superiors. Of course, on permanent posts, and in other spots where conscientious post and unit commanders and their wives were rightly jealous of the "old" Army and all that it meant, some of the garrison spirit of the past was reviving. One gallant lady single-handedly has for several years past kept up the distaff morale and instilled the spirit of the service, first in a division in Europe and later in an army area here. On the other hand, such things as the discouragement by 1st Infantry Division headquarters in Bad Tölz, during 1950, of the time-honored custom of exchanging calls, particularly with the divisional high command, were no help to morale.

At best, both abroad, where the Army was reliving again the "days of the Empire" along a new world-wide frontier, and here in our huge cantonments, the revival of Army spirit was more nearly akin to country club gathering than to the close-knit association of the past. The measured etiquette of military social intercourse was drooping, as it had earlier drooped in civil life.

This was unfortunate, for the biggest problem by this time was the assimilation into the officer corps once more of a large group of former emergency officers. Like their predecessors of 1920, these men could be divided roughly into two classes: those who had found a new vocation, and those to whom a life in uniform offered a better job than they could find in civil life.

But—and this is important—these newcomers were again divisible: those who were being integrated into the Regular service; and those who, retaining their Reserve status, were merely being kept on extended active service. These latter, and their families, could not help being imbued with an element of insecurity entirely incompatible with the rigid tenets of a lifetime profession.

Unfortunately, too, a generation of Americans brought up in cafeteria style found itself in our overseas stations living in luxury, surrounded by menials. Some individuals, particularly women, lost their heads. A certain degree of arrogance crept into their thinking, and there was not sufficient social intercourse with the older generation to correct this. The leaven was too thin; cracks were appearing in the moral fiber of the officer corps.

Abroad, in strange places, an Army Exchange Service provided all the necessities and most of the luxuries of life in the United States. All this was fine. But this Army, spick-and-span again physically, lacked soul; a moral inertia had gripped it. No one who has lived in our stations abroad, who has seen at close hand the little slimy, grubby tentacles of Black Market dealings wind themselves into Army lives, can deny this.

This Army traveled in reasonable comfort—by sea, by land, and in the air. Its families—officers and enlisted men alike—shared quarters on transports equipped beyond the wildest dreams of the "old" Army. Gone were the days when one queued up on a bath roster. Gone, too, were the days when a transport voyage for a small infant was really a risky performance. Baby food, baby formulas, adequate medical and nursing personnel, well-equipped dispensaries, replaced the one harassed ship's doctor of the turn of the century with his CC pills, castor oil and iodine. Our transportation people, it seemed, had learned that women and children were people!

Pay had crept up; never, of course, reaching either a comparable civilian level nor the ever-upward climb of the high cost of living. The officer, true, for a long time had been freed of the expense of providing his own personal arms and field equipment, and newcomers, except for West Point graduates and RÓTC honor students—barred from participation by the very fact that they were commissioned in the Regular Army initially—received an initial two hundred and fifty dollars clothing allowance. Theoretically the Regular, if he and his minded their pennies, could live as well as his forebears. Actually, this was not—and is not—so.

Not only had keeping up with the Joneses become a problem in this era of living in civilian communities, but the more urgent and very real additional expenses of the day—baby sitters, for instance— gouged holes in slim pocketbooks. No longer could the Regular and his wife leave the children home, confident that Private Jones, the family striker, would take charge. Now it was a case of paying seventy- five cents an hour for a sitter, when taking an evening off. Rentals in many areas ran well above the extra monetary allowance—"commuta- tion of quarters," the Army calls it—granted to its members forced to live outside government reservations; medical expenses, for those living off a post, became an urgent necessity in the family budget.

This was an Army of cosmopolites, as familiar with the Rue de la Paix, the Ringstrasse, the Ginza and the battered facade of Unter den Linden as it was with Main Street. It had experienced the Berlin Airlift, the Mozart Express, the North Atlantic Treaty. The stresses of an ever-increasing turmoil and tempo throughout the world were testing its soul as the wind of cold war blowing from behind the Iron Curtain's cynical, godless ideology sought every cranny and crevice in its fabric.

Professionally, the soldier had rubbed shoulders with diplomacy in a big way. The American officer, in occupied areas, in UN, in NATO, in Greece, in the frenzied Pentagon rabbit warren, had become not only a student but also a practitioner of world politics. He had so become, not because of any meddling of his own, but by official dictate. And he did a magnificent job.

The performance of our officers in tremendous vice-regal jobs of governing vast areas of occupation assigned them by the nation has never been equalled. MacArthur remade Japan. Lucius D. Clay in Germany and Mark W. Clark in Austria shepherded their flocks against the wolves of Soviet Communism and made bold, inflexible face against the Reds in the enclaves of Berlin and Vienna that some- how—contrary to all common-sense, military or civilian—had been foisted on the free world. The soldier in the ranks might shrug that situation off with a cynical "somebody goofed," but it was up to the military governor to salvage the pieces, the while maintaining his country's honor and prestige.

And all the while the Corps of Engineers, in addition to its duties with the armed forces here and abroad, was continuing in the civilian portion of its dual role, affecting the commercial, agricultural and economic well-being of the United States. We look on the Panama Canal as a monumental achievement of the Army Engineers, and it is. But the Engineers' other activities are so widespread and so inex- tricably entwined in the daily progress of the nation that they are sometimes lost sight of in the big picture.

Since 1824, when Congress passed the first Rivers and Harbors Act, the Corps of Engineers has been charged with ensuring safe entrance and egress of world water-borne traffic at our ports, its flow along our inland waterways, and with the harnessing of our rivers by flood control projects.

All our great harbors have been and still are the responsibility of the Army Engineers, who dredge and mark channels, and supervise enlargements of port facilities. They decide where and how bridges and piers should be constructed; impedence of traffic is not tolerated. They built the great Minot's Ledge lighthouse off Boston harbor, and the Delaware Breakwater. From Passamaquoddy on the Maine- Canadian border to the Gulf of Mexico and from Alaska to Southern California they have smoothed the path of water-borne transport and checked the ocean's ravages.

From the 1830s, when they started clearance of the age-old log- jam on the Red River just above its confluence with the Mississippi— the "Great Raft" as it was called—down to the present day the Engi- neers have been busy on our inland waterways. The networks of dams harnessing the Father of Waters itself, as well as the Missouri and the Colorado Rivers, all bear their stamp.

They made the surveys for the St. Lawrence Waterway; they built the Sault Ste. Marie locks making possible passage from Lake Superior to the other Great Lakes. They constructed, among many others, the great Bonneville and Fort Peck dams.

The intricate buffer-breakwater system on the Mississippi which, in 1838, saved St. Louis as a river port by forcing the current to scour in its own silt, was an Engineer project (Captain Robert E. Lee figured that one out).

On the land, the great Alcan Highway across Canada linking Alaska to the United States was an Engineer product of World War II. More than a century earlier the Engineers had smoothed our first pathway to the West, the so-called National Road from Baltimore, Md. to Vandalia, Ohio. The completion of the Washington Monument, the erection of the Capitol dome and wings in Washington, D.C., and the construction of the Pentagon were all chores of the Corps.

If and when the long-proposed Nicaragua Canal project becomes a reality, the complete surveys of the area—made back in the 1920s —are ready in the files of the Chief of Engineers.

So, in these post-war years the Engineers, the men who wear the castle as their ensign and on their buttons and whose quiet motto is "Essayons" (which we can translate "Let's Try"), were as usual going about their endless duties, so important to the nation.

Professionally, too, during the period, the Regular was struggling with the atom and its effect upon the art of war. In so doing he had to combat civilian dreams of pushbutton war, as well as the civilian's incipient panic. He was on the horns of a dilemma—on the one hand, how best to utilize the genii of the atom without throwing away the essentials of heretofore "conventional" war; on the other, to determine just what those essentials were in an atomic age. His deliberations were interrupted by the Korean explosion.

The enlisted man in 1950 had come far from his counterpart of 1904. His base pay of seventy-five dollars a month and "found" compared very favorably with the one hundred and eighty dollars of the just-joined second lieutenant. The "perpetual private" was long gone; milkshakes were more popular than whisky. The non-commissioned officer was a studious, serious-minded individual, probably married and bringing up a family. The stripes on his sleeve, unfortunately, were not necessarily tokens of ability to lead men in battle; every specialist wore chevrons. We had to add a little green shoulder tab to denote command status.

In addition to its own wide-ranging military educational system, the Army was now taking care of the individual needs of this soldier —if he so desired, and in his off-duty hours—through the correspondence courses and study centers of the United States Armed Forces Institute. These were set up in the United States and abroad. The gamut of general education ranged from high school to university; from liberal arts to purely technical subjects.

The company cadre, although it included a topkick, also included something new—a unit administrator of warrant rank, who was supposed to take from the commander the onus of the ever-waxing paperwork. This was all fine-and-dandy in theory. But what had happened was the insertion of an unnecessary idling gear between two essential pinions of the basic military machine. Like all idling gears, it reversed the direction of energy. The company commander was put out of touch with his men; his first sergeant—once his trusty right hand—was bypassed, his prerogatives clipped, his influence diminished. (One notes, *en passant,* that this situation has lately been corrected.)

Gone, too, in great part, were the days of individuality, when mess sergeants vied with one another for the reputation of the "best eatin' " outfit on the post. Like the post exchange, now become but one link in a great chain-store organization, the company mess was but a branch of a cafeteria system with a standardized daily diet and menu. However, this must be admitted: the new system protected the soldier from the less-than-mediocre efforts of a poor mess sergeant and an indifferent company commander. And it was still possible for an exceptionally conscientious commander, blessed with a good mess sergeant, to preserve some individuality in the mess.

This was your Army, Mr. Jones, when Korea flamed in 1950.

* * * * *

· · · ·

· · · · ·

17

THE MORNING IS NOT CALM

In 1947, the United States had reorganized its defense establishment. The Army, the Navy and the Air Force (divorced by the same legislation from the Army to become an entity), were incorporated into a Defense Department, their respective Secretaries subordinated to a Secretary of Defense. Under him, too, were gathered a War Council (the service Secretaries and their respective Chiefs of Staff), the Joint Chiefs of Staff (now become a permanent agency), the Munitions Board (industrial mobilization) and the Research and Developments Board. In theory at least, this amalgamation and integration was sound; the business of national defense had become a matter directly concerning the national survival in a world fast becoming one of tooth and fang.

For the services it was a shot-gun wedding. Old prejudices and old jealousies festered, their irritations not at all salved by the national demand—as always—for some economical solution to the problem.

By 1949, the Army, still staggering under the shock of the postwar disintegration, had climbed to a strength of six hundred and fifty-eight thousand. Its combat elements were scattered world-wide in occupation commitments, particularly in Germany, Austria and Japan. Louis A. Johnson, economy-minded Secretary of Defense, shook it back on its haunches by his announcement that in lopping one billion, seven hundred thousand dollars from expenditures for the coming fiscal year he had "cut the fat" from it.

The blow reduced its strength by some eighty-seven thousand men; perforce the Army pulled its belt in tighter. Except for the 1st Infantry Division and the armored constabulary regiments facing the Russian Bear along the West German border, most existing divisional units were partially skeletonized.

One of the three battalions in each infantry regiment was deactivated; in the remaining battalions a rifle company was dropped from each. Each battalion of division artillery had one battery—six precious guns—pruned away.

As further measure of economy the War Department decided to send the young West Pointers graduating in 1950 directly to their respective regiments, omitting the usual preliminary practical training courses at the schools of their arms.

In Japan, where four of these emasculated divisions stood, the situation was further strained. They had no supporting units, such as corps and army artillery and the various elements of other arms and services which go to make up a modern fighting force. Because Japanese bridges would not bear heavy loads, light tanks had been substituted for heavy ones. The manpower filling these cadres comprised for the most part draftees with less than eight-months' service, and only partly trained.

As for Korea, the "Land of the Morning Calm," all American troops had been withdrawn except for a military mission training South Korean constabulary. Korea didn't matter anyway, our pundits had announced, so it was not included in MacArthur's Far Eastern Command.

On June 25, 1950, Korea split wide open. A sudden thrust of disciplined Red North Korean troops, Russian-armed and Communist-trained, splashed southward through the scattered resistance of the South Korean constabulary. The United Nations screamed and President Harry Truman acted. He ordered General MacArthur to dam the Red tide.

MacArthur, immediately reaching into his skimpy resources, "managed," as he later said, "to throw in a part of two battalions of infantry, who put up a magnificent resistance before they were destroyed—a resistance which resulted, perhaps, in one of the most vital successes that we had."

That forlorn hope spearhead—Task Force Smith, a name to be added to Army annals—shattered itself against the Red blow July 5, 1950, while MacArthur, stripping his occupation forces in Japan, was pumping in more men to the danger zone, and at home the nation was hurriedly girding itself.

Once again the United States, in its traditional state of unpreparedness, was at war. From what President Truman, bold in his initial action, had so unfortunately christened—doubtless without intentional irony—a "police action," the Korean War developed into a major struggle of free world against Communism. The United States was the principal UN element. The war was fantastic in growth, frustrating in its end.

General William F. Dean's 24th Division, thrown in piece-meal, fought a "lieutenant's war," trading space for time in incessant little battles. They were thin-spread and outnumbered as they were forced back into that ever-shrinking perimeter around the port of Pusan, our vital foot-hold on the southern tip of the peninsula. Dean himself, captured in the forefront of this seemingly hopeless struggle, added one more tradition of leadership and devotion to the Army's records.

His was the battle of a strong man against fate, infusing by personal example the magic spark that leads men to pull themselves up by their own bootstraps and fight on when the world is crashing about them. As it turned out, his later behavior during the long months of captivity (he was returned only at the end of the war) presented his country with a never-to-be-forgotten example of the true American spirit.

Dean was subjected to continuous torture, both physical and mental, as the Communists strove to break down the will and mind of their prize prisoner. Had a Regular major general of the United States Army been brain-washed into a grovelling puppet, Communist propaganda would indeed have had something to tell the world.

But Dean, a University of California man who first started his military service in the Students Army Corps of World War I, would not break.

The grim scene in Korea changed September 26, 1950—just thirty-three years to the day from the launching of Pershing's great Meuse-Argonne offensive of World War I. MacArthur's Inchon landing, carried out with all the skill and vigor of a great captain, cut the Red assault of Pusan from its supply area north of the Yalu. The North Korean forces disintegrated and MacArthur's Eighth Army, led by Lieut. General Walton H. Walker, moved into the offensive. Three-dimensional warfare this master-move had been, for without the Navy to sweep the seas around the Korean peninsula and the Air Force to dominate the air above, it would have been impossible.

Red China's entry into the war, November 25-26, shifted the scene again. From their Manchurian sanctuary the Chinese poured across the Yalu and pushed MacArthur's troops back until finally braked both by dogged and skillful resistance and their own inability to keep up the offensive. Here the Army learned the valor of the token forces of the other United Nations fighting by its side and as part of its components.

Over here and in the rest of the free world a vast uneasiness began to spread, compounded both of honest apprehension that World War III might be just around the corner, and of the basic urge for self-preservation. On it the specious doctrine of appeasement began to thrive.

Now the Army man—firm in the soldier's belief and national tradition so well voiced by General MacArthur: "There is no substitute for victory"—found himself fighting with one arm tied behind his back, bound by artificial restrictions imposed through a welter of international fears and multi-national differing objectives.

From beginning to end the Red Manchurian bases, their sources of supply and springboards of attack, were preserved inviolate by Presidential order. The voice of Dennis Hart Mahan, crying, "Do the greatest damage to our enemy with the least exposure to ourselves," had at long last been stilled.

The violent to-and-fro of continued enemy efforts and counter-blows on our part continued until that fateful day of April 11, 1951, when President Truman suddenly jerked MacArthur from his command and General Matthew B. Ridgway took over.

Curious is the historical parallel here between Polk and Truman on the one hand and Scott and MacArthur on the other. Scott was relieved in 1847, at the moment of victory, to satisfy a political pique; MacArthur in 1951 in the midst of a struggle in which he had successfully withstood political handicaps limiting his combat power and at the moment when the fallacy of the administration's "limited war" policy was beginning to show. Both soldiers came home to thunderous popular acclaim. In neither case was the prerogative of the Commander-in-Chief to appoint or remove a subordinate in the field questioned. But each time the political party in power went down to disastrous defeat at the polls and an Army general became the next President of the United States—Taylor in 1848, Eisenhower in 1952.

For two years and two months following MacArthur's relief, the opponents continued in costly stalemate, while from July 10, 1951, to

July 27, 1953, when uneasy armistice was arrived at, Army representatives wrangled endlessly in peace conferences with their Communist
opposite numbers. Of more than four hundred and thirty-nine thousand casualties suffered by the United Nations forces, some one
hundred and forty-two thousand had been Americans, two hundred
and eighty thousand South Koreans, and seventeen thousand from
the other United Nations engaged. That tells the proportional story of
American participation in Truman's "police action."

From beginning to end the American soldier had forced upon
him in ever stronger doses a curious new concept of his mission, a
concept foreign to all that had gone before in our national history.
From the days of Washington's Continentals to World War II he had
gone to war—willingly or unwillingly—for the sole purpose of beating
his country's enemy. Now, it appeared, while war was still an extension
of diplomacy, American diplomacy was using the American soldier as
a pawn expendable in gambits labelled "limited war," dictated by
national fears and international power politics.

The frustrating withdrawals and retirements, the succeeding forward thrusts, the months of battling in the "Iron Triangle," carried
with them no promise of future reward. Soldiers fought and died to
take a hill or hold a ridge, well knowing that although failure might
be disastrous, success would not mean final victory. There was always
another hill or another ridge. War had become a matter of course for
our Army in the alternating mud and ice of Korea; a kill-or-be-killed
affair involving a mirage called the 38th parallel.

In such fashion evolved the magnificent Eighth Army, developed
under the leadership of MacArthur and Ridgway, of Walker and
James A. Van Fleet. It was a fighting machine which carried out the
nation's behest and left to the historian of the future the task of
putting the picture puzzle together.

Our Army learned other things in the Korean War. It learned that
it could still do what had been done before in the Philippines on much
smaller scale; it could train and assimilate in its ranks the soldiers of
an Asiatic nation and finally put them on their feet militarily.

It had learned, too, that its traditions and spirit—and the leadership of its officers—could carry it through vicissitudes which promptly
unravelled any undisciplined force.

We did add a new word to our military vocabulary as a result of Korea—a shameful word: "bugout." But galling though it may be to admit it, one must remember that bugouts had occurred prior to 1950. Panic is no respecter of persons. Once started, it is as hard to put out as a prairie fire in a gale. Leadership and discipline, though they will minimize its probability, cannot furnish guarantee against it.

The Shenandoah Valley, October 19, 1864, had witnessed the bugout of the entire VIII Corps of Sheridan's army. Before that, General Braxton Bragg's men on Missionary Ridge, November 25, 1863, had done just that. And on December 16, 1944, the Ardennes had witnessed mad panic in VIII Corps' sector.

Only leadership can curb panic—the personal leadership of strong men, known to their subordinates. "Turn, boys, turn!" shouted Sheridan to the fleeing rabble at Cedar Creek, and turn they did, because they knew him and relied on him. Any modern Sheridan, be he corporal or general, can do the same, provided his men know him well enough to rely on him. It was done in the Ardennes, on the Pusan perimeter, in the reel-back from the Yalu.

And to the credit of our "new" Army, remember that military historian S. L. A. Marshall declared he was unable to find, in all his exhaustive research in Korea, a single instance of mass bugout by an entire American unit.

But out of the backwash of the Korean War came in early 1956 an amazing allegation that one man in every three American soldiers made prisoner by the Communists had fallen prey to Red ideological indoctrination. These men had lost faith in their nation, in their comrades, and in themselves.

Already on the record was the indication that some thirteen per cent of our prisoners of war—including the twenty-odd men who had abjured their country and refused to return to the United States—had been found chargeable with serious military offenses of collaboration and of betrayal of their fellows while in confinement. This was something else.

The story, as unfolded, was a resume of the case histories of nearly one-quarter of the more than four thousand returned prisoners screened by Army psychological experts.*

---

* Copyrighted interview with Major William E. Mayer, M. C., in February 24, 1956, issue of *U.S. News & World Report,* an independent weekly news magazine published in Washington.

These soldiers, it was asserted, after being brainwashed in a carefully planned educational process, had proven to be of insufficient moral or mental strength to resist Communist arguments. Their patriotism had unravelled. Their comrades' sufferings became something to be shrugged off in an "every man for himself" attitude. Many of them turned informer on fellow prisoners; all spilled any military information they possessed. Some simply curled up and died. (These deaths were in addition to the brutal murder of six thousand, one hundred and thirteen American soldiers captured by the Communists in the early days of the war.)

All the more shocking to American ideologists was the further assertion that several hundred Turkish soldiers, who had been held under conditions of captivity similar to our men, survived "almost to a man." Their case histories indicated they had held themselves together in amazing discipline and devotion.

Here indeed was a challenge to leadership. Individual turncoats, traitors and informers are nothing new; all armies, including our own, have had such in their ranks. But no mass blight of such proportions had ever before threatened the United States Army.

The bright side of the picture, from the Army viewpoint, was that this screening process which had revealed the epidemic also revealed that in general the individual prisoner appeared to have been affected in ratio proportional to his service. That is, the officer and the long-time professional soldier were relatively immune; as for the other soldiers, the shorter their service prior to capture, the greater their susceptibility. The leaven of "Duty, Honor, Country" was, then, still good. The point was how best to instil it.

Another important revelation in this analysis was that the man of sincere religious conviction proved to have been better armed mentally and morally than others. Important this, to a nation whose motto is "In God We Trust."

But what all these things added up to was that in each barrel of one hundred shining American apples forty-six might be potentially rotten. This amazing situation appeared to indicate the necessity for a careful examination of national conscience. The assumption was a change in American behaviorism. If true, we were paying in a big way for the thirty or more years past of national indifference to our

American heritage. How far the worship of high living standards had overrun standards of character was worth consideration.

Our young men had been brought up in an atmosphere of TV and comic books, juke boxes and pinball machines, hot rods and drive-in movies, organized baseball and organized crime. Some of them came from families infected with the creeping paralysis of unemployment compensation turned into a racket. The nation itself, prosperous as never before, had become uninterested, it seemed, in anything beyond its creature comfort. Yet at that very time an element of fear was entering its consciousness: Soviet Russia had the atomic bomb!

With such background these young men, apparently lacking any moral incentive to stimulate their patriotism, were catapulted in Korea into the horrors of a warfare unparalleled since the days of Genghis Khan. Murder for the wounded, torture for the captive, was their lot.

And yet, despite the sorry showing of so many of those American soldiers captured by the enemy, the record of achievement was also there. American soldiers had met and fought and matched this enemy. To the older strains of our ancestry had been added the newer strains springing from the melting pot of the early days of the century. They too, it seemed, could raise staunch soldiers and leaders in this, their adopted country. Look at the roster of Medal of Honor winners. Here are a few names picked at random from men who earned the Medal of Honor in Korea:

Cafferata, Desiderio, Gomez, Jecelin, Kouma, Krzyzowski, Miyamura, Oullette, Rosser, Simanek—and even a Red Cloud, the only original American perhaps, but only one of a great host of true American men.

The difference between the old and the new American soldier, it appeared from the records of Korea, was that the successors of Calvin Titus and Alvin York needed an awful lot of indoctrination to convince them in the first place that the chips were down, and in the second, that they were their chips. Once convinced, they did write a golden page in our Army's books.

*   *   *   *   *

• • • •

• • • •

18

THE ARMY IN FERMENT

Following the uneasy armistice at the close of the Korean War, our Army was sucked slowly into the crosscurrents of a radical change in American mores, a part of the revolutionary spirit affecting the entire world. Disrespect for authority, savage racial and ethnic antagonisms, rising corruption in high places and low, all undermined the leadership, tradition and discipline essential to military efficiency.

These attacks on probity were all the more serious because upon the shoulders of American youth affected by them still lay the burden of compulsory military service.

In the Army, further unease came from an unhealthy interservice rivalry, exacerbated by the problems of the nuclear age; confusion and bickering over respective roles and missions in the national defense. To these were added—particularly in the officer corps— harassments brought about by creeping inflation, the decrease of so-called "fringe benefits," and early compulsory retirement.

It appeared also, to some men in uniform, that the Army's high command was drifting away from the troops, was losing the personal touch. This was a far cry from the "one for all, all for one" spirit of the old Army, as exemplified in 1921 by one courtly colonel on Corregidor who, discovering that the quarters assigned to an incoming captain (a complete stranger to him) were being reconstructed and were temporarily uninhabitable, met the transport and insisted that the officer, his wife and little son become guests in his own quarters until theirs were shipshape.

To put it mildly, the professional was caught between his own personal troubles and Pentagon interservice squabbles at the very time he, of necessity, was facing the tremendous problem of preparing the Army for possible nuclear warfare, while coping with "conventional" methodology. Experimentation was the order of the day, but to be meaningful, experimentation needed a concentration of energy.

Up in the rarified atmosphere of the Pentagon the Defense Department and its respective service components mushroomed into a multiheaded civilian "general staff" of sorts, with layers of undersecretaries, assistant secretaries, advisors and efficiency experts, many of them with high ideals and proven capacity in the rat race of civilian life, but ignorant of practical military know-how.

In 1956 this bedlam was compounded by an open clash between Army and Air Force, the so-called "revolt of the Colonels." A small coterie of ill-advised Army staff officers courted publicity with an open challenge to the Air Force doctrine asserting that national security lay mainly in air power.

As a result, Defense Secretary Charles E. ("Engine Charlie") Wilson, assessing national security in accord with his own lights, revised and drastically curtailed Army activities in the missile field. Attempting to transform the art of war into a parlor game of football, he prescribed who should carry the ball and how much yardage could be gained without penalty.

Later, clearheaded, efficient Robert S. McNamara, Defense Secretary from 1961 to 1968, was to accomplish a remarkable feat, by bringing the bickering Army, Navy and Air Force to heel. But McNamara's slide-rule mind never really grasped the fact that soldiers—being men and not machines—should be treated as human beings. Nor did the bickering cease; it was but muted.

McNamara's urge for efficiency changed the Pentagon into a vast, mechanized array of slide-rule operation and machine records, where —theoretically at least—round pegs went into round holes, square pegs into square holes. Correct in theory, in practice this presented many limitations and frustrations.

It must be remembered that this was the period of the "cold war," the stark, unceasing struggle of Communism to engulf the world. The USSR and Red China, although fearing one another, were yet both intent on eliminating the United States from its position as the dominant power of the non-Communist world.

We were already in the age of brinkmanship and tightrope diplomacy, with U.S. armed forces committed by President Eisenhower's administration to a policy of massive retaliation in the event of direct Communist attack.

Our Army was committed to maintaining itself in readiness for either nuclear or conventional war, while at the same time building up, at home, a striking force of regulars, mobile and ready to extinguish so-called "brush wars" instigated by the Communist bloc.

This was also a period of colossal research and development in weaponry and communications* in which the Army's magic wand brought the armament industry to the status of a major element in the national economy. Many eyebrows both in the Congress and among the general public raised as defense costs soared. President Eisenhower's warning against what he termed the "military-industrial complex" added fuel to civilian discontent.

It was during this time that the continental United States began to shiver in internal racial friction and violence. When, in 1957, Governor Orval M. Faubus of Arkansas barred Little Rock's Central High School to black students, calling out his own National Guard to put teeth into his rebellion against Federal law, President Eisenhower acted. Faubus' militia was promptly ordered out of his control and into Federal service, and troops of the 101st Airborne Division moved into the city to uphold the law. Kindred civil rights disturbances throughout the next few years necessitated Federal call-up of other National Guard units for short periods to quell disorders.

In 1957, the Army took a sensible step to stiffen morale by establishing the Combat Arms Regimental System. Taking a leaf out of Britain's military book, 165 selected regular Army infantry, armor and artillery regiments each became "parent" units of several battle groups. By this means, each battle group of a regiment was sustained by the tradition of the particular regiment from which it stemmed and whose battle honors it shared. There were so many proud traditions: Alexander Hamilton's Battery of the 5th Field Artillery, oldest unit in the Regular Army; the "Old Guard" 3rd Infantry (they used to call the 3rd the "Buffsticks," too); the 38th Infantry's "Rock of the Marne" label; and the 10th Field Artillery's equally proud "The Rock's Support." Preserved, too, were the "Brave Rifles" of the 3rd Cavalry, the "I'll Try, Sir!" of the 5th Infantry, the "Go for Broke" of the Nisei 442nd Infantry, and scores of similar stimuli to the pride

---

*See Chapter 19.

of American fighting men in both the Regular Army and the older outfits of the National Guard.

The stumbling block at this time was the ignorance and indifference of the youth, both black and white, among the thousands gathered into uniform by Selective Service. Some of them, affected like their elders in this age of permissiveness, appeared to neither know nor care for the responsibility of citizenship.

But the timing was ripe. For by 1961 the Army had begun a new organizational plan for its ground combat groupments: ROAD (Reorganization Objective, Army Division). Planned like an Erector set, each division comprised brigades, variable in number, to meet the needs of some particular situation.

And now the helicopter was adding a new dimension to ground combat. The "chopper" made possible the leapfrogging of men and materiel above the battlefield; sky-cavalry, operating on the principle of the knight's move in chess; the rescue of flyers brought down within enemy lines; quick evacuation of the wounded.

In 1958, the Army took the demands of the Lebanon crisis in stride, moving elements of its striking force from both Germany and the United States as promptly as the Air Force and the Navy could furnish transportation. By that time, too, its MAAGs (Military Assistance Advisory Groups) were training the armies of friendly nations menaced by Communist aggression in Japan, the Philippines, Thailand, South Korea, Taiwan and South Vietnam,* while its standing commitment to NATO constituted the backbone of the European free world's military shield.

In 1959, bearded Fidel Castro overthrew the Cuban government, and rapidly allied himself with the USSR, bringing active Communism within a stone's throw of the United States, and instigating ferment in Central and South America. A sadly mismanaged invasion of Cuba in 1961 by a small group of anti-Castro Cuban refugees, launched with the clandestine support of the CIA, ended in dismal failure at the Bay of Pigs. The Army was not involved in this madcap scheme.

In 1961, Soviet recalcitrance brought about another Berlin crisis. Lest the Communist world mistake United States promises to sup-

*See below for discussion of the war in Vietnam.

port NATO, the Seventh Army was reinforced and President Kennedy called upon 150,000 troops of both Army and Air National Guard and the Reserves—to replace for one year Regular units in the United States already earmarked for Europe. The airmen flew overseas directly in the largest mass overseas flight in peacetime history.

In 1962, infiltration of long-range missiles into Cuba by the USSR brought about a quick quasi-mobilization in the United States. President Kennedy's prompt, firm action faced down the Soviet threat. The Russian missiles were removed by November 1962, and Army regulars and National Guard units in the United States returned to their stations.

The Army was still deployed worldwide. In Europe was the Seventh Army, the principal element of NATO, with five divisions. In isolated Berlin an American garrison—the "Berlin Brigade"—boldly faced continued Soviet pricking. In the Pacific area the Eighth Army, reduced to two divisions, was in South Korea, with a reserve force in Hawaii, and a reserve battle group in Okinawa. The Panama Canal Zone held two more battle groups, as did Alaska, while in the continental United States lay the Strategic Army Corps—STRAC—with two airborne and one infantry division prepared—again, theoretically at least—for immediate service. And some 250 Nike missile batteries* dotted the United States as antiaircraft shield from coast to coast. For a short time, in 1965, the Army provided a 19,000-man force to stabilize the Dominican Republic, where an internal *coup d'etat* had ursurped civilian control, and bloody civil war was raging.

Global Army strength was now 868,632, of whom 86,364 were officers; an additional 150,000 civilians were in Army employ, a large proportion of them natives of friendly alien nations, hired locally in our overseas installations.

And then, over Southeast Asia, a small cloud, originally no bigger than the "man's hand" of Biblical lore,† swelled to awesome proportions.

---

*Missiles and space conquest are discussed in Chapter 19.

†1 Kings, 18:44.

The Army's role in Vietnam, the oddest, longest, most unpopular war in the United States history, was a phantasmagoria of savage combat, political and social entanglement and, above all, frustration.

Along the trail one finds no conventional give-and-take of campaigns and battles. It wasn't that kind of a war. It had no front. The enemy was here, there and everywhere in a bloody game of hide-and-seek over an almost roadless expanse of lush jungle, swampy rice paddies and innumerable waterways.

With few exceptions, the actual combat was one of small units—platoons, companies and battalions—in places with outlandish names: An Loc, Hue, the Drang Valley, Ninh, Quang Tri and a thousand others. There was even—shades of Korea—an "Iron Triangle." American soldiers fought and died in thickets, hamlets, ancient walled cities and in their own isolated fire bases.

In addition, some officers and noncoms also found themselves at the receiving end of hand grenades and tear gas bombs deliberately tossed in the night by men of their own commands. And that is not nice to think about.

Our involvement in Vietnam was the direct result of a solemn United States commitment, as a member of SEATO,* to check the tide of Communism which threatened, during the mid-1950s, to engulf Southeast Asia.

When France's colonial empire in Indo-China was dissolved in 1954, the little kingdom of Vietnam split. The northern portion, under aging Communist Ho Chi Minh, assumed the title of the Democratic Republic of Vietnam. The southern portion became the Republic of Vietnam, under Ngo Dinh Diem, national premier and later president of the new republic. A strip along the 17th parallel of latitude—arbitrarily set up in 1954 by international agreement†

---

*Southeast Asia Treaty Organization, established in 1954 by Australia, France, Great Britain, New Zealand, Pakistan, the Philippines, Thailand and the United States. Its objective was to provide collective defense and economic cooperation in Southeast Asia, and to protect the weak nations of the area against aggression. Later, on April 15, 1964, the SEATO Council, meeting in Manila, reiterated its objectives by voting (France alone abstaining) to support South Vietnam's military efforts against Viet Cong guerrillas.

†United States, USSR, Red China, Great Britain, France, with additional delegates from both Vietnam factions.

(the so-called Geneva Accords)—in theory separated the two Vietnams by a 10-kilometer-wide demilitarized zone (DMZ).

The United States, while refusing to sign the Accords, stipulated its recognition of the temporary division, provided that hostilities cease and the future of all Vietnam be decided by later popular general elections.

With the active support of both the USSR and Red China, Ho Chi Minh, in Hanoi, disregarding the DMZ, began a bloody campaign of aggressive terrorism against the Diem regime, spearheaded by a dedicated Communist guerrilla movement, the Viet Cong, long established in the southern area. The United States, to impede further Communist encroachments in Southeast Asia, continued military assistance to South Vietnam through a small MAAG, previously established in Saigon to aid the now-collapsed French regime.

This was the prelude to what grew into a colossal pyramiding of American military strength in Southeast Asia. From a MAAG of some 327 officers and men, it rose to a maximum of 543,482 before it began to ebb. When the last Army combat unit cleared Vietnam in August 1972, 40,000 Americans had been killed, an additional 195,601 had been wounded and some 1,600 others remained immured in Communist prison camps. In addition, the Vietnamese ulcer had created serious internal dissensions in the United States, lowered Army morale and efficiency, and besmirched Army honor in the mire of heretofore unheard-of corruption.

An undeclared war—Congress had never declared war upon North Vietnam—the conflict was to endure under the successive administrations of four presidents: Eisenhower, Kennedy, Johnson and Nixon.

One might liken our entry into Vietnam to President Truman's original "police action" in Korea, but there any similarity ends. In Korea, while President Truman's tight civilian control limited strategic objectives, United States commanders in the field ran their own tactical operations, and a unified command existed.

In Vietnam, on the contrary, the tail wagged the dog. Despite the massive American military involvement, control lay in the hands of a succession of amateurish, inept and corrupt South Vietnamese governments. No American military moves could be made without prior sanction of the Saigon regime. American officers were "guests."

They could plan, advise and recommend, but their command was limited to U.S. troops only.

Washington itself provided our military leaders with a further stumbling block by executive tactical meddling. President Johnson, in particular, so closely supervised operations that, it is alleged, he even designated the positions of individual American battalions.

South Vietnamese President Diem, in 1956, was an aesthetic dreamer, out of touch with his own people and hobbled by family influence. His officer corps, commissioned by favor, lacked the rudiments of military know-how; his army was a rabble. On the other hand, the Communist forces were commanded by General Vo Nguyen Giap, a capable soldier long accustomed to guerrilla warfare; Giap and his troops had defeated the French. So the Viet Cong initially were elusive fleas, here, there, everywhere—and nowhere at the same time.

In February 1961, President Kennedy, declaring that he would do his all to save crumbling South Vietnam from Communism, appointed General Paul D. Harkins to Saigon to head a reorganized Military Assistance Command.

Harkins, Patton's deputy chief of staff in World War II and later chief of staff of Van Fleet's Eighth Army in Korea, found himself holding a bag of snakes. His advice was flouted by Diem; he was sometimes at odds with United States State Department officials stationed in Saigon. Out in the field he seeded his Special Force detachments (Green Berets), with tough young volunteer officers and men, specifically trained in the United States in jungle warfare and survival tactics. They could and did indoctrinate the *Montagnards* of the Vietnam highlands—warriors all—who could understand warrior language. But the Green Beret advisors seemingly made but little impression on Diem's palace guards.

Riots in Saigon and Hue, stirred up by Diem's anti-Buddhist activities, made matters worse. In November 1963, a junta of South Vietnamese officers overthrew the Diem regime, and both he and his brother were assassinated. Frustrated, Harkins, nearing retirement age, was replaced in June 1964 by General William C. Westmoreland.

Then came the Tonkin Gulf "incident" of August 2-4, an attack by North Vietnamese light craft on U.S. patrolling vessels. In retaliation, President Johnson ordered naval air strikes against selected military targets in North Vietnam, and authorized Air Force assistance, from Thailand bases, to friendly ground forces. A joint Congressional resolution then warned the world that the United States was prepared to take all steps necessary to assist any SEATO member or protocol state requesting assistance in defense of its freedom. We had taken a major step further into Southeast Asia's morass.*

At the time, United States forces in South Vietnam had grown to 33,000, of whom only 13,000 were combat troops. But reinforcements were coming in, including contingents from Allied nations†

American strength rose and U.S. casualties also mounted: 189 were killed during the year, although our mission was still one of advice and support. Through it all, the Viet Cong grew stronger. A South Vietnamese government scheme to relocate its people in a series of "strategic hamlets" neared collapse. Daylight attacks upon deteriorating South Vietnamese troops were accompanied by sneak mortar bombings of American installations. In much of the South the Communist guerrillas were actually levying taxes on the terrorized civilian population.

Meanwhile, a new provisional government was established in South Vietnam, the eighth since Diem's assassination. General Nguyen Van Thieu became chief of state, with Air Force Marshal Nguyan Cao Ky commanding the government forces. However, the basic pattern still held: subordination of United States combat forces to South Vietnamese desires. No direct unified command existed.

As Viet Cong strength increased, North Vietnamese regular troops began appearing, as did sophisticated weaponry arriving in the North by ship from the USSR and by rail and motor across the Red Chinese border.

---

*Much controversy has since arisen in the United States over the authenticity of this alleged attack on our warships. Ex-President Johnson relates in detail the steps taken by him to verify the occurrence. See: Lyndon Johnson, *The Vantage Point: Perspectives of the Presidency 1963–1969* (New York: Holt, Rinehart & Winston, 1971), pp. 112–117.

†By 1968, Allied combat elements included troops from Australia, New Zealand, South Korea, Thailand and the Philippines, totaling more than 62,000 men. They suffered 8,500 casualties, of whom 2,500 were killed. Except for the Australia–New Zealand forces, which were under American tactical control, the Allied troops acted in cooperation with the South Vietnamese, as did other smaller noncombatant elements from Western Germany, Taiwan and Malaysia. All the Allied troops received U.S. logistical support.

This reinforcement of men and materiel flowed from North Vietnam above the demilitarized zone through two major channels: the mighty Mekong River and the Ho Chi Minh Trail. The Mekong and its tributaries flow in a maze of waterways through the southwestern corner of Laos into Cambodia, to debouch through the rich delta tip land of southern Vietnam into the South China Sea.

The Ho Chi Minh Trail, winding westward from North Vietnam, far above the DMZ, entered the sanctuary of Laotian territory, whence it wandered southward through dense jungle, with lateral branches jutting eastward, to cleverly concealed Communist caches and concentration points in South Vietnam.

This system of arsenals enabled the Viet Cong and later the North Vietnamese Army—replenished from their Soviet and Chinese sources—to engage in battle where and when they wished, despite the presence of ever-increasing American troops. The Mekong River artery was finally choked by the "Riverine Navy" of small craft manned by both U.S. Navy and Coast Guard personnel, but the incessant attempts of our Air Force to bomb out the Ho Chi Minh jungle path could never dam the enemy traffic flowing antlike through the jungles.

In this deteriorating situation, President Johnson poured more United States troops into Vietnam. By the end of 1965, American strength had mounted to 154,000 men. Our total combat deaths had risen during the year to 1,636, while 151 planes and helicopters had been downed by the enemy.

All this, while an enormous American support buildup blossomed: harbors, roads, airfields, cantonments and warehouses were crammed with munitions of war. By 1967 U.S. Army support was attending to the wants of more than a million men. A huge post exchange system was flourishing. At the same time, a black market grew, as thieving South Vietnamese, in collusion with equally corrupt wheeler-dealers in U.S. uniform, robbed blind our commissaries, munitions dumps and post exchanges.

So much did the Viet Cong prosper from this intolerable condition and from the quantities of American arms captured from South Vietnamese troops and militia home guards, that one might imagine some wag dubbing General Westmoreland the Viet Cong's "Mr. Commissary"—as Confederates called unfortunate Union Gen-

eral Banks in Civil War days. However, there was little levity in
Vietnam; no humor attended the death of an American soldier by
American land mines, American hand grenades or American bullets
fired from captured or stolen American small arms.

There was little that could be done about the black market.
Documented reports of robbery met a stock response from American
officialdom: we were "guests" in South Vietnam.

American troops had been in combat since June of 1966 when
General Westmoreland initiated a "search and destroy" policy in
conjunction with South Vietnamese forces. He met with no better
results than had his predecessor, General Otis, in the Philippines,
nearly 60 years previously.

An American infantry brigade, operating north of Saigon, drew
a tactical blank, despite furious fighting. So, too, did the 1st Cavalry
Division, striking into the Ia Trang valley. Belled cats catch few
mice: the Viet Cong knew what was going to happen long before
the troops started. A pattern had been established: momentary success in an initial sweep, followed by a lapping back of the enemy
tide when our troops withdrew.

By the end of 1966, 389,000 American soldiers were in South
Vietnam; monthly supply tonnage had risen to 600,000. Fifty-nine
airfields were in operation. But the enemy was still flourishing, and
Operation ATTLEBORO in Tay Minh province, hailed by the Pentagon as a victory, and including 22,000 U.S. combat troops, had
once more drawn a tactical blank.

The fact remained that American troops held only the ground
upon which they stood. They were harassed in their bases and cantonments by continual night bombings, their roadbound columns
were ambushed, and Saigon itself was assailed by guerrilla bombing
outrages.

On one thing our Army could pride itself: evacuation and care
for our wounded, those of the South Vietnamese Army, our Allies,
and such enemy casualties as fell into our hands. Thanks to the
ubiquitous helicopter, seldom was a casualty more than a half hour
from a field hospital, and the mortality rate among our combat
wounded fell to less than one percent—lowest in the history of warfare. The Army could also take pride in the speed and efficiency of
its gunners.

The war, of course, became national and international news. Correspondents for all media, foreign and domestic, swarmed in Saigon, accompanied troops in the field. There was no censorship insofar as United States forces were concerned. There being no front line, the ebb and flow of large forces simply didn't exist. Ergo, correspondents wrote as they wished, on what little they could find in the field, on rumor, and from the incessant flood of overoptimistic civilian and military briefings given in Saigon.

To establish some basis of comparison, the American command adopted a ghoulish "body count" of enemy dead, thus stigmatizing our troops as "killers" in the public eye. This further lowered Army morale; units began vying with one another to produce "kills." The flood of Micawberish official predictions of final success issued both in Saigon and at home contrasted sharply with what reporters in Vietnam could see for themselves.

GIs in the field, rotting in swamps and menaced night and day by an invisible enemy, read clippings sent from home and wondered. An aroused public opinion, fed by increasing antiwar sentiment, appeared to be trying to deny them all support.

All angles considered, both the Army's and the Administration's press relations concerning the war in Vietnam left much to be desired. The "body count" box score policy was in itself a colossal blunder.

Dissenters at home increasingly embraced not only a number of well-meaning people in high places but, above all, many young men of draft age. For the first time in our national history deserters from the draft, and prospective draftees, began fleeing the United States in droves, ostensibly for moral reasons; but a majority of them, sad to relate, were more interested in saving their own skins than in obedience to civic responsibility.

Soldier morale in Vietnam also suffered from the Army's system of rotating officers. Rarely did a company or platoon commander stay long enough with one unit to establish his personal leadership. Nor did the higher command in this overstaffed Army inspire the GI. His contacts with the indigenous population took further toll. In Saigon, in particular, the harpies of the underworld did their best to corrupt him. Drug traffic boomed, red-light ghettos thrived.

Venereal disease rates shifted from a rate of 277.4 per thousand men in 1965, to 281.5 in 1966, dropped to 170.8 by 1968, then soared to 326.4 in 1971. And worse yet, some responsible noncoms succumbed to the temptations offered by black market wheeler-dealing.

On January 30, 1968, all South Vietnam flamed with the Communist enemy's first full-scale stroke: the Tet offensive; coordinated assaults on bases and major cities, including Saigon and Hue. An estimated 84,000 enemy troops hit simultaneously 36 provincial capitals, 5 of the 6 autonomous cities, 34 district capitals and some 50 hamlets.

A major enemy objective was the former capital, Hue, an ancient walled city, where 3 U.S. Army, 3 U.S. Marine and 11 South Vietnamese battalions were involved. Before it was over and the enemy driven out, Hue was a shambles. At Khe Sanh, a Marine base, and at a Special Forces camp in the Central Highlands, particularly, sanguinary combats raged.

But none of these actions were battles in the sense of collisions between armies. The fighting, and it was bitter, was one of battalions, of companies and of individual platoons.

In the midst of the Tet offensive, with the initiative still in the hands of the enemy, Secretary of State Dean Rusk naively announced that the Communists had rejected United States terms for entering into peace negotiations!

President Johnson forwarded reinforcements, among them a brigade of the 82nd Airborne Division, which dropped in the combat zone direct from South Carolina, the longest air deployment of a large combat unit in military history.

When the Tet offensive ebbed at last, on February 29, 1968, United States battle deaths stood at 1,825; the South Vietnamese Army had lost 3,557 more, and the "body count" box score of enemy dead was 45,000. More than 7,000 Communist prisoners had been captured. General Westmoreland announced that his troops had defeated a concentrated North Vietnamese effort to "cut the country in two."

By this time U.S. troop strength in Vietnam had waxed to 495,-000, the South Vietnamese Army to some 500,000. Vague estimates put Communist strength at over 222,000 (CIA later estimates were

500,000). But since January 1, 1961, 18,799 American soldiers and airmen had died in combat; a grim toll indeed. At this point General Westmoreland asked for 206,000 additional U.S. troops.

Psychologically, the Tet offensive ended in a Communist victory, since it fired fierce antiwar sentiment in the United States. Tactically, however, it was a Communist defeat. Ho Chi Minh's all-out bid for battlefield victory had failed.

But the enemy was still here, there and everywhere in tormented South Vietnam, and the sophistication of his weapons—flowing in from the USSR and Red China—had vastly increased.

In March, President Johnson called up 51,400 reservists, among them 22,000 Air and Army National Guard; by May the first Air National Guard unit to deploy in war since World War II had arrived in South Vietnam. Most of these units returned home after a year's hard service in the field. New Hampshire's field artillery complement brought back—much-needed comic relief—a report of having been charged by an elephant, an irate mother who felt the rumbling self-propelled guns were threatening her baby.

In July, General Westmoreland returned to the United States to become Chief of Staff of the Army, and General Creighton W. Abrams, his deputy in Vietnam, succeeded him. Abrams, a hard-boiled veteran of the 4th Armored Division in Patton's World War II Third Army, with the relief of Bastogne under his belt, was hailed by some military folk as a breath of fresh air. But whether he could improve the situation was a moot question. By this time, another enemy offensive—one of many to follow—had broken, and fighting had reached Saigon itself, with nightly rocket attacks. Throughout all South Vietnam our bases and other installations were under sporadic enemy fire.

By the end of 1968 these enemy offensives had been momentarily checked, and a concerted effort began to hinder further reinforcement of Communist forces through Cambodia; enemy supplies still moved in great quantities down the Ho Chi Minh Trail. (The Royal Cambodian government, after admitting Communist use of its terrain for supply purposes, was recognized by the United States in 1969, and the South Vietnamese government agreed to open discussions on disputed national borders.)

The United States had received a shocking jolt early in this period. The skipper of the USS *Pueblo,* a lightly armed reconnaissance ship cruising off the Korean coast, tamely surrendered his ship to a North Korean gunboat attack on January 24 without firing a shot. Neither this nor another later incident off our own Eastern coast— when a Coast Guard cutter skipper permitted a Soviet boarding party to drag from his ship a defector seeking refuge—had any direct connection with the war in Vietnam, but they lowered American prestige throughout the world.

In January 1969, President Nixon was inaugurated, Melvin R. Laird became Secretary of Defense and Henry Cabot Lodge headed for Paris, where a Communist delegation had already arrived, to continue a fruitless succession of negotiating efforts initiated by Averell Harriman the summer before. In February, North Vietnam's aggression recommenced, in a series of four strikes against more than 100 South Vietnam cities and troop bases. Enemy strategy was evidently focusing on protracted war.

At home the antiwar movement had reached a violent peak: riotous demonstrations and active sabotage fell on Selective Service offices, while a concerted activist onslaught on ROTC had not only rocked college campuses but resulted in its abolition in a number of collegiate institutions. The "stop the war" advocates hitched their wagon to racist and minority groups wherever possible.

President Nixon, with the din of dissidence ringing in his ears, announced his intention to withdraw United States forces from Vietnam, dependent always upon improvement of South Vietnamese military capability, return of American POWs, cessation of enemy activities and progress in the Paris peace talks.

United States policy became one of "Vietnamization"; transfer of the brunt of land battle to reorganized South Vietnamese armed forces equipped with the latest in U.S. arms, planes, river gunboats and—above all—realistic combat training. President Thieu and Marshal Ky read the message loud and clear: "sink or swim."

By this time—April 1969—U.S. forces in Vietnam had reached peak strength: 543,482. Their combat structure had burgeoned into two corps headquarters, seven divisions, two separate infantry brigades, an airborne brigade and an armored cavalry regiment. Marine strength (under Army command) amounted to two additional divisions and a separate regiment. All this was supported by .

an enormous logistical "slice," supplying our own and Allied troops, and the entire South Vietnamese war effort.

True to his announced intentions, President Nixon began progressive reduction of Army strength during the next two years— although Navy and Air Force operations continued in hot tempo. At the same time, Communist aggressiveness increased once again, in the hope of breaking down South Vietnam resistance.

In the spring of 1970, a joint United States–South Vietnam drive crossed the Cambodian border, aimed at dislocating the Ho Chi Minh supply artery and destroying enemy depots which all too evidently nestled within Cambodian sanctuary. The move brought increased roars of indignation from dissidents at home. United States participation in the drive was limited to a 22-mile-deep incursion, but the South Vietnamese troops penetrated further. Immense caches of enemy arms and munitions were discovered, and the behavior of South Vietnamese units in combat had apparently improved, much to the satisfaction of their American instructors and advisors.

However, the supply route could not be effectively cut, and enemy counteractivities far to the east along the South Vietnamese littoral proved definitely that the infiltration of North Vietnamese supplies would not cease until the pipelines from the USSR and Red China could be throttled at North Vietnam's eastern frontier, an opinion loudly voiced for some time by many military men in the United States.

Nevertheless, though U.S. troops had been withdrawn from Cambodia by June 30, South Vietnam operations there and in Laos continued, while Thailand's government in June announced its intention to aid with large-scale military assistance in Cambodia itself.

Meanwhile massive transfers of U.S. materiel to the South Vietnamese forces continued. U.S. Army combat troops dwindled to a minimum. So the war dragged on, while at home our involvement had become a political football in the coming Presidential elections. And early in 1972, while the Paris peace talks bogged down in seemingly irrevocable disagreement, North Vietnamese General Giap launched a full-scale assault straight south through the DMZ. Overrunning South Vietnamese ground resistance, the enemy tide captured Quang Tri city, swirled around Khe Sanh and threatened battered Hue.

It was then that President Nixon, reiterating his determination that American participation in the war would not cease until our unfortunate POWs could be returned from their living death in North Vietnam, turned to the controversial plan of throttling the enemy war supply by the mining of Hanoi and other North Vietnamese ports and the bombing of supply routes debouching from the Red Chinese border. The gauntlet, one could assume, had been thrown down. Both USSR and Communist China refused to pick it up. Giap's offensive lost its momentum for the moment, an amazingly rejuvenated South Vietnamese Army counterattacked, and the invasion ground to a halt, with the invaders clinging defensively to the medieval citadel of Kwang Tri.

But Giap, it seemed, was far from through. Summer came and went, with the South Vietnamese forces engaged in dingdong fighting, not only against the enemy troops clinging to Kwang Tri's citadel, but also against renewed enemy activity flaring throughout South Vietnam.

On August 12, 1972, in the midst of this turmoil, the last U.S. Army combat unit—the 3rd Battalion, 21st Infantry, and its attached elements, cleared Danang port. The Army's ground force combat role in Vietnam, the Pentagon announced, had officially ended. This statement was somewhat puzzling.

An estimated 40,000 or more Army personnel remained in Vietnam, for the Army was still providing logistical support to the South Vietnamese combat units. Army helicopter pilots were still under fire, as were Army medics and communications men. In Thailand, to the west, Army troops in numbers never fully disclosed stood in Thailand bases.

To sum up, the situation in Vietnam by September 1972 was that the Army might be officially out of the ground combat, but the U.S. Air Force was strenuously raking North Vietnam, the U.S. Navy in the Gulf of Tonkin was playing out a similar part on the surface and in the air, while American soldiers, sailors and airmen were in enemy hands—hands of a foe who scoffed at Geneva Conventions concerning prisoners of war. The Vietnam ulcer was still gnawing at the American body politic, for the heartwrenching question of POWs and of men missing in action was still unresolved. Defense Department figures in April 1972 listed 489 Americans known to be held prisoner in Southeast Asia, 75 of them Army men. But the Defense Department rolls also carried the names of 1,146 others—353 from the Army—missing in action. Many of these men, it was believed, were still alive, hidden in the Communist limbo of the lost. But how many were there and in what condition? Only the enemy could answer, and the enemy refused to tell.

We leave it at that, and turn to an examination of just what did happen to the Army as an entity, during the war in Vietnam.

Many unpleasant things happened to the Army during the war in Vietnam; far, far too many. And the worst of it was that the resultant defacement of the Army's image in the public mind came about through sins of commission and omission of some of its own officers and men.

Take, for instance, My Lai 4.

On March 16, 1968, a task force of the American Division conducted one of General Westmoreland's "search and destroy" sweeps in Quang Tri Province on the northeast coast of South Vietnam, long a Viet Cong stronghold. The operation was a U.S. Army affair, since the area was a "free-fire zone" (enemy-held terrain) and no sanction by the Saigon regime was necessary.

The objective was the eradication of a Viet Cong battalion reportedly operating out of "Pinkville," the GI nickname for a cluster of four hamlets: My Lai 1, 2, 3 and 4. All enemy materiel and installations found there were to be destroyed. My Lai 4 was the key target and Charlie (C) Company, 1st Battalion, 20th U.S. Infantry Regiment, was the assault element. Captain Ernest M. Medina commanded Charlie Company, and 2d Lieutenant William L. Calley, Jr., led its spearhead, the 1st Platoon. Both officers were products of OCS (Officer Candidate School).

Charlie Company poured out of its helicopters, blazed its way through My Lai 4, razed the hamlet, and before nightfall reported its mission accomplished at the cost of two American soldiers killed and ten others wounded. The gruesome "body count" register rang up 128 dead Viet Cong. General Westmoreland, hailing the affair as a "heavy blow" to the enemy, officially congratulated the officers and man of Charlie Company for "outstanding action," and My Lai 4 went on the record as a U.S. Army victory.

Not until September 5, 1969—a year and a half after the event—did the American people learn that at My Lai 4 Charlie Company, 20th U.S. Infantry, had not cut down 128 Viet Cong guerrillas in a fire-fight. Instead, it had callously murdered between 450 and 500 helpless Vietnamese peasants: men, women and children who had offered no resistance and who bore no arms. It also learned that Lieutenant Calley was facing court-martial charges alleging that he had personally murdered 102 of the victims.

National shock was followed by a wave of disbelief, excepting among the radical fringe of antiwar, antimilitary fanatics, who seized on the atrocity to spur their campaign. For most Americans the initial reaction was that American soldiers could never have been guilty of such an act; the tale must be Communist propaganda.

But as the petals of this stinking flower of evil were peeled slowly off, one by one, the evidence became indisputable. To make matters worse, it appeared that an effort, running through successive layers of command, had been made to sweep the whole affair under the rug.

Before the rumpus died away, both Major General Samuel A. Koster, the commander of the Americal Division at the time of the massacre, and his deputy, Brigadier General George Young, were entangled in the investigative net. Both received letters of censure and were stripped of their decorations. Koster, in addition, lost one star. Both officers were permitted to retire. On the murder charges, separate courts-martial acquitted Medina, a proven liar, and several enlisted men of Charlie Company. Medina left the Army. Calley, convicted, received a life sentence, later commuted to a 20-year term.*

But the question of basic responsibility still remained moot insofar as the public was concerned. If and when the report of a board of inquiry, headed by Lieutenant General William B. Peers, is made public, the puzzle may be solved. That report, admittedly the basis for the spate of courts-martial and other disciplinary actions, still lies in Pentagon classified files, protected by a Federal Court order handed down in August 1972 denying Congressional access to it.

Meanwhile, in the court of world opinion, the entire United States Army must stand branded as ruthless killers, and the honor of the military profession lie besmirched.

*In 1972 Calley's case was still under appeal.

Remembering ex-President Harry S. Truman's classic aphorism: "The buck stops here," the pessimist wonders just where the buck on My Lai 4 does stop.

However, one may speculate on the causes leading to the atrocity. Certainly it was not for lack of orders. As the record shows, General Westmoreland had laid down the strictest of injunctions upon the treatment of civilians—women and children especially. And he had prescribed incessant inspections throughout.

But somewhere along the road the essential follow-through must have been neglected. True, higher commanders—regimental, brigade, division and above—in Vietnam did from time to time hover over ground combat in "choppers" or light planes. Several brave men wearing stars died under enemy fire in so doing. But the impression persists that rarely did these commanders go down into the mud beside their GIs; that there was neither the desire nor the opportunity to study junior officers and their ability to lead men in battle. Furthermore, had not laxity crept into OCS training and selection, it does not seem possible that men of the caliber of Medina and Calley ever would have been commissioned.

Nor did the Army's short-term rotation policy help. Good combat leaders—and there were many—had little opportunity to impress their men with their personality and to instill the spirit of team play. In turn, the doubting Thomases of Selective Service watched the unending procession of officers through their units and drew their own conclusions. They knew that without a tour of duty in Vietnam the prospects of selective promotion for line officers above the grade of major were bleak. In consequence, not a few GIs scoffed at authority.

For some of these soldiers—misfits cast from the same mold as their brethren at home, who were wrecking draft board offices, burning American flags and waving Viet Cong emblems in the name of peace—the next step was "fragging": a hand grenade or a tear gas bomb flung into an officer's quarters, a booby trap rigged in his bunk.

At home, the courts-martial resulting from My Lai 4, as well as from other substantial brutal excesses, agitated the general public. This was nothing new; military justice, as history shows, has always been under unfair criticism from the unthinking. But the drumfire now from civilian legal lights, as well as the man in the street, was heavy indeed. The clamor was abetted by tongue in cheek reporting, outrageous cartoons and off-the-cuff tongue-lashing editorials in newspapers and news magazines, on radio and TV, throughout the United States.

It remained for one prominent criminal lawyer to break a lance in defense of military justice: Melvin Mouron Belli, who had defended many military men brought before courts-martial. Said Belli, as quoted in the magazine *Soldiers,* July 1971: "I am tremendously impressed with the paternalism of military justice. . . . Right now in the military we've got the most protective of the individual systems of law in the civilized world. And Lee Bailey [another famous criminal lawyer] and I have said that if we were ever picked up on a criminal charge and had a choice of forum, we'd pick the military court, military justice."

Between 1968 and 1971, to the disgust and chagrin of the great majority of Army officers and men conscientiously performing their duty according to the accepted tenets of the Army, and to the glee of detractors, other nauseating things began crawling out of the Army's wainscoting.

One concerned a former Provost Marshal General—the service's chief policeman—who, following his retirement, was tried and convicted in a Federal District Court on five counts of soliciting gifts and one of income tax evasion. Former Major General Carl C. Turner, his Distinguished Service Medal citation revoked, went to the Lewisburg, Pennsylvania, penitentiary on May 10, 1971, to serve a sentence of three years and three months. With Juvenal one can well comment: *"Quis custodiet istos custodes?"*

Another case concerned the indictment of five high-ranking non-commissioned officers, including the former much-touted, highest-ranking enlisted man in the entire Army—Sergeant Major William O. Wooldridge. The five men, who actually formed a corporation and divided its stock among them, were allegedly bilking noncoms' clubs and post exchanges worldwide; big business while it lasted. In 1972, they were still awaiting trial in the Federal District Court, Los Angeles, California.

And then there was the case of Brigadier General Earl F. Cole, AUS, onetime boss of Post Exchange purchasing in Vietnam. Charged with favoring certain merchants, by giving their products a monopoly at the expense of competitors, Cole was stripped of his Distinguished Service Medal on July 30, 1970, and demoted to colonel. The Secretary of the Army's official letter demoting him commented that he ". . . had failed to maintain the high degree of personal decorum and exemplary conduct the Army and the American public have the right to demand of a general officer." Legal action followed.

The case of Lieutenant Colonel Anthony B. Herbert lies in a different category. Herbert, whose personal bravery in Korea and while in brief command of the 2nd Battalion, 503rd Infantry, 173rd Airborne Brigade in Vietnam had won him the unofficial accolade of the fightingest man in the United States Army, was suddenly relieved of command in early April 1969. The cause given: unsatisfactory performance of duty, accompanied by a derogatory efficiency report. Quite properly, Herbert demanded redress of his wrongs (we used to call it a court of inquiry), but ensuing investigations upheld the original action.

Then Herbert lashed out. Proclaiming in the press and on radio and TV that he had been relieved of command because he had presumed to report war crimes committed in his brigade, he preferred charges against both his former brigade commander and deputy commander. Both officers were cleared by further investigations.

Will Herbert become the Fitz-John Porter* of the Vietnam war? Probably not. But meanwhile his case remains a part of the fog of innuendo dimming the Army's record in Vietnam.

Drab reading, all this. But the historian, to be worthy of his salt, must keep the record straight. It is time now to turn to the bright pages of valor, tenacity and devotion to duty displayed in the Army in Vietnam. In sum, despite the blemishes inflicted by the few, the Army as an entity can feel proud of its record along that *via dolorosa*. The vast majority of its personnel—regulars, reservists and draftees, officers and men alike—responded to the call of duty in a fashion comparable to their predecessors.

Up to mid-1972, the record shows that 134 Medals of Honor[†] had been awarded, many of them posthumously. Some of these men

---

*See p. 125 for the famous case of Major General Fitz-John Porter, unjustly accused by Pope of disobeying orders at the second Battle of Bull Run. Cashiered from the Army, Porter's wrongs were not redressed until twenty years had passed.

[†]See pp. 140-141 for a brief discussion of the nation's highest combat decoration, awarded only for documented evidence of valor displayed "above and beyond the call of duty."

died, as did Sergeant Brian L. Baker, rallying a South Vietnamese
strike force. Others died as did 2d Lieutenant Robert L. Leisy, protecting an ambushed convoy. Still others, such as Sp.4c. Joseph C.
La Pointe, Jr., medical aid man, died under enemy fire while dragging
wounded comrades back to safety.

Manifestly, there is not room here to call a complete roll of these
men. Manifestly, also, the quality of valor, like that of mercy, is not
strained. So one picks the saga of one man to epitomize Army dedication to duty, honor and country in Southeast Asia.

On October 29, 1963, twenty-three-year-old Lieutenant James
Nelson Rowe, Texan-born, Green Bereted member of Special Forces
Group 5, was captured when a Viet Cong raid overran the South
Vietnamese unit he was coaching, down in the Mekong Delta. In
early January 1969, an Army "chopper," cruising low over a clearing
not far from Quan Long in the Ca Mau area of that same lush
Mekong River delta in South Vietnam's southern tip, espied a figure
in black pajamas, waving a mosquito net. The pilot stooped. Before
the dust roused by his swirling blades had subsided, Jim Rowe—
bearded, gaunt, but smiling—had been hauled on board.

When Rowe graduated from West Point in the class of 1960, the
first act of the artillery "shavetail" was to volunteer for Special
Service duty. Once the gruelling indoctrination course in jungle combat and survival training had ended, he found himself in Vietnam.

The Special Forces knew that Rowe had been alive when captured, and he was officially listed as missing. As time passed, intelligence reports, rumors, admissions of Viet Cong prisoners and hearsay
garnered from defectors brought to Saigon tales of an American
prisoner who was making life miserable for his captors. The trickles
of information added up to an individual who attempted several times
to escape, and who at all times defied his captors. The Viet Cong had
a nickname for this man: they called him "Mr. Trouble."

"Mr. Trouble," the grapevine ran, simply couldn't be dominated.
He was, asserted one defector from the Viet Cong, "stubborn, sneaky
and very smart." Was this man James Rowe? Green Berets thought
so, but incessant search and investigation brought no tangible evidence. Now Jim Rowe, his shackles loosened through his own indomitable effort, had appeared in person. Major Rowe he was now;
he hadn't realized that automatic promotions throughout the years
on the Army list had raised him from first lieutenant to major.

Hustled away by his captors in 1963, Jim Rowe had spent five long years in a Viet Cong secret jungle hideaway, enduring insult, privation and a continuous flood of brainwashing. Most of the time he spent in solitary confinement; never did he see more than a handful of fellow prisoners. For the last 14 months of his captivity his efforts to escape had brought his confinement in a wooden cage, from which he was permitted to grub during daylight hours—within a radius of only 125 feet—for snakes, mice and other small creatures to eke out his ration of fish and rice.

Always he was subject to propaganda: endless lectures, pamphlets, films and a constantly blaring radio in his hovel, which sought to prove the degeneracy of the United States and the imminent collapse of its government through domestic revolution. Apparently he was never threatened with death—contrary to the experiences of the handful of other POWs who were exchanged. His was mental torment, designed to break the spirit of a man of intelligence, and to inculcate the spirit of defeat.

This procedure is worthy of note, for it indicates the careful ingenuity of Communist brainwashers in cutting their propaganda cloth to fit the mentality of the subject.

But Rowe refused to collaborate. Keeping his mind and body busy, he concentrated on escape. Several attempts failed. His final opportunity came on December 31, 1968, when one of the Allied sweeps in the delta threatened the discovery of his jungle prison. The immediate transfer of the POWs to a safer hiding place brought momentary turmoil. Rowe, in the custody of a single Viet Cong prison guard, shook himself free and dove into the jungle. A few days brought him to the clearing and the clatter of a helicopter. "Mr. Trouble" was back in his Army again.

On the bright side of the ledger, too, must go the Army's efforts to restore the soldiers' morale. USO shows—with a tip of the hat here to Bob Hope, Martha Raye and their thespian associates— brought much-needed laughter into the hearts of men who, not without reason, sometimes felt that they were forgotten, despised even, by the nation they were serving.

An extensive Recreational and Recuperation Program (R&R) afforded leaves—one week for each tour of duty—spent in Manila, Hong Kong, Bangkok, Tokyo, Taipei, Singapore, Penang, Kuala Lumpur, Sydney and Hawaii.

The ubiquitous Red Cross also played a prominent part in recreational assistance, in addition to its aid to men's domestic relations with their home folk. Nor should it be forgotten that special pay was granted soldiers engaged in combat zones, together with reductions in income tax.

So much for Vietnam. The Department of the Army has now begun a drastic reorganization of its structure within the continental United States, discarding both the existing Continental Army Command (CONARC) and Combat Development Command (CDC) concepts.

Instead, all deployable (i.e., mobile) combat elements in the Army of the United States—regular, reserve, and National Guard— are to be amalgamated within Force Command (FORSCOM) in a group of three Armies: the First, Fifth, and Sixth, with the mission of immediate readiness for field service.

A Training and Doctrine Command (TRADOC) will control all service schools, training centers, ROTC, and combat development activities. The Army Materiel Command (AMC) will continue in its present support role but with some consolidation of its scattered elements.

This sweeping reorganization, aimed at attaining efficiency, economy, and elasticity, is to be completed by the end of 1973.

Let's turn now to the Army's most significant contribution to American scientific advances during the entire twentieth century.

*   *   *   *   *

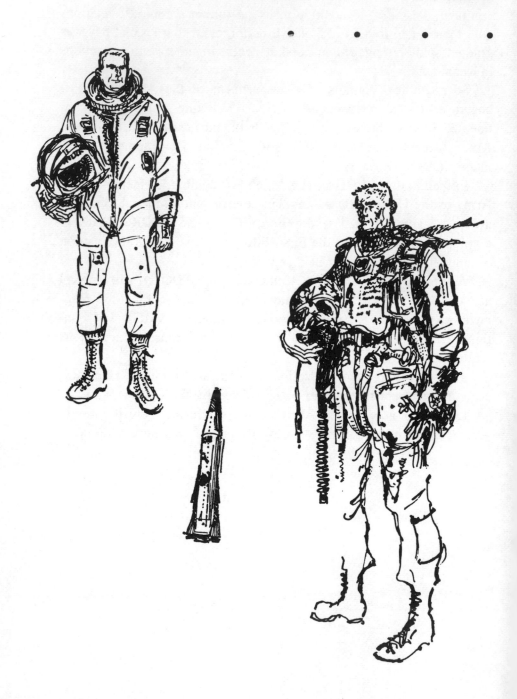

• • • •

19

THE ARMY IN THE SPACE AGE

Once upon a time, when "I'd just as soon fly to the moon" denoted the height of impossibility, the Army's sprightly little monthly house organ, *Recruiting News,* unceasingly reiterated the Regular Army's peacetime activities under the standing head: "What the Army Does Besides Fight."

Today we fly to the moon. So let's look at the Army's role in the space conquest of which we Americans are so justly proud.

The stark fact is that the Ordnance Corps of the United States Army laid the foundation on which the National Aeronautics and Space Administration (NASA) has performed its magnificent job. For the mighty Jupiter rocket engine, invention of the Ordnance Corps, has provided the basic thrust for all our manned spacecraft.

How this came about is worth the telling. It is particularly interesting, since the leadership, drive and tenacity of two men in particular, scientists both, made it possible. They are German-born Dr. Wernher von Braun, wizard of rocketry; and Major General John B. Medaris, Ordnance Corps genius, who from 1956 to 1960 commanded the Army's Redstone Arsenal at Huntsville, Alabama, and the Army Ballistic Missile Agency.

Immediately following the close of World War II in Europe, Eisenhower's AEF launched twin operations—British DUSTBIN and American ASHCAN—to sweep up, ahead of the Soviets, the German scientists who had produced the deadly V-1 and V-2 missiles that plagued London and Antwerp. Most of these men were gathered up at Pennemunde, the German rocket base, now in the Russian zone, but the mastermind among them—von Braun—in early April 1945, gathered up his group, moved west, and deliberately surrendered to the Americans. As soon as possible the entire American share of these German scientists was delivered to the Army's Ordnance Corps, together with a fragmentary assortment of their materiel removed from Pennemunde for research purposes.

Von Braun, who later became an American citizen, soon headed the Army's missile-building research and development team at Redstone. And in 1956 General Medaris, who had been most interested in rocketry developments, came there to command the Arsenal and the newly formed Army Ballistic Missile Agency.

When Medaris first assumed command, the Redstone personnel consisted of some 350 military and 1,700 civilians. Before he left, it had become a vast establishment manned by approximately 25,000 soldiers and civilians.

By the time Medaris arrived, von Braun's team had already developed the Redstone rocket engine, prototype of what was to become a huge family of missile engines. Now the team was wrestling with an improved rocket engine labeled Jupiter.

There is no room here for detailed discussion of the obstacles in Medaris' path as he pressed the development of Jupiter. But one should note that on October 4, 1957, the Jupiter-C engine was already an accomplished project. It was on that day that an astonished world learned that the USSR's Sputnik I was orbiting the earth in space, the first earth satellite. Soviet advances in rocketry, already a definite "cold war" challenge to the United States, had become an awesome threat.

Medaris and his ABMA met it. On January 31, 1958, Explorer I, their brainchild, thrust up through earth's atmosphere by its Jupiter-C booster, went into orbit around the globe.

President Eisenhower announced to the world that the United States had successfully launched an earth satellite. But neither in his broadcast nor in later official releases was there mention of the Army, the Army Ballistic Missile Agency or of any Army individual responsible for the feat.

This deliberate omission foreshadowed a new development, a policy to mute any military connection with United States space operations. In 1959 NASA was established. Its first major move was to absorb the von Braun task force at Redstone.

Later, when manned spacecraft became fact, our pilot-astronauts —most of them Air Force and Navy men—appear to have lost their respective service identities in the public mind, as have other service people connected with NASA.

But the United States Army, now out of the picture in space exploration, likes to remember that six of the early pilot-astronauts were graduates of West Point, and that one of these men, Edward H. White of the Gemini IV space crew, in 1965, became the first human being ever to really walk in space. (White died in the Apollo spacecraft disaster of 1967.)

During those years the Redstone Arsenal had been busy with other developments of the Space Age. An entire series of missiles—large and small—evolved, the most important being Nike, backbone of strategic antiaircraft defense. Its sites, manned by both regulars and National Guard, were dotting the American countryside. And von Braun's wizardry had developed the one antimissile missile as yet proven to be effective, Nike-Zeus, which in 1959 destroyed another rocket missile in flight. Nike-Zeus production in mass is still debatable because of the pros and cons of its usefulness, contrasted with the enormous expense involved in mass production.

Redstone's developments in the field of tactical mobile missiles must also be noted. Ground-to-air, ground-to-ground, short range and intermediate range, the Redstone families, successively improved, play their part in the equipment of United States ground forces still deployed worldwide.

Side by side with the Ordnance Corps, the Signal Corps—under the Army's Department of Communications and Electronics—played a most important part in linking our space vehicles to the earth. Guidance and control of the satellites was but one part. The fantastic two-way electronic devices which brought moon probes to earthlings' eyes and which enabled instantaneous communication to bounce from earth to satellite and back again, worldwide, had their birth in the great laboratory at Fort Monmouth, New Jersey. There, too, were developed ingenious instrumentalities facilitating military reconnaissance via satellite to all parts of the earth's surface.

Such, in a nutshell, was the Army's contribution to the Spage Age. It was a pretty good contribution.

*   *   *   *   *

• • • •

ENVOI

Still licking the wounds incurred during the Vietnam era, the Army, in 1972, shouldered another task. By mid-1973, the crutch bolstering its strength to an approximate 830,000 men would be removed, for the Selective Service Act would then die. So, by Presidential directive, the Department of the Army would then recruit and train sufficient volunteers to fill the gap and to provide for the maintenance of that strength by replacements estimated at 50,000 men per annum.

The concept, hailed by the American people as a transformation of our regulars to an "all-volunteer" Army, was really no transformation at all. The Regular Army had always been an all-vounteer force. Selective Service, inaugurated in national emergency, through the years had become a reservoir to fill the regular ranks, for the simple reason that volunteers in sufficient numbers to meet immediate demands were not obtainable.

Even in those long-gone days when the Regular Army strength quota was set at 25,000 men, the record shows that in peacetime there had always been difficulties in obtaining that minuscule number. Those were the days when the recruiter invoked a simple appeal to patriotism, guts and tradition: "The Army Builds Men."

In 1972, when sentimentalists and detractors alike joined to depict the career soldier as a brutal killer, something more, it seemed, would be needed to spur potential recruits.

The problem necessitated consideration from several angles: the definite change existing in American mores, the higher mental caliber of a large segment of today's youthful citizenry, and solutions to the thoughtful queries being posed by serious-minded young men and women not only with regard to their own personal futures but also to the future of the nation.

The recruiter, then, must step out of the "fool's paradise" feared by Major Burns in 1937* and sell the Army as a career with an appeal that will meet all of the above points. So someone conjured up an oriflamme:

"The Army Wants to Join You!"

. . . And the Army, with a hope, a prayer and an offer of "$332 and found per month" for the private soldier, went into the market-place under the banner of "The Army Wants to Join You!" to compete with civilian demands for manpower.

Will the scheme work? Only time will tell. Already opposition has arisen. Some of the very people who clapped hands joyously when the "all-volunteer" mirage first loomed were voicing qualms that the result might be the semi-cloistered Praetorian Guard so feared in 1638 by Governor John Winthrop of the Massachusetts Bay Colony: ". . . a force which might easily in time overthrow the civil power."

Such mumbo jumbo is, of course, poppycock, refuted by the Regular Army's 183 years of service in upholding and defending the Constitution of the United States.

The real stumbling block is the cost attendant upon the plan. That solution rests with the Congress, which also has a Constitutional directive: to raise and maintain armies.

Meanwhile our Army has received its directive. Its answer, as always, is summed up in the 5th Infantry's immortal motto:

"I'll Try, Sir!"

*   *   *   *   *

---

*See p. 10.

SELECTED BIBLIOGRAPHY

General

Adams, James Truslow, *Epic of America*, Garden City Books, 1931.

American State Papers, Military Affairs, 7 vols., Gales & Seaton, Washington, 1838-1861.

Army Almanac, Department of the Army, Washington, 1950.

Army Lineage Book, vol. II, *Infantry*, Department of the Army, Washington, 1953.

Birkhimer, William E., *Historical Sketch of the U. S. Artillery*, Chapman, Washington, 1884.

Cullum, George W., *Biographical Register of Officers and Graduates of the U.S. Military Academy*, New York, 1968. 2nd Edition 1879, 3rd Edition 1891. Supplemental vol. since 1900.

Dupuy, R. Ernest, *Where They Have Trod*, Stokes, New York, 1940.

———, *Men of West Point*, Sloane, New York, 1952.

———, "Hamilton's Battery," *Blue Book*, July and August, 1950.

———, "Pass in Review," *Army Combat Forces Journal*, October, 1954.

———, and Trevor N. Dupuy, *The Encyclopedia of Military History*, Harper & Row, New York, 1970.

———, *Military Heritage of America*, McGraw-Hill, New York, 1956.

Edmonds, James E., *Fighting Fools*, Appleton-Century-Crofts, New York, 1939.

Ganoe, William A., *History of the U.S. Army*, revised ed., Appleton-Century-Crofts, New York, 1942.

Haskin, William M., *History of the First Regiment of Artillery*, Portland, 1879.

Herr, John K., and Edward S. Wallace, *Story of the U. S. Cavalry, 1775-1942*, Little, Brown, Boston, 1953.

Heitman, Francis B., *Historical Dictionary and Register of the U. S. Army*, Government Printing Office, Washington, 1903.

Hume, Edgar E., *Victories of Army Medicine*, Lippincott, Philadelphia, 1943.

Hurd, Charles, *The Compact History of the American Red Cross*, Hawthorn, New York, 1959.

Morris, Richard B., *Encyclopedia of American History*, Harper & Row, New York, 1953.

Mahan, Dennis Hart, *Advanced Guard, Outpost . . . and Essential Principles of Strategy and Grand Tactics*, Wiley, New York, 1863.

Moss, James A., *Officers' Manual*, Banta, Menasha, Wis., 1911.

Paullin, Charles O., *Atlas of the Historical Geography of the U.S.*, Carnegie Institute and American Geographical Society, New York, 1932.

Pierce, Philip N., and Frank O. Hough, *The Compact History of the United States Marine Corps*, Hawthorn, New York, 1960.

Pratt, Fletcher, *The Compact History of the United States Navy*, Hawthorn. New York, 1957.

Puleston, William D., *Mahan*, Yale University Press, New Haven, 1939.

Riedler, A., *American Technological Schools*, H. R. Docs., 2nd Session, 53rd Congress. Vol. 5, Part I. Washington, 1895.

Rodenbough, Theophilus F., and William L. Haskin, *The Army of the United States*, Maynard, Merrill, New York, 1896.

Register of Graduates and Former Cadets, U. S. M. A., West Point Alumni Foundation, New York. Annually since 1947.

Spaulding, Oliver L., *The U. S. Army in War and Peace*, Putnam, New York, 1937.

Steele, Matthew F., *American Campaigns*, 2 vols., War Department, Washington, 1909.

Todd, Frederick P., and Fritz Kredel, *Soldiers of the American Army—1775-1954*, Regnery, Chicago, 1954.

Upton, Emory, *Military Policy of the United States*, Government Printing Office, Washington, 1904.

War of the Revolution; the Continental Army and Early Days of the U.S. Army:

Bolton, Charles Knowles, *The Private Soldier Under Washington*, Scribner's, New York, 1902.

Dupuy, R. Ernest, and Trevor N. Dupuy, *The Compact History of the Revolutionary War*, Hawthorn, New York, 1963.

Jacobs, James Ripley, *The Beginning of the U. S. Army*, Princeton University Press, Princeton, 1947.

Freeman, Douglas S., *George Washington*, 6 vols., Scribner's, New York, 1948-1954.

Ward, Christopher, *The War of the Revolution*, 2 vols., Macmillan, New York, 1952.

Weigley, Russell F., *History of the United States Army*, Macmillan, New York, 1967.

War of 1812:

Adams, Henry, *The War of 1812*, H. A. DeWeerd, Ed., Infantry Journal Press, Washington, 1944.

Tucker, Glen, *Poltroons and Patriots*, Bobbs-Merrill, Indianapolis, 1954.

Mexican War:

Elliott, Charles W., *Winfield Scott*, Macmillan, New York, 1937.

Kirby Smith, Ephraim, *To Mexico with Scott*, Harvard University Press, Cambridge, 1917.

McClellan, George B., *Mexican War Diary*, Princeton University Press, Princeton, 1917.

Smith, Justin H., *The War with Mexico*, 2 vols., Macmillan, New York, 1919.

Civil War:

Billings, John D., *Hard Tack and Coffee,* George M. Smith, Boston, 1887.

Catton, Bruce, *Mr. Lincoln's Army,* Doubleday, New York, 1949.

————, *Glory Road,* Doubleday, New York, 1952.

————, *A Stillness at Appomattox,* Doubleday, New York, 1953.

Dupuy, R. Ernest and Trevor N. Dupuy, *The Compact History of the Civil War,* Hawthorn, New York, 1960.

Freeman, Douglas S., *Lee's Lieutenants,* 3 vols., Scribner's, New York, 1945.

————, and *R. E. Lee.* 4 vols., Scribner's, New York, 1947.

War of the Rebellion; Official Records of the Union and Confederate Armies, 130 vols., War Department, Washington, 1882–1900.

Wars Against the Indians:

Bourke, John G., *An Apache Campaign in the Sierra Madre,* Scribner's, New York, 1886.

————, *On the Border with Crook,* Scribners, New York, 1891.

Custer, Elizabeth B., *Boots and Saddles,* Harper, New York, 1885.

————, *Tenting on the Plains,* Webster, New York, 1889.

————, *Following the Guidon,* Harper, New York, 1890.

Downey, Fairfax, *Indian-Fighting Army,* Scribner's, New York, 1941.

Pelzer, Louis, *Marches of the Dragoons in the Mississippi Valley,* State Historical Society of Iowa, Iowa City, 1917.

Spanish-American War, Philippine Insurrection and Boxer Expedition:

Millis, Walter, *The Martial Spirit; A Study of Our War with Spain,* Houghton, Mifflin, Boston, 1931.

Sexton, William T., *Soldiers in the Sun,* Military Service, Harrisburg, 1939.

Titherington, Richard H., *A History of the Spanish-American War of 1898,* Appleton-Century-Crofts, New York, 1900.

War Department, *Reports of the Major-General Commanding the Army,* 1898 (2 vols.), 1899 (3 vols.), and 1900 (7 vols.), Government Printing Office.

World War I:

Dupuy, R. Ernest, *Perish by the Sword,* Military Service Publishing Co., Harrisburg, 1939.

Graves, William S., *America's Siberian Adventure,* Cape and Smith, New York, 1931.

Palmer, Frederick, *Bliss—Peacemaker,* Dodd, Mead, New York, 1939.

Stamps, T. Dodson, Vincent J. Esposito and associates, *A Short History of World War I* (with Atlas), 2 vols., Department of Military Art and Engineering, U. S. Military Academy, West Point, 1950.

Between World Wars:

MacArthur, Douglas, *Annual Reports of the Chief of Staff, U.S. Army, to the Secretary of War, 1931-1935,* Government Printing Office, Washington.

World War II:

Bush, Vannevar, *Modern Arms and Free Men,* Simon & Schuster, New York, 1949.

Craven, Wesley Frank and James Lea Cate, *The Army Air Forces in World War II,* University of Chicago Press, Chicago, 1948.

Dupuy, R. Ernest, *St. Vith-Lion in the Way,* Infantry Journal Press, Washington, 1948.

————,*World War II: A Compact History,* Hawthorn, New York, 1969.

Greenfield, Kent R., Robert R. Palmer and Bell I. Wiley, *Army Ground Forces, Organization of Ground Combat Troops,* Historical Division, Department of the Army, Washington, 1947.

Marshall, George Catlett, *Biennial Report of the Chief of Staff, U.S. Army, to the Secretary of War, 1943-1945,* Government Printing Office, Washington, 1945.

Marshall, Samuel L. A., *Bastogne,* Infantry Journal Press, Washington, 1946.

Omaha Beachhead, Historical Division, Department of the Army, Washington, 1945.

Pogue, Forrest C., *European Theatre of Operations; the Supreme Command,* Historical Division, Department of the Army, Washington, 1954.

Sherwood, Robert E., *Roosevelt and Hopkins,* Harper & Row, New York, 1948.

Stamps, T. Dodson, Vincent J. Esposito and associates, *World War II,* with Atlas, 3 vols., Department of Military Art and Engineering, U. S. Military Academy, West Point, 1950.

Stimson, Henry L., and McGeorge Bundy, *On Active Service,* Harper & Row, 1947.

Korean War:

Marshall, Samuel L. A., *The River and the Gauntlet,* Morrow, New York, 1953.

Mayer, William E., "Why Did Many GI Captives Cave In?" *U. S. News and World Report,* February 24, 1956.

Stamps, T. Dodson, Vincent J. Esposito and associates, *Operations in Korea,* Department of Military Art and Engineering, U. S. Military Academy, West Point, 1952.

Voorhees, Melvin B., *Korean Tales,* Simon & Schuster, New York, 1952.

Whitney, Courtney, *MacArthur,* Knopf, New York, 1956.

Vietnam:

Hersh, Seymour M., *My Lai Four: A Report on the Massacre and Its Aftermath,* Random, New York, 1970.

Johnson, Lyndon B., *The Vantage Point: Perspectives of the Presidency,* Holt, Rinehart & Winston, New York, 1971.

Lederer, William J., *Our Own Worst Enemy,* Norton, New York, 1968.

Mecklin, John, *Mission in Torment,* Doubleday, New York, 1965.

Westmoreland, William C., *Report on the War in Vietnam,* Government Printing Office, Washington, 1968.

The Space Age:

Gavin, James M., *War and Peace in the Space Age,* Harper & Row, New York, 1958.

Medaris, John B., *Countdown for Decision.* Putnam, New York, 1960.

Ridgway, Matthew B., *Soldier,* Harper & Row, New York, 1956.

INDEX

(For the reader's convenience, service units referred to in the text are listed at the beginning of this index in numerical order.)